CUNNINGHAM & C<u>o</u>.

CUNNINGHAM & CO. Copyright © 2022 by John Basalto.

Published by the San Joaquin County Sheriff's Foundation
7000 Michael N. Canlis Boulevard, French Camp, CA, 95231
www.sjcsfoundation.org

Cover and interior by Lisa Basalto.

All rights reserved. This book or any portion thereof may not be reproduced or used in any manner whatsoever without the express written permission of the publisher except for the use of brief quotations in a book review.

ISBN: 978-1-958051-01-6
LCCN: 2022913658

To all members of the San Joaquin County Sheriff's Office, past, present and future.

CUNNINGHAM & Co.

STORIES OF SAN JOAQUIN COUNTY, CALIFORNIA,
SHERIFF THOMAS CUNNINGHAM
& HIS DEPUTIES

1872 TO 1899

JOHN BASALTO

CONTENTS

Maps i

Acknowledgments v

Introduction ix

1. Leather Crafter Becomes Lawman 1

2. One Year In 19

3. Hunting Bandits 37

4. A Dark Time 57

5. Burglars, Robbers and Murderers 77

6. The Daily Grind 93

7. Trouble on the Moquelumnes 113

8. The Sheriff's Last Execution 139

9. A High-Profile Case 163

10. Routine 189

11. Dealing with Industrials	221
12. Death of a Deputy	247
13. Embezzlers, Stick-Up Men and Thugs	267
14. The Train Wreckers	281
15. End of an Era	295
16. An Honorable Name	311
NOTES	323
BIBLIOGRAPHY	349
INDEX	354

MAP OF SAN JOAQUIN COUNTY

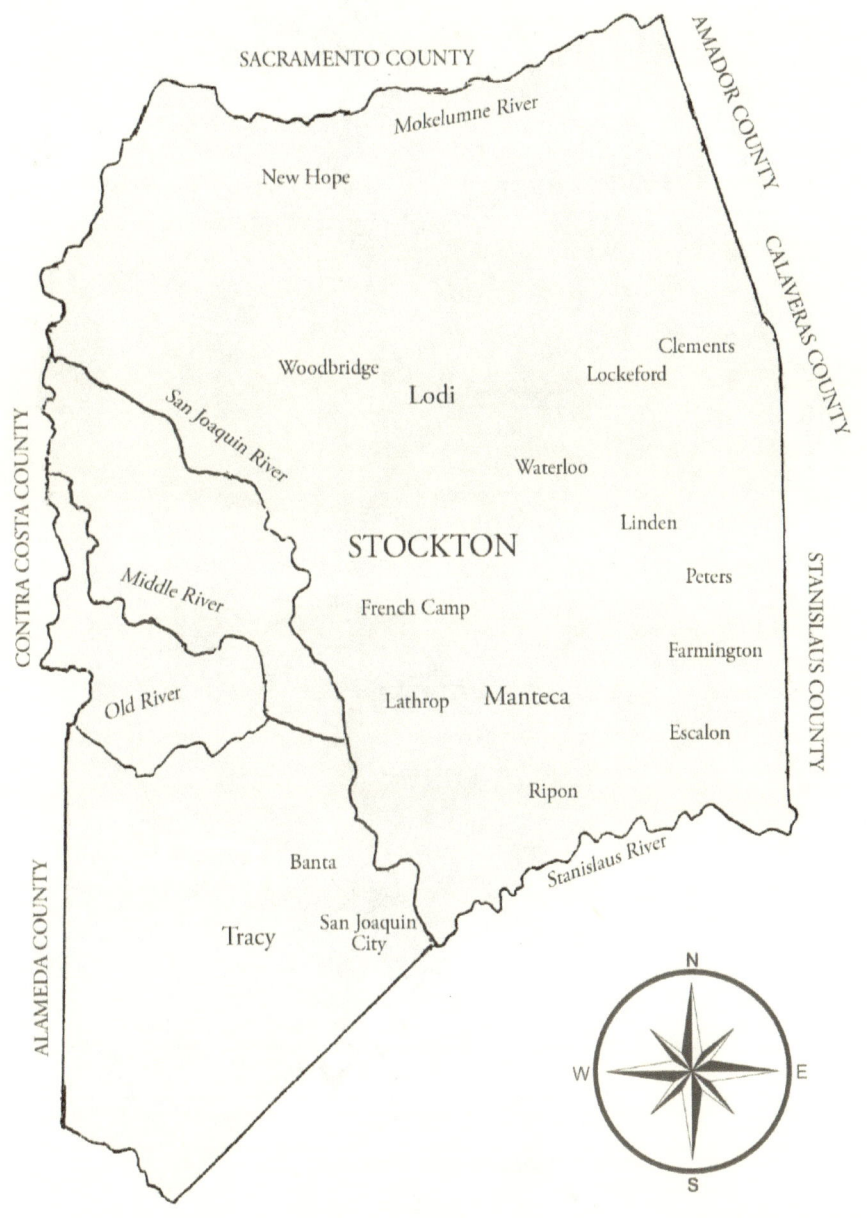

* not drawn to scale

Map of San Joaquin County c. 1895
[*Library of Congress*]

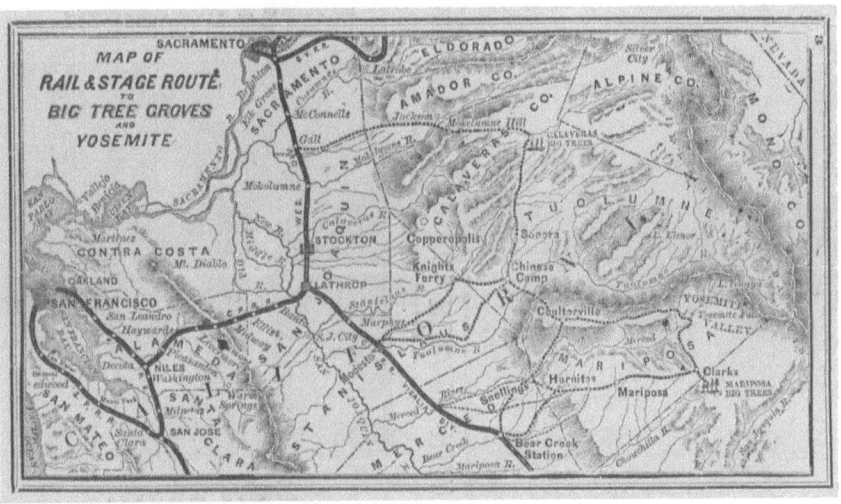

Railroad map showing San Joaquin County and the Mother Lode.
[*In Time and Place*]

ACKNOWLEDGMENTS

I owe a lot of people thanks for helping me with this project. My daughter Lisa is a talented author in her own right and formatted this book and did the cover art. Lisa, thank you.

I have several long-time friends who share my passion for the history of the San Joaquin County Sheriff's Office. The late Terry Eproson was a retired deputy sheriff who was an A-lister. Terry hunted down bad guys with the best of 'em. He would have felt right at home working for Thomas Cunningham.

R. Tod Ruse, the historian for the Office, has helped me with this project in both big ways and small. His book on the history of the Stockton Police Department was invaluable in helping me research this book. Tod, your friendship means a great deal to me.

Tod and Marlene Von Berg read through the manuscript with a critical eye. Both Tod and Marlene have spent their lives in education as teachers and school administrators, and their knowledge and experience was very helpful. Thank you both.

My old friend Ray Moreno, another retired San Joaquin County deputy sheriff, gave me several illustrations and photos which are presented in the book. Thank you, Ray.

Alyssa Benz, the corporate historian for Wells Fargo, was very gracious and generous when I reached out to her for information. Thank you, Alyssa; I appreciate your help.

Laurence Valterza is a native Stocktonian and local historian. Although I have never met Larry in person, he has always generously shared his photographs with me, and several are shown in the book. Thank you, sir.

I had a friend, the late Horace Spencer, who was a Stockton elementary school teacher and local historian. He preserved much of Stockton's history through his photographs, and he was very enthusiastic about my projects. He served on the Sheriff's historical board at one time, and he was always willing to share any materials he had from his vast archives.

Back in the 1990s, I met a lady named Nancy Lea Schmer, who was a member of the Lodi Historical Society. She shared a picture of Deputy William Wall with me. Billy Wall is one of my heroes, and I hadn't been able to find a photo of him anywhere. Thank you, Nancy.

I want to thank all of the men and women I worked with at the San Joaquin County Sheriff's Office. A better bunch of people you will not meet on this earth.

Thank you to all of the members of the San Joaquin County Sheriff's Foundation Historical Preservation Committee, without whose support this book would not have happened.

I thank all of the people in the Technical Services Unit, who always take photos for us whenever they are asked.

A big thank you goes to the families of retired deputies, who generously donated items to the Historical Preservation Committee.

Sheriff Patrick Withrow has been a particular friend to me. Pat is a people-person, and he possesses many of the qualities that Thomas Cunningham had. Thank you, Sheriff Withrow, sir, for your love of the history of your Office, for your support of the Historical Preservation Committee, and, most of all, for your friendship.

Thomas Cunningham
[*R. Tod Ruse*]

INTRODUCTION

Like many people, I have always been fascinated by the stories of the lawmen of the Old West. Names like Wyatt Earp, Bat Materson and Wild Bill Hickock live on in legend and folklore, but these men were gamblers and itinerant lawmen of the Midwest and Southwest who were hired by towns primarily for their reputations. The real nineteenth-century lawmen of California had been mostly forgotten through the mists of time and its only been until relatively recently that they have gotten their due, thanks to researchers like William B. Secrest, John Bossenecker and Kevin Mullins. Men like Ben Thorn of Calaveras, John Adams of Santa Clara, Harry Morse of Alameda, and Doc Standley of Mendocino were highly regarded in their time, but were virtually unknown in modern times until the last 20 or 30 years. One of those forgotten lawmen was Thomas Cunningham, who served as the San Joaquin County sheriff from 1872 to 1899.

The officers of Sheriff Cunningham's time didn't enjoy the amenities that law enforcement officers know today, things like climate-controlled patrol cars, radio communications, body armor, and computer-generated information at the touch of a button. Back then, the tools of the trade were a six-shot revolver, a rifle, a bulky pair of handcuffs, leg irons and belly chains. Many officers carried a double-barreled shotgun, which provided maximum firepower at close range. The only way to get around in those days was by horseback, wagon, steamboat or train. Prior to the advent of the telephone, communications were limited to the telegraph or mail. Many officers, including Sheriff Cunningham, sent out wanted information on penny postcards.

San Joaquin County is located in the middle of California's fertile San Joaquin Valley, and is bordered to the west by the inner Coastal Range mountains and on the east by the Mother Lode foothills of the Sierra Nevadas. Stockton, the seat of San Joaquin County, sits at the head of a deep-water channel which extends from the San Joaquin River, and this made travel by boat to and from San Francisco the most convenient mode of travel in the early days. The area west of Stockton is comprised of a series of rivers and sloughs which make up the San Joaquin Delta. Chinese laborers were used in the mid-1800s to create levees, forming islands of nutrient-rich farm land.

Because of the ease of river travel and its proximity to San Francisco, Stockton was a major supply hub during the California Gold Rush, and from its earliest days Stockton was populated by a darker element, men who preyed off of others. Thomas Cunningham was inexperienced as a lawman prior to taking office. Because of his kind demeanor, many thought he did not possess the mettle it would take to be sheriff, but he quickly established himself as a tough law enforcer.

Sheriff Cunningham did not play favorites, and over his career he arrested and jailed a county treasurer and a member of the county board of supervisors; he jailed a deputy U.S. marshal; and he served an arrest warrant on a justice of the U.S. Supreme Court.

He carried out the execution of a man he served with on the fire department. He consistently enforced gambling laws, even when it was unpopular to do so.

Cunningham learned early in his career that in order to stay alive, an officer had to pay very close attention and not get distracted when taking a prisoner into custody. That philosophy was illustrated by a comment made by a man named George Robbins in 1899, after Cunningham's retirement. Robbins had served as a town marshal in San Luis Obispo County, and was having a conversation with some other men after a San Diego County deputy sheriff had been assaulted while transporting a prisoner to San Quentin on a steamer off the coast of Port Harford.

A newspaper reporter was present in the group and reported on what was said. One of the men in the group mentioned, "Officers take too great a risk in handling prisoners." Robbins replied, "That is a fact," then related an experience he had with Sheriff Cunningham while searching for a wanted criminal. "In 1879, while I was serving as marshal, Tom Cunningham, the veteran sheriff of San Joaquin County, came to this county to arrest a murderer whom he had located in the Rinconada Valley. The man, who had been an outlaw for three years, was known to be a desperate character. I accompanied Cunningham on a trip and about eight miles beyond Santa Margarita on the Pozo road, we met the man coming toward us. I merely spoke to him and in an instant Cunningham was out of the buggy and had a gun leveled at his head. The man was handcuffed and brought back to town, but Cunningham never took his eyes off his prisoner."[1]

Through his hard work and even-handed approach to the job, Cunningham was returned to office by the people during every election between 1871 and 1898, serving as their sheriff for over a quarter of a century and becoming the longest tenured sheriff in the history of the San Joaquin County Sheriff's Office. Over time, Cunningham became widely renowned for his humanitarian approach to the job of sheriff. He never shied away from his duties when called upon, but was always willing to treat people with respect and dignity, including his prisoners, once they were in custody. His ability to connect with people endeared Thomas Cunningham to the public he served.

One evening in 1890, Cunningham spoke with a reporter from the *San Francisco Call*. He had held the sheriff's job for nearly 20 years at that point. Wrote the reporter: "The genial sheriff walked into the Grand Hotel last night, and as he sat by the fire warming his feet, spoke of his record:

> "'It's rather hard,' he said with a smile, 'to sell people out of their house and home as a sheriff is required to do and still retain their friendship, but I have managed to do it. I always remember that it is an officer's duty to tell a defendant his rights under the law when he is ignorant of them, and that is the best I can do. The Democrats have long since given up nominating anyone to oppose me, so that gives me an advantage, but this year the Prohibitionists got after me. They put up a candidate and he got 900 votes out of 6000. It was about as close a shave as I've had in a number of years.'"[2]

Sheriff Cunningham was considered an innovator in the field of law enforcement, as evidenced by a number of methods and techniques he brought to his profession. He created a large library of criminal photographs, descriptions, and criminal accounts. This library proved very useful and became widely renowned by law officers.

Cunningham felt that it was very important for California's

lawmen to work closely together, communicating freely and sharing information. In an effort to accomplish this, he annually published a booklet listing the names and addresses of all of the state's sheriffs, constables and police chiefs, furnishing it to all of these officers free of charge. Because horse and cattle thefts were such a problem, Sheriff Cunningham published a booklet with outlines of horses and cows. Ranchers and horse owners could then draw on these figures to indicate ear-marks, physical markings and brands to more easily identify their animals.[3]

Sheriff Cunningham was a charter member of the California State Sheriff's Association when it was formed in 1894. He was a student of the newly developing science of criminology, studying the habits, methods and motivations of the criminal. As mentioned before, he and his deputies compiled a library of large volumes of mug-shot photographs, news clippings and other data on American crime. His rogue's gallery reportedly contained between 14,000 and 40,000 photos. Cunningham's criminal record collection was not a static display—he routinely studied the materials and made many arrests over his career because of his memory for the wanted outlaw. He also created a museum in the front lobby of the Sheriff's Office from a large collection of weapons and other curiosities from early California's criminal history.[4]

Then as now, California sheriffs were charged with carrying out a number of varied duties, including maintaining the jail, attending the courts of record, serving subpoenas for the grand jury and criminal cases, carrying out court orders, serving civil process, transporting inmates to the state prisons and state asylums, and preserving the peace in their respective counties. Sheriffs also had the unenviable task of carrying out the executions of condemned prisoners in their jurisdictions until an 1891 law transferred that duty to the wardens of San Quentin and Folsom prisons.⁵

Cunningham was required to carry out the executions of two men during his time as sheriff. Because of mishaps that occurred around the country during hangings, Thomas designed the gallows that Uzza French was hanged on in 1886. In his 1994 unpublished book *Death Without Honor, Legal Executions in the History of San Joaquin County*, retired San Joaquin County Deputy District Attorney Eual Blansett, who worked on the homicide prosecution team, wrote about Sheriff Cunningham's approach to this unenviable job:

> "One cannot help but appreciate the sensitivity shown by Sheriff Cunningham in the performance of his duties. When the law demands that a life be taken for the slaying of another, the execution of that sentence should always be done with the utmost gravity. Sheriff Cunningham's concern for every detail of the execution was exemplary. He foresaw the needs of the citizens, the victim's family, fellow law enforcement officers, and the condemned. He set a standard for his peers throughout the state."⁶

Although Cunningham's jurisdiction stretched over 1400-plus square miles, he had arrest powers throughout California like any other peace officer, and he did not confine his investigations and manhunts to San Joaquin County's borders. Like other lawmen of the time, Sheriff Cunningham could be seen assisting with criminal investigations in many areas of California, and over his career Cunningham logged thousands of miles investigating crimes and bringing criminals to justice. He took part in most every major investigation or manhunt in the state during his time as sheriff, to one degree or another, and his assistance and counsel were always appreciated by his fellow lawmen. Because he spent so much of his time in the field, he left many of the administrative duties of the job to his undersheriff.

California lawmen routinely worked with each other to resolve criminal cases. Town marshals and their deputies, city police chiefs and their officers, sheriffs and their deputies, U.S. marshals and their deputies, and Wells Fargo and railroad detectives were often seen working shoulder-to-shoulder while chasing down a bandit. One classification of officer was the constable. Counties in California were divided into townships, each of which had a Justice Court, presided over by a justice of the peace. Constables were elected for each township to serve the justice courts, and they were responsible for carrying out duties similar to that of the sheriff at the County and District court levels. Constables were also often seen assisting other officers with criminal cases, and many were also deputized by the sheriff.

No diaries or personal letters left by Thomas Cunningham are known to exist, but luckily, he was widely written about in the newspapers of the time. Using these contemporary newspaper accounts, court documents and other available primary source materials, one can get a sense of what life was like back at that time.

My goal is to present Thomas Cunningham to you in the way that he was presented to people in his time. These, then, were the conditions and circumstances in which Sheriff Cunningham and his fellow peace officers carried out their duties. Often in the saddle in freezing cold or blistering hot temperatures, these men did their work to enforce the law.

1

LEATHER CRAFTER BECOMES LAWMAN

Born in Longford County, Ireland, on August 17th, 1838, Thomas Cunningham was the youngest of seven children. He immigrated to the United States with other family members when he was ten years old. The Cunninghams settled in Brooklyn, New York, where Thomas attended school. As a young boy, Thomas learned the trade of harness making under the guidance of one of his brothers-in-law.

In 1855, Thomas and a friend set out for California, embarking on the long and treacherous journey from New York aboard the steamer *Illinois*. After crossing the Isthmus of Panama and taking a ship up the Pacific coast, they arrived in San Francisco on June 16th, 1855.[1]

Cunningham immediately left for Stockton to start a new life. Two of his sisters, Elizabeth (Mrs. Charles Dewitt Benjamin) and Catherine (Mrs. Hartman Littebrandt) also made Stockton their home. Thomas partnered with Henry F. Horn making saddle trees, the raw-hide covered wood frame that is the foundation of a saddle.

That partnership dissolved on October 31st, 1857, and Cunningham bought out Horn's share of the business and continued by himself in a shop on Channel Street. He later moved his saddle tree business to a location on Hunter Street.[2]

Many exciting things were happening in young Thomas's life around this time, one of those events occurring on August 21st, 1860, when he obtained his United States citizenship.[3]

On July 1st, 1861, Thomas bought out the saddle and harness shop of Joseph W. Scott, setting up business for himself in Scott's former shop on Main Street near the corner of El Dorado Street. Thomas's business thrived and grew to the point that at one time he employed eight men, producing harnesses, saddles, bridals, lashes, whips, and other leather-made goods. Receipts for the business reportedly totaled $28,000 in 1871, an amount equaling almost $600,000 in 2020 dollars.[4]

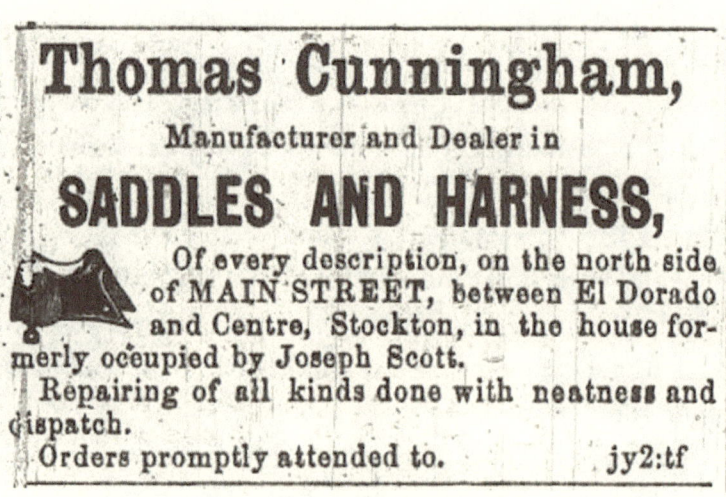

Advertisement in the *San Joaquin Republican*, July 2, 1861
[*California Digital Newspaper Collection*]

Cunningham was interested in public service and politics from a young age, becoming actively involved in public life, and he became a member of the local Republican party shortly after arriving in Stockton. His name was seen on all of the petitions that were circulated dealing with civic improvement projects.

One of the biggest threats to public safety at that time was fire. Because the threat was so great and resources so scarce, cities and towns across the country formed volunteer fire companies. Fighting fire was the primary duty of these volunteer companies, but membership in a fire company was also a sign of prestige, and political power and influence ran right through the fire houses. Each fire company ran its own organization, and although Stockton city government made some funds available to them, each company was responsible for raising much of the funds it took to maintain their organizations. They did this by hosting fireman's balls, picnics and other events. Firemen and their equipment took part in parades, and they were at the center of civic pride.

Cunningham applied to and was voted in to the Eureka Engine Company Number 2 on January 7th, 1857. He spent a lot of time at the firehouse and was voted into leadership positions by fellow company members, serving first as assistant foreman in 1861 and then as foreman in 1862, a position he retained with the company until being voted chief engineer of the Stockton Fire Department in October 1864 by members of all of the fire companies in the city. He held the job for two years, then resumed his position as foreman of Eureka Engine Company 2 until August 1868, when he was once again voted chief engineer of the department. He would remain a leader in the fire service for many years.[5]

Thomas was married to Catherine Quirk in January 1866. Members of Eureka Company 2 and the Stockton Coronet Band took advantage of the occasion to march to the Cunningham's house on Weber Avenue and serenade the couple. The *San Joaquin Republican* reported:

> "After the band had been exercised sufficiently in a melodious way, all hands, headed by the Chief, proceeded to the nearest establishment, where 'spiritual comfort' could be obtained, and amid song, laughter, and general good feeling, many a flowing bumper was quaffed in honor of the occasion, and to health, happiness, and prosperity of the happy couple. And all the fire companies in this city over whom Tom is Chief, cannot more heartily wish him happiness than we do."[6]

The young couple bought a home at 320 Market Street to start their family. The location of the house was convenient for Cunningham; his saddle shop was located about three blocks away, the firehouse was about a block and a half distant, the courthouse just over a block, and the jail was within a block's distance. Thomas and Catherine had three daughters: Lillian was born on October 13th, 1867. Margaret graced her happy parents by making her entrance on July 25th, 1870, and Katherine would be born five years later.

On December 6th, 1870, after having once again been unanimously voted the foreman of Eureka Engine Company 2, Cunningham was presented with a memento in the form of a beautiful solid-gold medal by company president Abraham B. Bennett. The local paper printed Bennett's remarks:

> "In the responsible position of Chief Engineer of the Stockton Fire Department, notwithstanding you were most exacting in your demand for prompt and skillful service, yet these demands were free from partiality and immunity to individuals and were freely acquiesced in by the gallant firemen of the Department;

and none will deny that on all occasions you made a judicious use of all the means at your command. As Foreman of the company, your labors have been unremitting. Your head, your heart, your hands and your purse, have equally and largely contributed to the advancement of its interests."[7]

After Bennett was done speaking, Cunningham, who had been standing in front of the assembly, humbly thanked the company.

Thomas Cunningham and Eureka Co. 2
[R. Tod Ruse]

Thomas was nominated by the Republicans to serve as an alderman for Ward 3 on the Stockton City Council in April 1865, winning the seat in an election held on May 1st by one vote![8] He held the position for one year. He was again elected to the city council in May 1870. He was nominated by his party for the office of sheriff in 1871, and was elected to the position during the September elections that year.[9]

Thomas Cunningham was sworn in as San Joaquin County's sheriff on March 4th, 1872. He appointed his friend Abraham Bennett, a local businessman who served with him in Eureka Engine Company 2, as his undersheriff. George Perry, a Stockton constable, and D. O. Harelson, who later served as Stockton's police chief, were appointed as his deputies. A. J. Tibbetts, a local carpenter and also a member of Eureka Company 2, was appointed deputy in charge of the jail. Cunningham tendered his resignation to the Stockton City Council the next day.[10]

A.B. Bennett,
Undersheriff
1872-1875
[*R. Tod Ruse*]

Leather Crafter Becomes Lawman

When Cunningham took office, he brought with him a Colt revolving belt pistol of Naval caliber. This gun is known today as the 1851 Colt Navy. A .36 caliber, six-shot revolver, it was developed by Samuel Colt between 1847 and 1850, and was based on earlier models of revolvers being manufactured by the Colt's Patent Firearms Manufacturing Company, in Hartford, Connecticut. A percussion revolver, it was very cumbersome to load. The user was required to pour a measured amount of black power into each cylinder, then ram a round lead ball or conical bullet into the cylinders. A firing cap was then placed on a knob on the front-side of the cylinder before it was ready for use.[11]

The sheriff and his deputies wore plain clothes, wearing their badge on the inside of their coat lapel. They would carry their handgun in either a reinforced coat pocket or in a holster on a belt under their coat.

Sheriff Cunningham wasted no time and hit the ground running. Within a week of taking office, Cunningham had made a couple of arrests. His first was on a man named James Satterlee, who had stabbed another man in the neck on March 6th, 1872. Then, on the evening of March 10th, Cunningham took the engineer of an east-bound Central Pacific Railroad passenger train into custody at the Banta station, outside of Tracy in southern San Joaquin County, on a warrant charging bigamy. These were just routine arrests, and were just the first of many Cunningham would make over his career.[12]

The following month, Sheriff Cunningham caught up with a jail escapee who had been on the lamb for a year. Arthur "Al" Elmore was a slippery sort of fellow. He had been indicted by a San Francisco grand jury for larceny in 1871, but had escaped from San Francisco's jail yard. San Francisco officers caught up with him at the Banta train station a short time later, but he escaped them too.

Even though he was only thirty-three years old at the time he took office, Thomas was already bald, and this was an identifying trademark of the sheriff to both his friends and criminal adversaries, so Thomas often wore disguises to get close to his prey.

Sheriff Cunningham received information that Al was working in the area of Hill's Ferry, along the San Joaquin River in south San Joaquin County. Dressing in old and ratty clothes and blackening his face, Cunningham went into the area acting as an out-of-luck sheep herder. He found Al in the kitchen of a farm house and had no trouble taking his man into custody.

Al did not believe the sheriff when he identified himself until Cunningham took off his hat, revealing his "skating rink." With that, Al blurted out, "I know you now!"[13]

Sheriff Cunningham and his deputies worked out of the county's first courthouse until 1888.
[*SJSO collection*]

Although he was already spending a lot of his time in the field, one of Sheriff Cunningham's first priorities was to mitigate the conditions at the county jail. Built in 1854, by 1872 it had become inadequate to house the numbers of prisoners that were lodged there, and there were numerous problems with its operation.

The two-story jail, located on the north side of Market Street between Hunter and San Joaquin streets in Stockton, had seventeen cells—eight on the ground floor and nine on the second. Constructed with a brick exterior facade and interior wood planking, sheet iron was placed in between the interior and exterior walls to help prevent escapes. The cell doors were constructed of heavy metal and had small openings covered with iron wickets. Iron bars covered the windows and the front door was made of heavy steel.

The front door opened into an area known as the reception room, where prisoners were searched and their property taken for safekeeping. A hallway ran the length of the building, south to north, on both floors, with cells on both sides. Police officers utilized three cells on the first floor to confine city prisoners. The first cell on the left on the first floor was eight-by-twelve feet in size, and was used as the "drunk tank." The cell directly across from it was the "trustee's" cell, where inmates who worked inside the jail were housed. The women prisoners were confined in a six-by-eight-foot cell to the north of the trustees' cell. Upstairs, the jailer's room was located in the southwest corner; the undersheriff's office was located in the southeast corner. The room across from that was equipped as a kitchen. The first cell on the west side of the hallway housed the condemned prisoners. The other cells housed men awaiting trial on their charges, or sentenced to do time in the county jail. A door off the north side of the second-floor hallway led to a platform area, where gallows would be erected to carry out executions.[14]

A few days after taking office, Cunningham put the Board of Supervisors on notice about conditions in the Sheriff's Office, located in the county courthouse, and the jail, in a letter he wrote to them:

> "To the Honorable Board of Supervisors of San Joaquin County—Gentlemen: On entering the duties of the office of Sheriff of San Joaquin County, I must confess to feeling myself somewhat repelled by what on the surface appears to be an unfriendly discrimination against the office of Sheriff of this county. I sincerely indulge the hope, however, that this is only in the seeming, and that it is simply necessary to call your attention to existing facts to secure such recognition as will place the office on a footing with the most favored. The room set apart for the use of the Sheriff, in its original proportions (13x23 feet) was hardly adequate, and illy adapted to the proper discharge of his duties; for it must be remembered that the office of Sheriff is by no means an office of secondary importance in the county. He is an immediate officer of every court of record, and is himself required by law to hold Court, and by jury try any claim upon property seized or levied upon by him. It is also apparent that the Sheriff's office should contain two apartments, for of all the officers of the county the Sheriff is most frequently importuned for private interview, not only by clients and attorneys, but by the detectives at home and from abroad for the purpose of subserving the ends of public justice. Indeed, it needs no argument to show that secrecy is an essential element in the discharge of much of the duty he is called on to perform. Small and inadequate as the office was originally, it has recently been reduced in size to give additional room actually required by the Recorder; and it would hardly be believed by men acquainted

with the exigencies of the office that a single room of 12x13 feet is all that is apportioned to the Sheriff of a county, second in importance to none in the State, after those of Sacramento and San Francisco. From conversations with the occupants of the very important county offices, I learn that the office, furniture and fixtures have been supplied at a county expense. On examining the inventory of the late sheriff to ascertain the apportionment of which I should be in receipt, I could not resist the inference that the office of the Sheriff had in a measure been overlooked in the distribution. As to expense, this apparent omission is a matter of but little consequence, and can be remedied at my own cost; but it's the moral aspect to one who is about entering upon the discharge of the duties of an office involving great responsibilities, and is in need of friendly recognition from those whose duty it is, in a sense, to supervise his administration of its affairs, seems quite formidable; for if, as appearances would seem to indicate, he is placed at a disadvantage upon the threshold of his duties, how is he to know but than other and more formidable obstacles may present themselves as he advances, from the same extraneous source? If in this recital I have in anything misjudged, or have taken undue counsel of my fears, I hope its merit of frankness and this disclaimer of any intention of placing the matter considered therein in a false light, will receive due consideration."[15]

Cunningham then gave a detailed and graphic description of conditions in the long-neglected county jail:

"I beg leave, also, to your attention to the present condition of the County Jail. There is ample testimony that the jail is infested with vermin. From this and other considerations, it cannot be said to be in a sanitary condition. Various causes have contributed to bring about this state of affairs; among them may be considered the lack of proper ventilation, the use of buckets in the cells in place of earth closets, lack of personal cleanliness on the part of the prisoners (the latter evil, I am glad to perceive, may be remedied by the enforced use of a bath tub and artesian water provided for use of the officers of the jail, and which can and should be turned over to the use of the prisoners.) But I have yet to name the most fruitful source of danger to the health and well-being of the prisoners confined in the jail cells. The walls and partitions of these cells are made of plank six inches thick, laid one upon another for the whole height, and spiked through. The natural shrinkage of timbers admit of the circulation of the fetid air of the cells, arising from the bodies of the prisoners and the before-mentioned buckets, through the interstices of the walls. From an approximate calculation, the smallest cell has in its walls and ceiling a superfice of not less than 1,500 square feet. As these surfaces cannot be reached for the purpose of cleansing them by any known process short of taking down the jail, measures should be instituted for effectively closing the interstices between them. This has been partially accomplished by a coat of rough plaster upon the walls and partitions in the upper portion of the building, but, on the lower floor this sanitary precaution has been entirely overlooked. The common wash usually employed does not adhere properly and is continually scaling off, leaving passages for the mephitic gasses and vermin; and if under existing circumstances, the small-pox, now gathering headway through the State, should find lodgment within our county jail, death would lurk within its walls for a long time and the county would be subjected to great expense in temporarily providing for the safe keeping of its prisoners; and, what is still greater moment, it would serve to extend the contagion in our midst. The remedy seems to be in the thorough renovation of the entire jail, first by scraping all the interior walls and partitions on the lower floor, so that they shall present a proper surface for the adhesion of a superior wash or cement that will not crack or peel off; secondly, by cleansing and scrubbing all floors with water charged with cleansing and disinfecting agents; and, thirdly, by painting all the cell doors, joints and contiguous parts usually covered with that article. The walls surrounding the jail are sadly in need of like attention, which they will receive at the earliest practicable moment. To the accomplishment of these objects, and procuring facilitating for the creditable administration of my office, I earnestly bespeak the interest and cooperation of your honorable body."[16]

Sheriff Cunningham took immediate steps to improve living conditions in the jail. Repair work was done in areas where repairs were needed, the interior was painted, and the sheriff made sure that the jail was kept clean. One of the biggest improvements was in the food provided to the prisoners; the sheriff's personal cook prepared all meals for the inmates.[17]

Market Street Jail
[*SJSO collection*]

Cunningham was diplomatic in his approach to the issues, but he never shied away from anything he viewed as his duty. This was but the first time Sheriff Cunningham took the county to task; he would sue San Joaquin County government officials a number of times over his career for issues that he felt they were responsible for.

Cunningham left the rehabilitation efforts at the jail in the hands of his able jailer, Deputy A. J. Tibbetts. Meanwhile, back in the field, Sheriff Cunningham was often on the trail. In April 1872, in addition to arresting the San Francisco fugitive Arthur Elmore, Cunningham hunted down a robber named Farney in the small Amador County settlement of Launcha Plana, on the north side of the Mokelumne River, about nine miles southeast of Ione.[18]

The month of May kept the sheriff on the road after thieves. On Saturday afternoon, May 18th, Cunningham learned that a horse and buggy belonging to a man named Fairbanks had been stolen from the streets around courthouse square, virtually outside of the Sheriff's Office. The sheriff obtained a description of the stolen property, but not finding any witnesses, he headed south out of town on a horse. He rode to French Camp, a distance of about ten miles, and not finding any trace of the animal or buggy, turned around and started in the other direction. His search took him back through Stockton and north to the town of Woodbridge, about fourteen miles distant. Stumped, Cunningham returned home empty handed, getting back into Stockton about eleven that night.[19]

Two days later, Cunningham was on the train to Oakdale, in Stanislaus County, after a vagabond who had stolen money from a local Stockton store owner. The vagrant had been hanging around the business of Thomas Barnes for a few days, and when Barnes left a young boy to look after the store for a short time, the tramp took the opportunity to sneak some money from the till while the boy was busy trying to work out an arithmetic problem. Barnes swore out a warrant for the man, who had given the name of Greenwood, and the sheriff started in search of the thief.[20]

The sheriff had not forgotten the horse and buggy theft, and a few days later he was back on the road, looking of clues. The search would be a long one. This time, Cunningham took the road east out of Stockton, heading for Calaveras County. He located the stolen property in Salt Spring Valley, where the scoundrel sold the horse and buggy to a man for $50. Obtaining a description of the culprit, Sheriff Cunningham traced him through Chinese Camp, Altaville and Murphys. Along the way, Cunningham picked up information on the outlaw which led him to give up his hunt at that time. He returned to Stockton with Mr. Fairbanks' horse and buggy, having ridden over 150 miles in all.[21]

Less than a week after the sheriff got back to town, another horse and buggy was stolen from around the courthouse. These thefts, in broad daylight and in front of the very symbol of law and order, was a big affront to the local lawmen, and Stockton constable Orrin Langmaid immediately started out after the thief, heading east out of town towards the Mother Lode country. Langmaid located his man, along with the stolen horse and buggy, in the town of Columbia, in Tuolumne County. The thief made an attempt on Langmaid's life by striking him in the head with a rock during an escape attempt while Langmaid was escorting him back to Stockton, but the attempt failed and the outlaw was successfully lodged in the jail on Market Street. Initially trying to make the officers believe he was insane, the thief eventually confessed to the crime, saying he was also the one who had stolen Mr. Fairbanks' property.[22]

If the lawmen were thinking they had resolved the issue of

horse and buggy theft around the courthouse, they were wrong. In mid-June, yet another horse and buggy were stolen from in front of the courthouse. Sheriff Cunningham headed east, in the direction of Milton, in Calaveras County, but a short time after he left, information came in to the Sheriff's Office that the thief had actually left heading north out of town. Deputy D. O. Harelson started in pursuit in that direction. Two days later, the Sheriff's Office received the following telegram from Harelson: "Galt, June 20, 5:27 p.m. Sheriff Cunningham—I have boy and property—Harelson." This time, the culprit was a ten-year-old boy. Amazingly, he was lodged in the Market Street jail because at that time, juveniles were treated just like adults.[23]

At the end of July, word of a shooting at the Foreman's Ranch, located along the Gold Rush era Mokelumne Hill Road in the area of present-day Linden, reached the Sheriff's Office. Sheriff Cunningham made the 12 to 14 mile ride and found that a man named Patrick Gibbons had been shot with birdshot from a shotgun by James Duncan. Duncan was arrested by Cunningham and lodged in the Stockton jail late that night. Duncan was a prominent name in the area and Gibbons was a troublesome sort, having been previously tried and acquitted of the shooting death of another man. Duncan was released on bail.[24]

In early September, Sheriff Cunningham received word of a stabbing at a sheep ranch near San Joaquin County's western border with Alameda County, near a place called Midway, on the road to Livermore. He arrived at the ranch, and for some reason decided to arrest not only the man who did the stabbing, but also the victim. The suspect, a man named L. Garcia, was held on a $500 bond on a charge of assault with a deadly weapon. The interesting part is that the victim was held on a $100 bond as a witness! Apparently, Sheriff Cunningham's instincts were right.

In the 1870s, rough play and general Tom-foolery was known as "skylarking." Generally occurring after a good drinking session when men were full of rot-gut and lacking in good judgment, these impromptu wrestling matches would sometimes result in tragedy. Such was the case for Frederick Horber. Two men, Richard Johnson and Alfred Anderson, were implicated in Horber's death, which occurred a few months after a skylarking incident.

Richard Johnson and Alfred Anderson were half-owners of a schooner named the *Caroline Z*, and were engaged in the shipping business between San Francisco and the river towns located along the San Joaquin and Sacramento rivers.

It seems that skylarking was a favorite past-time of Richard Johnson. Sometime in June of 1872, there was some sort of incident on the *Caroline Z* involving Richard Johnson and Frederick Horber that newspapers reported as a friendly wrestling match between friends. During the incident, Horber was forcefully thrown to the deck, landing on his head and sustaining severe injuries. Horber's injuries caused him to start acting strangely, and he ended up being committed to the Insane Asylum in Stockton for a couple of months before succumbing to his injuries.

Sheriff Cunningham received the report of the incident upon Horber's death in late September and he began investigating. The sheriff secured a warrant for Richard Johnson's arrest, after Cunningham received information implicating him. Sheriff Cunningham traveled to San Francisco, where he arrested Johnson. After delivering Johnson to Stockton's jail, Cunningham headed out again, this time in search of Johnson's partner, Alfred Anderson, and the *Caroline Z*, after the sheriff received information, more than likely from Johnson, that led him to believe Anderson was also involved in the fight that caused Horber's subsequent death. The *Caroline Z* was tracked to Joice

Island, in Solano County, about 15 miles from Suisun City, where Sheriff Cunningham put the irons on Alfred Anderson.

When Sheriff Cunningham got back to Stockton with Anderson, he found that Richard Johnson had been released after an examination by Justice Martin for lack of evidence. Undoubtedly, Johnson and Anderson pointed the finger at each other, and without any corroborating witnesses or evidence to go on, Anderson also never faced charges in Horber's death.[25]

In October 1872, Sheriff Cunningham made another of his frequent trips to San Francisco to make the arrest of a forger who had defrauded a victim out of $1,500 the previous May in San Joaquin County. The victim had located the suspect in San Francisco, and swore out a warrant for his arrest before a San Francisco police judge. Sheriff Cunningham went to San Francisco and made the arrest, intending to bring the suspect back to Stockton to face the charges. As part of the process, Cunningham delivered the suspect before a San Francisco magistrate, who promptly released the forger for lack of evidence when the forged check could not be produced.[26]

Like as not, Sheriff Cunningham was disappointed by the outcome of some of these cases, but he knew his job was to deliver the accused; it was up to somebody else to judge them.

That Thanksgiving, Sheriff Cunningham treated the inmates in the jail to a turkey dinner, starting a holiday tradition that lasted throughout his administration.

All of these varied cases, as well as the routine duties of the job, were gaining Thomas Cunningham invaluable experience in a short amount of time. Learning from successes and failures, he would put this hard-earned experience to good use over the next quarter of a century.

2

ONE YEAR IN

Sheriff Cunningham approached his one-year anniversary in office as the calendar page turned to the year 1873. The job kept him busy throughout the year. In addition to all of his various duties as sheriff, Thomas also remained very active in the fire company, and he was also involved with several civic committees. With all of his time monopolized, Thomas turned over the management of his saddle business to an employee.[1]

Early on in his time as sheriff, Thomas filed suit against San Joaquin County over the issue of mileage fees. Cunningham was a shrewd businessman, and as he read the law, he was entitled to mileage fees in both directions when serving subpoenas, transporting prisoners, and summoning jurors. The case was heard in the District Court in February 1873, and was appealed all the way to the California Supreme Court, which sided with Sheriff Cunningham.[2]

Thomas spent his one-year anniversary in office searching for a horse thief. In the middle of this investigation, on March 3rd,

Sheriff Cunningham escorted a prisoner to San Quentin.[3]

The horse theft case had its start on February 5th, 1873, when a riding horse belonging to the daughter of a French Camp area rancher named G. W. Sampson was stolen. Around the same time, a mare belonging to French Camp resident Franck Douillard went missing. A man named John Ward was suspected of the thefts. G. W. Sampson was a prominent citizen and had served as the Castoria Township constable since 1869. He first tried to track down Ward on his own, but after being unsuccessful in his search for about eleven days, he notified Sheriff Cunningham of the thefts. While Cunningham was leaving the Sampson's house after receiving the report, he asked if he could borrow one of Sampson's Winchester rifles, remarking that he wished that he had one himself.[4]

Over the next three weeks, Sheriff Cunningham made three successive trips down the San Joaquin Valley, travelling through Stanislaus, Merced, Fresno and Tulare counties in search of John Ward and the stolen horses. Initially unsuccessful in picking up any leads, on his third trip Cunningham located the stolen horses. After returning the horses to their owners, Cunningham returned to Stockton and learned that the wanted John Ward was actually staying in town. Officers kept an eye out, and on the evening of March 5th, Sheriff Cunningham and Deputy Tibbitts tracked Ward to a vacant house on the south side of Stockton, where he was arrested. Ward was convicted and was sentenced to three years in San Quentin.[5]

A few weeks later, on the evening of March 25th, a man named James Smith, who lived in an area known as Nightengale, southeast of Stockton on the road to Sonora, got into an argument with a brother-in-law named Michael Quinn over a long-standing disagreement. During the argument, Quinn pulled out his shooting iron. Smith out-drew Quinn, shooting him in the left side. James Smith was arrested by Sheriff Cunningham and Stockton Police Chief Jerome Myers and lodged in jail that evening.⁶

Long-time Stockton lawman Jerome Myers
[*R. Tod Ruse*]

Later that night, at about 11:00 p.m., J. P. D. Wilkens, the Stockton harbor master and city tax collector, was found unconscious on a downtown street. He had been beaten in the back of the head by some type of blunt object. The blow fractured his skull and left him clinging to life. His pockets were rifled and left inside-out.

Sheriff Cunningham and Chief Myers immediately began an investigation. Cunningham called in deputies Tibbetts and Harelson to assist. Officers determined that it was Wilkens' habit to work late into the night at his office. That night he had stopped into the Independence Saloon for a beer before walking home. He paid for his drink, taking the money out of a coin purse that had a substantial amount of money in it. Other patrons in the bar had noticed this and had commented that it wasn't safe for Wilkens to walk around that late at night with that much money on him.

Conversation turned to the shooting in Nightengale earlier in the evening, and Wilkens had replied that he had walked the streets at all hours of the night and had never been bothered, and said that he never carried a weapon.

The lawmen studied the scene of the crime and noticed some well-defined shoe prints near a boxed tree where Wilkens was found. Measurements were taken of the prints and their shape and any peculiarities were noted.

Suspicion fell on two strangers, who were wearing similar shoes. The two gave their names as George Gifford and John Russell. They were arrested on suspicion and were walked to the jail by the officers, followed by a large crowd of people.[7]

Michael Quinn lingered for a day and a half, dying on the morning March 27th. Wilkens died on the following morning.[8]

James Smith was released on April 1st after his preliminary hearing, where Justice Martin ruled the shooting was done in self-defense.[9]

The two men arrested for the Wilkens murder, who initially gave their names as George Gifford and John Russell, were actually Ira Hall and Bob Durkin. Both were wanted out of Sacramento for burglary. Stolen property from the Sacramento crime was located on both men when they were booked into the Stockton jail. The grand jury in Stockton found that there was not enough evidence to try them for the Wilkens murder, and they were sent to Sacramento on warrants charging those crimes.[10]

During the Wilkens murder investigation, Sheriff Cunningham learned that a Stockton saddle maker named George Bennett had been intimate with both Wilkens' wife and her adult daughter. Wilkens had confronted Bennett, forbidding him from coming around the Wilkens' house.

Bennett left Stockton immediately after the murder, first traveling to Salt Lake City and then to San Francisco. Evidence led Sheriff Cunningham to believe that Bennett and Wilkens' wife, Lizzie Wilkens, had conspired to kill Mr. Wilkens. The sheriff arrested George Bennett off of a San Francisco street on May 26th, 1873. Lizzie Wilkens was also arrested for the murder. Both Bennett and Lizzie Wilkens were later found not guilty after separate jury trials.[11]

A couple of weeks after those two homicide investigations, a jail escape occurred during the early afternoon of April 13th, causing Sheriff Cunningham and local officers to move into high gear. Because of his good work, Sheriff Cunningham had the escapee back in custody within three-and-a-half hours.

At about 1:00 p.m. that afternoon, Deputy Tibbetts left the jail to go pick up the meal for the prisoners. While he was gone, an inmate named Racardo, who had one month left of a six-month sentence and who had the run of the jail, forced a lock to a door leading to the jail yard. Once in the yard, Racardo stacked firewood against the outer wall and made his escape.

Deputy Tibbetts returned a short time later, and discovering the escape right away, put out the alarm. Sheriff Cunningham mounted his horse and started east out of town on the Copperopolis Road in search of Racardo. After travelling some distance and not finding any clues of the fugitive, Cunningham turned around and re-directed his search. The sheriff went to the Central Pacific Railroad station in Stockton, where he spoke to a little girl who had seen a man matching Racardo's description walking south out of town along the railroad tracks.

Sheriff Cunningham rode the tracks south out of town, following them into the area of French Camp, where he came across G. W. Sampson and his family, who were returning home from a visit to friends who lived along the San Joaquin River. Sampson reported seeing the man sitting in some tall weeds on the other side of a small vineyard, about a mile father west.

Cunningham urged his horse forward, coming across Racardo in a short time. Racardo immediately gave up when he saw the sheriff. The fugitive told Sheriff Cunningham that he would come along peacefully, but Cunningham, reassuring Racardo that he would, in fact, come peacefully, threw a lariat around his shoulders, securing the other end to his saddle horn and leading his prisoner along the road in a sort of a trot. When he got back to the Sampson place, G. W. was very amused at the sight he saw. Sampson hooked up a buggy and assisted the sheriff by returning Racardo back to jail.[12]

During these manhunts, Sheriff Cunningham undoubtedly was thinking about something that had to weigh heavily on him; Cunningham's jail held an inmate named John J. Murphy, who was scheduled to be executed on April 25th, 1873. To add to this, the condemned prisoner had been a member of Eureka Engine Company 2 at one time, and he considered Thomas Cunningham a friend.

Murphy's case had its start on October 13th, 1868, when Murphy claimed that during an argument with a brother-in-law named Patrick Murray, he shot Murray with a shotgun and killed him in self-defense. Murphy said the argument stemmed from Murray's cruel treatment of his sick wife, who was John Murphy's sister. Murphy came into town the next day and turned himself in to Sheriff Freeman Mills. He had been in custody since that day.[13]

Murphy's trial commenced on February 22nd, 1869, and was conducted over the next four days, concluding at about 4:00 p.m.

on the afternoon on February 25th. During the trial, witnesses testified that Patrick Murray had returned home on October 13th, 1868, after working all day, and was sitting by the fireplace with his bedridden wife and young son in the room when Murphy burst through the front door, leveled a double-barreled shotgun at him, and shot him without provocation.

Closing arguments started at about 7:00 p.m. on the evening on February 25th and went until 1:00 a.m. the following morning, at which time the jury was given the case. After deliberating for 50 minutes, the jury returned with a verdict against John Murphy for murder in the first degree. Judge J. M. Cavis, who presided over the trial, set over the case until the afternoon of February 27th for the pronouncement of judgment. At that time, Judge Cavis ordered that Murphy be hanged.[14]

The case was appealed and was sent back to the trial court, where Murphy was tried a second time in August 1871. He was once again convicted by a jury of murder in the first degree, and was once again sentenced to death by Judge Louis Ramage, who presided over the second trial. The conviction and death penalty were affirmed by the California State Supreme Court in June of 1871. After more appeals by Murphy's lawyers, the execution date was set for April 25th, 1873.[15]

The day before his execution, John Murphy spoke with a reporter from the *Stockton Independent*. Sheriff Cunningham stood by at Murphy's cell during the conversation:

> "'I have been four years, six months and ten days in jail. When I first came here, Mr. Collins was jailer; that man treated me as kindly as a man could desire, and his wife was like a mother to me. The next who came in was Sheriff George H. Castle. No man could be treated better than I was by Mr. Castle—be used

(sic) me kindly in every respect. Castle's jailer, C. L. Woods, was as kind to me as a man could be; he treated me like a brother. Under this administration, that is Sheriff Cunningham's, I have been treated kindly and respectfully both by him and his officers. I have known Mr. Cunningham about eighteen years, and he is and always has been a kind friend of mine, and we have had many pleasant hours together. I do not regret anything I have done that has placed me in my present situation. I think I did nothing more than brotherly love required.

"'I have a sister and brothers in the East. I came to the United States in 1842, and will be either 50 or 51 years of age on the 24th of next June. I am twenty-three years married. I believe that is all I have to say.' Turning to Sheriff Cunningham, Murphy said, 'I wish my friends to be cheerful when the last hour comes; I do not want them to show any feeling as it would disturb me—particularly you, Mr. Cunningham.'"[16]

Sheriff Cunningham had been accused by a Sacramento newspaper editor of showing preference to Murphy by allowing him freedom in the jail and actually allowing him to do errands around town without a guard or any shackles. The Stockton newspaper editor fired back, basically calling the allegations preposterous and stating the Murphy had not been allowed out of his cell during Cunningham's administration.[17]

On the day of the execution, the gallows had been erected in the jailhouse yard. The *Independent* gave details about the events of that day:

> "The sheriff, knowing his duty, terrible as it was, softened its execution by investing it with all the decorum and solemnity that befitted the taking of human life by order of the law…"[18]

At 1:00 p.m., Sheriff Cunningham led the approximately 50

invited witnesses into the jail yard.

> "About fifteen minutes after one, the Sheriff, his deputies and officers in charge of the condemned man, who was accompanied by Father Spellman, his spiritual adviser, emerged from a rear door of the jail, and, descending a few steps, took their places on the platform. The prisoner, though pale from long incarceration, appeared firm, calm, and dignified—conscious of his immediate fate, and neither daring nor dreading it.
>
> "When the condemned man was placed upon the platform, and advised that he could say anything he desired to say, he remarked in a subdued voice, substantially, 'I stand here convicted of the murder of Mr. Murray. That I killed him, there is no doubt and I have never denied it. I did it in defense of my sister and myself.'
>
> "The persons concerned being on the platform, Mr. Bennett, Undersheriff, proceeded to read the death warrant in a singularly clear, impressive and solemn manner. The prisoner stood erect, and all the witnesses uncovered. The reading done, Father Spellman, in a most impressive manner, performed the functions of his holy office, the condemned man devoutly joining. While the law officers were discharging their painful duty of preparing the condemned man for his death, the Rev. Father Spellman was upon his knees, begging Infinite mercy to do what finite justice could not do."[19]

Sheriff Cunningham bound Murphy's hands and adjusted the noose around his neck.

> "The last moment having come, the sheriff placed the sable cap over the face of the sufferer—gave the signal, and the drop fell…The act of execution took place at twenty-four minutes after one o'clock p.m. The drop was about eight feet. There was no perceptible motion of the body after the fall. The attending surgeons immediately examined the condition of the

victim…Ten minutes after the body was taken down, placed in a coffin, and taken away and consigned to the care of those who loved it while living and who treated it gently and reverently in death."[20]

Three of John Murphy's jailers and three members of Eureka Engine Company 2 acted as pallbearers. A large delegation of Eureka Engine Company members attended his funeral and his remains were interred at the Catholic cemetery in Stockton.[21]

May 1873 saw Sheriff Cunningham busy in the field. The first week of that month, Cunningham travelled to Sacramento to bring a man named Frank Brown back to Stockton on a grand larceny charge. The following week, Cunningham travelled to Oakdale to arrest John S. Tipton, a Farmington area rancher, for assault with a deadly weapon. Later that week, Sheriff Cunningham was in Lockeford, taking charge of a burglary suspect.[22]

On May 15th, Sheriff Cunningham and Stockton Police Chief Jerome Myers attended the Sacramento execution of Charles Mortimer, a life-long criminal convicted of the murder of a Sacramento saloon owner named Mary Gibson.[23]

A week later, on the afternoon of May 22nd, 1873, Sheriff Cunningham was sitting at his desk when he was summoned to the district attorney's office, where a surprise awaited him.

Emma Sampson was the young daughter of G. W. Sampson, and was the owner of one of the horses that Sheriff Cunningham had recovered and returned that March. Emma was very grateful to the sheriff for the return of her horse, and she had not forgotten the remark that Cunningham had made to her father about his desire for a Winchester rifle. Emma had urged her father and her neighbor, Franck Douillard, who had also been a victim and who had his horse returned to him by the sheriff, to purchase a rifle for Thomas Cunningham in appreciation.

Sheriff Cunningham was taken aback when he was greeted by Miss Samson and her father, Mr. Drouillard, and a contingency of Thomas's friends. His eyes then went to a beautifully engraved, 44-caliber, 1866 Winchester Yellowboy rifle. The engraving said: "Presented to Thomas Cunningham as a testimonial of our esteem for him as an officer and a citizen. Emma J. Sampson—F. Douillard, Stockton, May 15, 1873." Cunningham was very humbled by the gift of the beautiful firearm.[24]

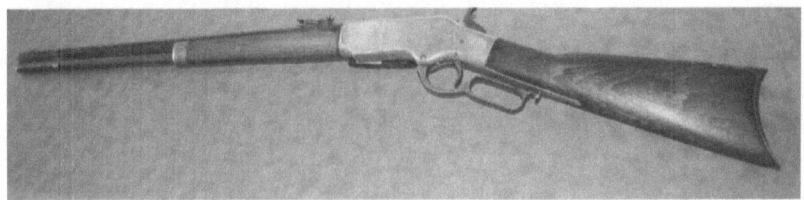

Sheriff Cunningham's 1866 Winchester
[*SJSO photo by P.J. Ruiz*]

Close-up of 1866 Winchester inscription
[*SJSO photo by P.J. Ruiz*]

Sheriff Cunningham and his deputies remained busy throughout the summer, investigating homicides in July and August, recovering stolen horses and other property, conducting a sheriff's sale, escorting prisoners to San Quentin, and investigating a stabbing and shooting incident in early September.

The July homicide occurred outside of Lockeford, in northeastern San Joaquin County, when a man named John Edgerton drove a wagonload of wood across a neighbor's field. The neighbor, Mathew Cooper, said that he had warned Edgerton not to cross his property in the past, and when confronted this time, Edgerton refused to turn around and leave Cooper's property. Cooper said that Edgerton pulled a pistol on him. With that, Cooper let loose with both barrels of his double-barreled shotgun, striking Edgerton in the head and shoulder, killing him instantly. The gunshots spooked Edgerton's horses, and he was thrown from the wagon and run over. Cooper was subsequently convicted of manslaughter after a jury trial, and was sentenced to ten years in prison.[25]

On August 23rd, 1873, Sheriff Cunningham was called to the area of Waterloo, a small settlement about eight miles northeast of Stockton, where a man was hit in the head with a crowbar during a fight. The culprit, a man named Charles Dial, had a reputation as good man and a hard worker. He owned a wheat threshing machine and had hired the victim, John Brannon, to load wheat into sacks and sew them shut. Brannon was drunk and was spilling wheat grain all over when Dial confronted him. During an argument, Brannon rushed Dial, who picked up a crowbar and struck Brannon over the head. He died later that day and Dial fled the area.[26]

Sheriff Cunningham traced Dial to Linden, where he was seen obtaining a horse and leaving the area. He told locals he would not be taken alive, but he ended up turning himself in the following day. Dial apparently didn't face charges in the case, because in May of 1880, he was reported to own over 2300 acres which were planted in wheat, and he was considered an upstanding citizen in Lockeford. Dial later served as the town's constable.[27]

Early on Sunday morning, August 31st, 1873, Sheriff Cunningham was called to an old-fashioned donnybrook that happened at McFee's Saloon in Woodbridge the previous night, where gun smoke hung in the air and a man was stabbed. It all happened as the result of a card game gone astray. Six-guns were drawn and at least one shot was fired at a man named Augustus Adams. Adams drew a knife and proceeded to the bar, where a young man named Lafayette Woods was sitting, and stabbed him in the back, inflicting a near-fatal wound. Interestingly, Augustus Adams had been employed as a wood cutter for the Woods family for about three months. Even more interestingly, Lafayette Woods' father was killed in the very same saloon eight years earlier. After sorting out the details, Sheriff Cunningham arrested Augustus Adams that morning.[28]

As if Cunningham wasn't busy enough that summer, he was also in the middle of a campaign for re-election. His efforts were successful, and he beat out a challenger named P. W. Dudley in the September elections.[29]

That fall, on October 19th, 1873, Sheriff Cunningham was called in to investigate the theft of a horse and buggy from in front of a house on El Dorado Street in Stockton. After taking the report, Cunningham and Stockton Police Officer J. J. Evans set out in search of the culprit.

Officer Evans was a good man to have along. He had been a Stockton police officer since 1868, and consistently made the most monthly arrests among Stockton's police officers. The sheriff would later name J. J. Evans as one of his deputies.³⁰

One of Sheriff Cunningham's re-election campaign posters
[*R. Tod Ruse*]

The officers caught up with the thief, Jim Williams, about eight miles outside of Stockton, where Williams was in the process of changing horses.³¹

In November, Sheriff Cunningham arrested San Joaquin County Treasurer U. S. Harrold in Sacramento, after he had been indicted by a grand jury on a misdemeanor charge of not residing in the county seat. Harrold was allowed by the court to post bail, and he was released in Sacramento.³²

On Monday, January 12th, 1874, local officers received

information that a man wanted in connection with an 1871 homicide outside of Tuolumne City was in the Stockton area.

The body of a man named Al Bryant was found on March 6th, 1871, in the Tuolumne River, about four miles below Tuolumne City, in Tuolumne County. The back of Bryant's head was crushed in and it appeared that he had been murdered. Bryant had been chopping wood in the area with a man known only as "Charley." The day after the body was discovered, Charley had bought some bottles of whiskey in Tuolumne City and got drunk. He next broke into a house, took some clothes, then stole a horse, saddle and bridle, and disappeared. A detailed description of "Charley" had been circulated, but he had not been seen since.

Stockton Police Officer R. C. Wells received the information about the suspect being in Stockton from a young man, who told him that the man wanted in the homicide had been seen in town. Following up, Wells discovered that a man fitting "Charley's" description had departed on a train for Lodi.

Intent on catching the next train to Lodi, Wells headed to the train station, where he met Sheriff Cunningham, who was waiting for the train to Sacramento. Wells told Cunningham the story and the sheriff sent a messenger to his office, instructing Undersheriff Bennett to assign Deputy Harelson to assist Officer Wells. The Undersheriff then located the young man who had initially given Officer Wells the information, and after getting the story for himself, sent the lad over to jailer Tibbetts. Tibbetts immediately recognized the description of the killer as matching that of a man he currently had in custody for public drunkenness.

Stockton Police Officer William Collins was detailed to immediately take the prisoner, who had identified himself as George Cunningham, to the police court, where he was sentenced to nine days. This gave officers the chance to investigate.

Deputy Tibbetts realized that the prisoner had been in his jail the previous spring for drunkenness, and at that time had given his name as McCarthy. In addition to Cunningham and McCarthy, he had also used the names Hunt and Greenhorn, but it was believed that his true name was Charles Everson.[33]

Sheriff Cunningham's 1851 Colt's Navy
[*R. Tod Ruse*]

Shortly after Bryant's murder was discovered, Governor Haight had authorized a $300 reward for Everson's arrest and conviction, but the outcome of the case wasn't reported.[34]

On Tuesday, January 13th, Sheriff Cunningham met with Alameda County Sheriff Harry Morse in San Jose. The nature of their meeting was not reported on, but it would come into focus in the following months.[35]

Three days later, on the afternoon of February 16th, 1874, Sheriff Cunningham was summoned to the Lodi area, where a man named J. Q. A. Williams had knifed his step-father, Daniel Crist, cutting his face. Williams ended up pleading guilty, and received a fine of $100 in gold or 50 days in the county jail.[36]

Back when Thomas Cunningham was sheriff, all county officials' salaries and fees were regulated by state law. The amount of money granted to the sheriff was the Office's operating budget for the year, and included salaries for his deputies. At the beginning of his time in office, Cunningham's annual salary was set at $5,500. Travel expenses were also regulated. These numbers had been adopted for the San Joaquin County sheriff's position by a legislative act of 1871-1872, known as the Woodward Bill.[37]

In February 1874, Sheriff Cunningham petitioned the legislature to increase his salary, fees and travel expenses, listing all of his expenses of office and giving a snapshot of the Sheriff's Office at the time:

Salary for an Undersheriff, at $150 a month..........................$1,800
Salary of an outside Deputy, at $125 a month.......................$1,500
Salary for principal jailer, at $100 a month............................$1,200
Salary of assistant jailer, per year..$800
Retaining fee of attorney, per year...$500
Total $5,800
Sheriff's salary for self and all deputies, under Woodward's bill....$5,500

The sheriff reported that he kept three horses in livery for the use of the Sheriff's Office, and hired vehicles as required. Travel expenses included all expenses for each officer and his animal, railroad fares, boat fares, and tolls over roads and bridges. Office expenses also included hiring extra help when needed, telegraph expenses, and any other expenses relating to running the Office.[38]

Back on the road in early March 1874, Sheriff Cunningham made two trips to San Quentin; one trip on March 4th to return a prisoner named J. H. Smith to testify before the grand jury in Stockton, and a March 10th trip to deliver a prisoner named William Briggs, sentenced to seventeen months for housebreaking.[39]

Cunningham made it back to town just in time to take part in the longest manhunt of his career.

3

HUNTING BANDITS

California was plagued by bands of roaming bandits at the time Thomas Cunningham became sheriff. These loosely-knit groups of marauders included gangs of Mexicans and native Californians of Mexican descent who operated throughout the state, pillaging, terrorizing and killing citizens. Outlaws the likes of Joaquin Murrietta had operated freely all over California since the Gold Rush era. These bandits were very difficult for law officers to deal with because they would often do one or two crimes together and then go their separate ways, and they operated over vast geographical areas. They often stayed in very isolated places where outsiders were easily detected, making it very difficult for local lawmen to successfully follow and apprehend them.

Citizens in San Joaquin County became very familiar with the brutality dispensed by these criminals when five men were murdered at the Medina store, a roadside store and way-stop along what would become modern-day Shelton Road, near Bellota, in December 1869. The victims had been marched across the road from the store and shot execution-style in an area of tailings from a nearby mine. San Joaquin County Sheriff Freeman Mills and his men cut the killers' trail and followed it to a small settlement along the Stanislaus River called Langwarths, but lost it there.[1]

Officers determined the identities of the three men suspected in the murders through witness interviews. They were identified as Jesus Tejada, alias Peres, described as tall and thin with curly hair, high cheek bones, narrow chin, slightly marked with small pox, with a gunshot wound scar on the arm, about thirty-nine years old; a man named Isodor or Isodoro, described as being about twenty-two years old, light complexion, round, smooth face, red spot in the corner of the left eye, with a very small foot. Isodore was later identified as Isadore Padilla, also reported as Isodoro Padillo and Ysidoro Purdillo, who had been raised in the Marysville area and who had connections to Stockton. The third suspect was named as Antone or Antonio, an Indian, five-and-a-half-feet tall, heavy set, round face, about twenty-two years old. Antone was later identified as Antonio Garcia, but Garcia was never brought to justice.[2]

Jesus Tejada (left) and Isadore Padilla
[*Terry Eproson*]

Alameda County Sheriff Harry Morse had been seeking information on the killers since hearing of the Medina murders. Morse spoke Spanish and utilized informants, and in May of 1870 came across some information regarding the whereabouts of Jesus Tejada. Harry and his deputy, Lewis Morehouse, made a trip from San Leandro to the Los Banos Creek area of the Coast Range mountains, a one hundred and fifty mile one-way trip, in search of their prey.

Morse made a very risky trip into the canyon and spied a man he thought to be Tejada in a camp full of hard-looking outlaws, but the original description circulated on Tejada did not match. Morse returned home to firm up his understanding of Tejada's actual description before he and Morehouse made a second trip to the canyon. Morse was successful this time, grabbing his man just after dark and getting out of the area before Tejada's confederates were able to mount an assault.[3]

Alameda County Sheriff Harry Morse was a lifelong friend of Sheriff Cunningham
[*Author's collection*]

Five months passed before officers in Marysville located and arrested Isodore Padilla. Interestingly, Marysville officer Henry McCoy had been in Stockton in 1869 when word of the Medina murders had reached town, and he had volunteered to assist in the original search for the killers. McCoy was one of the officers who finally located Padilla, and slapped the irons on him on October 12th, 1870. He escorted Padilla on the train to Stockton the following day.[4]

Trials for Tejada and Padilla commenced in the Stockton courtroom of District Court Judge Samuel Booker in May 1871. After separate trials, both men were found guilty and sentenced to hang. Both convictions were subsequently overturned on appeal. Jesus Tejada died in the Stockton jail on April 10th, 1872, while awaiting a new trial. Several of the key witnesses used in Padilla's first trial were no longer available, and he was acquitted after a second jury trial. Sheriff Cunningham released him from custody on May 20th, 1872, but the two were destined to meet again.[5]

The most notorious bandido of them all in the 1870s was Tiburcio Vasquez, a native Californian of Mexican heritage who was born to a respectable family in Monterey in 1835. Despite this, Tiburcio took up with the wrong crowd and became troublesome as a young teenager. He was sentenced to San Quentin prison in November 1857 for grand larceny from Los Angeles County. He took part in a massive prison break where a number of people were killed in June 1859.[6]

Authorities caught up with Vasquez that August, when he was arrested in Amador County for larceny and sent back to San Quentin. When he was released from that stretch in the prison, he took up with his old pals in the area around Sonoma County, where he was thought to be part of a cattle theft ring operating in

Napa and Sonoma counties, and he was arrested for a July 4th, 1866 Petaluma burglary, where he received a four-year sentence.[7]

Soon after his release from prison, Tiburcio fell back into his criminal ways. He became a member of a roving pack of robbers and thieves headed by Procopio Bustamonte. He was named as a participant in a robbery of the San Benito stagecoach south of Hollister in April of 1872, where the coach and all of its passengers were separated from their valuables. After their load was lightened, the driver and passengers were bound together with one rope and left face-down in the road. One of the robbers, Jose Castro, was reported to have been caught and summarily hanged. The rest of the gang fled south.[8]

Tiburcio Vasquez was not named in the papers again for about ten months, but by mid-1873, his name was on every tongue in California after he and a small band of outlaws committed a number of crimes around the central state. Their depredations were such that by the end of 1873, the sensation and panic created by Vasquez and his men caused reported sightings of them all around the state. Every stage holdup or other violent crime in California was attributed to the brigands.

Many of the state's most hardened criminals and ex-convicts joined Vasquez's group. One man, Cleodoveo Chavez, became Vasquez's lieutenant. A young vaquero of about twenty-four, he apparently had never been in trouble before he fell in with Tiburcio. He quickly became one of Vasquez's most trusted soldiers.

Vasquez and his cohorts would commit crimes in settlements and then retreat into the mountain ranges along the California coast and those north of Los Angeles. These areas were very sparsely populated, with no means of communication. Those who did live in the mountain canyons were either allies of Vasquez or were deathly afraid of him. The movements of any strangers were immediately reported to Vasquez.

In early 1873, Vasquez started a violent crime spree that lasted into 1874. On February 26th, 1873, Tibercio Vasquez, Cleodoveo Chavez and four other men rode up to the store at Firebaugh's Ferry, along the San Joaquin River in Fresno County, and simultaneously robbed the store and an arriving stagecoach. The men were apparently feeling chivalrous at this time, as detailed in the *Fresno Expositor* of March 19th, 1873:

> "...They made their appearance in the store about dark, all masked save one, and commanded those in the store to lie down on the floor and keep quiet. Enforcing their demand by presenting cocked revolvers, they proceeded to tie the captor's hands... The robbers then began to search for coin and valuables. About this time the stage drove up, which startled the outlaws somewhat, but a deputation went out and took charge of what money the driver had and also the Wells Fargo and Co.'s box. Mrs. Hoffman's watch was also returned upon her entreating them so to do, the robber having it saying that they didn't come there to rob women..."[9]

The March 20th edition of the *Sacramento Daily Union* reported, "The people at San Benito have been greatly excited ever since the last bold robbery at Firebaugh's Ferry. The gang of robbers had its headquarters in the neighboring mountains and the people are afraid of another raid."[10]

Some time in July 1873, a number of Mexican thieves made a raid on a herd of cattle near Firebaugh's Ferry, and, along with the drover of the cattle, fled into the nearby Diablo Range mountains.[11]

On August 26th, 1873, the gang rode into the tiny village of Tres Pinos, near San Juan Bautista, intent on robbing a store and hotel there. In the process, three bystanders were shot and killed.

The *Daily Alta California* printed an account of what happened in its August 28th, 1873 edition:

"HOLLISTER—August 27—At 8 o'clock, eight Californians rode up to the store of Mr. Snyder, about twelve miles from Hollister at the crossroad from Tres Pinos to the San Benito River. No suspicions were aroused, because the native Californians are very numerous... They dismounted and entered the store. Some engaged in conversation, and others occupied the attention of the clerk, John Utzrath, until all seemed to be in readiness, when they drew their revolvers and ordered the inmates of the store, some three or four in number, to lie down, which they did. So quietly did they proceed that the clerk was surprised when he turned around to see the prostate forms, and was still more so when requested to lie down himself, with two or three revolvers aimed at him. He laid down, and part of the robbers proceeded to bind their hands behind their backs and pinion their legs together. While this was going on within, the terrified prisoners were startled at the report of three pistol shots without, which proved to be the death-knell of Mr. L. Davidson, proprietor of the hotel, Mr. Redford, a teamster, and a Portuguese sheep herder, name unknown. It seems that these three men, being outside the building, did not readily obey the commands of the assassins or attempted to escape, and were instantly killed, two of them being shot through the breast and the other in the mouth. The robbers then proceeded to search for plunder and money. Mrs. Snyder lives in the house adjacent the store, and the robbers ordered her to deliver up all the money she had, which she did readily. They then went to Mr. Snyder and released him on his promise to give up all his money, which he did, amounting to some $500 in coin, and several hundred dollars in checks and drafts. After completing their search for money and jewelry, having ransacked the money drawers and pockets of all their victims, they proceeded to divest themselves of their clothes and dressed up in Mr. Snyder's best clothes, of which he has plenty upon his shelves. Only one of the bands was masked and two or three of them are well-known. All the time they conducted themselves in a cool and intrepid manner, proving themselves to be the desperate band that Vasquez has so long been credited with leading. But little was said, and that in a whisper. Vasquez himself remarked that $5000 reward had been offered for his head. After completing the robbery, they took all the horses they could find and left, most of them going toward the San Benito."[12]

Tres Pinos was still within the boundaries of Monterey County at that time, and Monterey County Sheriff Andrew Wasson and Santa Clara County Sheriff John Adams arrived in Tres Pinos at about noon the next day. They organized a posse and headed out of the settlement at about 5:00 p.m. that afternoon. Governor Booth offered a $1000 reward for the arrest and conviction of Tiburcio Vasquez and his gang members. Sheriff Morse was reported to be searching the San Joaquin Valley, along the Diablo Range mountains, for the gang.[13]

The sheriffs learned that the robbers had been seen at a place called Willow Creek, about forty miles from Tres Pinos, by some campers at daylight that morning. Wasson and Adams split up, doubling the amount of territory they could cover. Adams popped out into the San Joaquin Valley, travelling through Visalia and Bakersfield. He received reports that Vasquez and his men were many hours ahead of him and heading to the Elizabeth Lake area in Los Angeles County.[14]

Sheriff Adams teamed up with Los Angeles County Sheriff William Rowland and continued pursuit, following the gang eastward through the mountains of Los Angeles County. Sheriff Rowland stayed with Sheriff Adams and his party to Canyon Pass, in San Bernardino County, before turning back. Adams' posse continued across the Sierra Madre, coming upon an abandoned camp left by the Vasquez gang. Adams and one of his possemen ended up in a gunfight with a couple of the robbers at Little Rock Creek Canyon before they lost the trail in very difficult terrain.[15]

Santa Clara County Sheriff
John Adams
[*History San Jose*]

During their retreat and while in the Elizabeth Lake area, one member of Vasquez's gang, Abdon Leiva, found his wife in a compromising position with Tiburcio Vasquez. Raging and wanting revenge, Leiva drew a revolver on Vasquez and threatened to shoot him, but was prevented from doing so by Cleodoveo Chavez. Leiva then did the next-best thing; he left the group, turned himself over to Sheriff Rowland, and began squawking like a parrot. Leiva talked about all of the gangs' crimes, and he named names.[16]

The group's depredations continued through that year and Vasquez recruited new members, reportedly to include Isadore Padilla; yes, that Isadore Padilla, the same one Sheriff Cunningham had released from jail in May 1872 after he was acquitted of the Medina murders.[17]

Tiburcio Vasquez
[*California State Library*]

Nearly every person who crossed paths with these bandits fell victim and were robbed of whatever thing of value they had on them. The bandits were back north on November 10th, when members of the gang raided Jones's store near Millerton, along the river in Fresno County. There were about a dozen men congregated in the store around six that evening, smoking and playing cards, when the front and rear doors were opened simultaneously and three men walked through, each with revolvers drawn and cocked. The guns were pointed at each of the victims, while the bandit leader ordered them to cough up their valuables, lie down, and keep quiet, on the peril of their life. The men had their hands tied, then the store clerk was ordered to open the safe, the bandits taking everything from within it. The leader then invited each of his men to help themselves to whatever clothing they wanted, along with all the firearms in the place, and a new saddle each. The gang stayed at the store for an hour or more, leisurely ransacking and enjoying themselves before departing.[18]

Two days later, on November 12th, a sheep herder was shot several times by Cleovaro Chavez, who then cut his throat. This happened near New Idria, in Monterey County. Chavez had been accompanied on that crime by another unknown outlaw. Chavez's partner in the crime was chased down by a citizen's posse. He confessed and was summarily hanged, but Chavez got away.[19]

Vasquez's gang staged their biggest and boldest crime yet on the day after Christmas 1873, when they raided two stores and a hotel, tying up and robbing thirty-five people in a place called Kingston, in Fresno County.

About a dozen outlaws tied their horses along the bank of the Kings River across from the settlement and walked across the bridge into town that evening. The bandits were heavily armed, Tibercio Vasquez himself reported to have been carrying four Navy revolvers. The cut-throats took possession of the hotel and two stores, tying up about thirty-five men, then rifling through all the safes and cash drawers. All of the victims were relieved of their valuables. A stagecoach rolled into town during the raid, and all of the passengers and driver were gone through.

An alarm was spread of the takeover, and armed men began appearing. A shootout commenced, forcing the bandits to flee towards the Coast Range mountains with armed citizens in pursuit. The next morning, traces of blood were found on the bridge, indicating that one of the outlaws had been hit. The posse was successful in capturing one of the bandits, but the others fled into the mountains.[20]

Vasquez's crimes had been widely reported on throughout the state in both English and Spanish newspapers and his description had been widely publicized. Californians were completely up in arms and outraged by Tiburcio Vasquez and his followers. Public outcry was succinctly summed up in a *Los Angeles Herald* editorial, which said:

> "Though almost a week has passed away since the unparalleled outrage at Kingston, in Fresno County, and although this is the second raid made by the desperado Vasquez, we have not yet learned of any decided measures being taken by the authorities to bring this band of ruffians to justice. That a town can be captured, and its citizens turned over to plunder, is a disgrace to the whole State, and the authorities at Sacramento should take such action as will ensure the utter extermination of this band of cut-throats. Rewards for these criminals, dead or alive, ought to be offered in an amount that will fill the mountains with eager pursuers. Extermination is the only cure for these marauders."[21]

The legislature was quick to act, passing a bill authorizing Governor Newton Booth to spend $15,000 from the state treasury for a manhunt. The governor also authorized a reward for the capture of Vasquez: $3,000 alive and $2,000 dead![22] A slight incentive to bring him in still kicking.

The job of heading the posse charged with capturing Vasquez was highly coveted, and many of the state's sheriffs were hoping for the appointment, including Santa Clara County Sheriff John Adams and Los Angeles County Sheriff William Rowland. The governor ultimately chose Alameda County Sheriff Harry Morse to head the expedition, and authorized an eight-man posse. Morse immediately picked his friend Thomas Cunningham as his second-in-command. Although Cunningham had only been in office for less than two years at that point, Morse cited Cunningham's reputation as a stellar lawman in choosing him.

The other members of the posse were former Santa Cruz County Sheriff Ambrose Calderwood, deputy sheriffs Harry Thomas and Ralph Faville, and Morse's son, George Morse. A man named David Davids acted as the group's cook and general utility man. Rounding out the posse was Ramon Romero, a prison convict who was also an accomplished vaquero, acting as a guide. Romero was thoroughly familiar with the mountain ranges the posse would need to traverse. Morse also allowed a newspaper correspondent with the *San Francisco Chronical*, A. B. Henderson, to accompany the group.[23]

Ramon Romero's story is an interesting one, and in many ways his appointment to the posse was a surprise. Romero had been convicted of killing two men in two separate incidents in the 1860s. The first murder occurred in a dance hall in Oakland in 1860, where Romero killed a man named John Doane. Romero was convicted of first-degree murder and had been sentenced to death, but the California Supreme Court had overturned the conviction, and after a second trial, Romero was found not guilty. Five months later, Romero stabbed Luis Gamboa to death in a Sacramento dance hall. He was convicted of second-degree murder and was sentenced to twelve years in San Quentin. Romero was pardoned in March of 1872. (He was sentenced to life in San Quentin in 1877, after killing another man in Contra Costa County, but his sentence was commuted in 1898 by Governor James Budd, partially on the recommendation of Thomas Cunningham. Cunningham wrote the governor a letter, talking about the valuable service that Romero had provided Harry Morse's posse during the hunt for Tiburcio Vasquez.)[24]

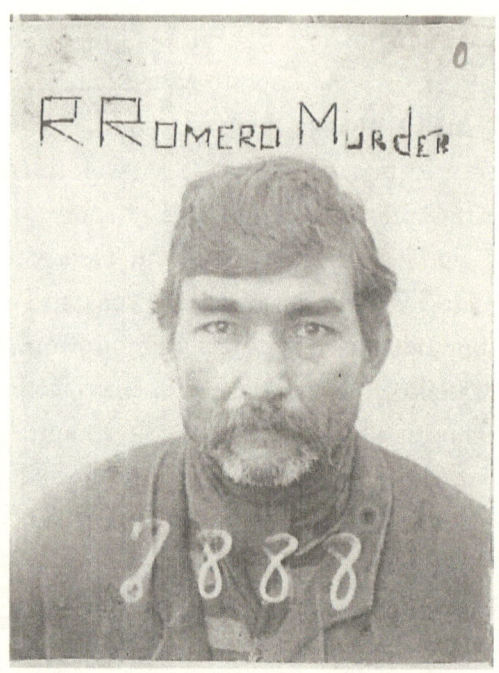

Ramon Romero in 1877
[*Cunningham's mug book, SJSO collection*]

Sheriff Morse spent nearly two months preparing for the manhunt. Morse sent two of his men ahead to Firebaugh's Ferry with a wagon full of provisions. He and the other possemen left Oakland about two weeks later, on March 12th, taking a train to Lathrop to meet up with Sheriff Cunningham.[25]

The lawmen rode the train down to a place called Berenda, then met up with the others at Firebaugh's Ferry. From there, they began a search that led them from the San Joaquin River to the coast, from Fresno and Monterey counties in the north, to Los Angeles County in the south. They scoured the Coast Range mountains, back and forth, going into isolated and remote places that were very dangerous for lawmen to venture into. They recovered many stolen horses and cattle, but their prey eluded them.

The posse continued on with the manhunt, driving south and searching the desolate canyon areas of the Coast Range, but they were having trouble picking up leads. Sheriff Morse wrote a dispatch to Governor Booth, saying, "It is going to be hard work to find Vasquez, he has so many friends among the Mexicans; they hide him and feed him, and lie to the officers."[26]

Morse and his posse met many dead ends, the people living in the mountain canyons sending them on false pursuits. Henderson wrote of their challenges for his newspaper:

> "Morse believed it would be an easy matter to find Vasquez if he could only induce the Mexican settlers in this region to disclose his lurking place. He therefore offered to them a reward of $1,000, in addition to the entire sum offered by the state, if they would simply furnish him information that would bring him in sight of Vasquez; but...there is some sort of glamour about the character and career of Vasquez in the eyes of the Mexican settlers and they all, with one accord, professed to have no knowledge of the bandit's whereabouts and declined to furnish any information concerning him. Vasquez's Mexican friends will not betray him, and his friends numbered most of the Mexicans in this region, who all admire the doughty robber in greater or less degree."[27]

At the end of March, the posse cut the trail of gang member Manuel Lopez, who was reported to have slain six men. They pursued him for several days through the Santa Lucia mountains, hampered by cold and hunger, but Lopez eluded them.[28]

Morse's posse reached the Tehachapi mountains on April 12th, from where he sent a wire to Governor Booth: "Have been in the saddle every day, sleeping out from our wagon with only one blanket and about half the time without eating. Our greatest trouble is in getting fresh horses, every new lot of horses are grass fed and they don't stand our riding very long."[29]

Newspaper reporters kept very close tabs on the lawmen who were searching for Vasquez, keeping the bandit chief abreast of their every move. The *Stockton Daily Independent* of April 17th talked about the events of that time:

> "LOS ANGELES—April 15—The Sheriff (Rowland) this morning about eight o'clock received information that Vasquez, with four of his men, was at San Gabriel Mission, where they took up an Italian named Alexander Reparto and compelled him to sign a check on a bank here for $800, and sent his son with the check to draw the money, threatening him with death if he divulged anything about it. The cashier mistrusted that something was wrong and the boy told the story. The Sheriff immediately left with a posse of fifteen men. He has just returned, and reports that it was Vasquez. His men are after them, and he is now getting ten additional men to assist. The man was tied up, but upon the appearance of the Sheriff they untied him and fled. The Sheriff's party are about one mile behind them. Rogers, one of the party, has just returned. He saw Reparto, who said they were all Mexicans. The boy drew $500 on the check, and the Sheriff sent him ahead with the money. It is not known yet if Vasquez got the money. They have gone towards San Fernando Pass. The Sheriff has gone again with reinforcements."[30]

Showing unbelievable audacity, while on the run with Sheriff Rowland's posse in pursuit, Vasquez and his men took the time to stop three men along the road near the head of the Arroyo Seco, relieving the victims of everything of value. As the Vasquez gang rode out of sight of their victims, the sheriff's posse rode into view, being only about a half-mile behind the bandits.³¹

A later dispatch told the following story:

> "The excitement over the Vasquez pursuit continues. At sundown, four more mounted men started to join the pursuers. Sheriff Rowland's party are following closely in Soledad Canyon. Morse and eight men were at Elizabeth Lake last night coming south. There is no doubt as to the identity of Vasquez. The last robbery at the Arroyo Seco, was committed within three miles of this city."³²

On Monday, April 20th, Sheriff Morse and Sheriff Cunningham made a visit to Los Angeles. A *Los Angeles Herald* reporter described their appearance:

> "On Monday night, Harry Morse, Sheriff of Alameda County, and Thomas Cunningham, Sheriff of San Joaquin County, were in this city. They came unheralded and in such questionable shape that their most intimate friends had to take a square look before recognizing them. They looked more like a couple of dilapidated sheep herders than the High Sheriff's of two of the most wealthy and populous counties. Both wore old thread-bare coats and flannel shirts without collars; their hats could be changed to any desirable shape without damage to the article or great exertion on the part of the owners. The hair of each was cut short and their faces were tanned...
>
> "These two sheriffs have been in the Coast Range since the 8th of March, and no doubt know more of the habits of Vasquez and his gang than any other two men in the State. They left yesterday as they came—quietly and without saying where they thought they were going. That they had a party of armed men not over thirty miles from this city, we chance to know; and that they will keep the bandit on the move, if they do not capture

him, we confidently believe. Both Morse and Cunningham are brave as lions, keen on the scent of outlaws and well acquainted with the desperate Mexican characters in the State. They know the Coast and Sierra ranges from the Shasta Butte to San Gorgonio Pass. If but once they are on Vasquez's trail while it is warm, the people of California may expect to hear of some desperate fighting and of the bandit's death or capture."[33]

The Stockton newspaper reported on April 23rd about Sheriff Morse's posse's movements:

"Los Angeles, April 22—Vasquez, followed closely by Major Mitchell and the men of Sheriff Rowland's posse, abandoned his horses at Little Tejara Canyon and took to the mountains on foot yesterday morning. The party, reinforced by Sheriff Rowland and four men, started last night from this city. Sheriff Morse and Sheriff Cunningham and men probably join with the Los Angeles parties in hunting the bandits down. Morse is supposed to be on the other side of the mountain. Vasquez's camp was captured, and also all his horses."[34]

Los Angeles County Sheriff William Rowland
[*Santa Clarita Valley History*]

On the morning of April 30th, Morse and Cunningham arrived at El Tejon and received a tip that Vasquez and Chavez had left Los Angeles County and were headed north to the New Idria mines. The information ultimately turned out to be bogus, but the lawmen immediately sunk spurs and headed in that direction, trailing two riders to the area of Zapato Chino Creek. Here, the sheriffs split the posse, Morse and Cunningham taking different routes and meeting up at New Idria on May 7th. From there they moved north and east, searching the mountains and canyons and arriving at the San Luis Rancho on May 10th.

The following morning, the posse headed north to Banta, where they caught the train for home. Cunningham arrived back in Stockton on May 12th.[35]

Two days later, information came from Los Angeles that Sheriff Rowland and his posse had Tiburcio Vasquez in custody. Acting on information, the sheriff located Vasquez and two of his men in the cabin of a man known as Greek George, in Nicholas Canyon, southwest of Los Angeles. Vasquez was shot and wounded by a posse member and was taken into custody.[36]

Vasquez was taken to San Jose, where he stood trial for the Tres Pinos crime. Convicted of murder, he was hanged by Santa Clara County Sheriff John Adams on March 19th, 1875.[37]

Sheriff Morse and Sheriff Cunningham were disappointed that they were not the ones to slap irons on Tiburcio Vasquez. Still in all, they were professionals and knew of their valuable contribution to the hunt. Sheriff Morse reported to the governor that he and his posse had ridden for 61 days, covering over 2700 miles in that time. The grueling trip had taken them through heavy rains and swollen rivers at times, with the hunt taking place not only during daylight hours but sometimes at night. Morse said that they broke up many dens of reputed murderers and thieves in places where officers had never ventured to go before. For his part, Cunningham later said that this was the most grueling manhunt he ever took part in.[38]

Sheriff Cunningham did not have a long rest period when he got back to town; there was always something else to do.

4

A DARK TIME

Deputy Tibbetts assisted with a felony arrest during Sheriff Cunningham's long absence. The incident occurred in Stockton late on Saturday night, April 4th, 1874, when Fernando Lastreto struck Arthur Hussey over the head with his revolver for no apparent reason, causing a deep cut. A warrant was issued for Lastreto, but he had disappeared.

Officers kept up the search for Lastreto, and on Monday, April 6th, they received a tip that he was hiding in a house near the railroad depot on the east side of town. Deputy Tibbetts and Chief of Police Jerome Myers went to the house, but Lastreto wasn't there. They searched the area and found him hiding in the middle of a nearby field. Lastreto was held to answer by the court and was lodged in the jail.[1]

On May 30th, 1874, Sheriff Cunningham took a report from a young man who came into the courthouse, saying that $100 had been stolen from his pants pocket while he was staying at a house east of Stockton. The victim suspected two strangers that had stopped at the house. Cunningham obtained a description of the two men and rode out to the area to investigate. Not finding any trace of the strangers, Cunningham returned to town but kept his eyes open.

Two days later, the sheriff was out on the street when he saw a man who matched the description of one of the thieves. Cunningham approached the man, and, using a ploy, asked if the man might be interested in a job. The man said he was, but he needed to tell his partner that he was leaving. The sheriff said that he was actually in need of two men, and inquired as to if the partner might also be in need of work. They met up with the partner, who matched the description of the second thief. Instead of heading out to the country for some manual labor, the two found themselves in the county jail for some rest and relaxation.[2]

That July, Sheriff Cunningham became involved in a four-year-old murder case. On August 10th, 1870, a Chinese man was murdered in Stockton by two other Chinese men who attacked the victim with a hatchet and knife. The two killers fled as a Stockton police officer ran into the area, responding to the victim's cries.

Stockton has always had a large Chinese community, and the people of the community trusted Thomas. In early July 1874, Sheriff Cunningham got word that the two killers, Ah Shoo and Ah Nam, had returned from China and were working at a cigar factory on Clay Street, in San Francisco. The following day, the sheriff left for San Francisco, accompanied by his informant, who could identify the killers. With the assistance of San Francisco Police Officer Edwin Eaton, Cunningham took the two into custody on July 3rd. Both were armed with revolvers at the time, but they were disarmed and taken without incident. They were returned to Stockton on the train the next day.³

San Joaquin County saw a number of horse thefts during the summer of 1874, and the sheriff and his deputies were kept busy arresting horse thieves and recovering stolen horses. One of the victims was Deputy D. O. Harelson, who had his horse stolen on August 1st. The suspect in that case, John Brown, alias Douglas, alias Foster, was arrested eight miles outside of Oroville, and was returned to Stockton on September 2nd by Sheriff Cunningham.⁴

Later in September, Thomas made back-to-back trips to San Quentin with prisoners. He was in San Francisco on September 16th with William Kennedy, sentenced to a two-year stretch for grand larceny. Two days later, Cunningham was escorting Emma and George Beyer, sentenced for bigamy and grand larceny.⁵

Just before Christmas in 1874, Sheriff Cunningham was involved in another long manhunt. During the previous two years, a card sharp named James Russell, but who was widely known as "Slim Jim," led a group of con men who fleeced people out of thousands of dollars in crooked card games on long-distance trains. This group operated in three or four western states on the Central Pacific Railroad, and they generated a lot of publicity.

One member of the group, a monte-sharp whose last name was Lewis, alias Roper, was arrested by railroad officers in Salt Lake City for theft, but he broke jail. Lewis travelled west and rejoined his group, traveling on trains between Sacramento and San Francisco. He was arrested by railroad officers in Stockton on Thursday, December 10th, on an escape warrant from Utah.

Lewis turned over a large amount of watches and jewelry, plunder from his crimes, to his attorney, and he was released on $500 bail.

Railroad officers, fearing that Lewis might make such a move, had already secured another warrant for his arrest and they re-arrested him as soon as he was released. A deputy U.S. marshal from Utah was on his way to Stockton with a requisition from the Utah governor to take Lewis back with him, but Lewis was turned loose by Justice Buckley before that could happen. One member of the gang was waiting for Lewis outside with a team of horses and a wagon, and they high-tailed it out of town.

Railroad officers quickly obtained a third warrant for Lewis and placed it into Sheriff Cunningham's hands. Lewis and his cohort had about a thirty-minute start on the sheriff, but Thomas grabbed his trusty mount and started in pursuit.

Lewis kept the team on the run until he reached a point about eighteen miles east of Stockton, known as Messick's Bridge, where the sheriff was crowding them closely. Seeing Cunningham, Lewis jumped out of the wagon and headed for nearby brush, while his partner turned around and started back to Stockton with the jaded team. Darkness had fallen by then, so Sheriff Cunningham posted some local men in the area and returned to Stockton to organize the chase.

Accompanied by railroad special agent F. F. Burke, the sheriff returned to the area the following morning, tracing Lewis to a ranch about four miles from the bridge. Lewis had purchased a horse from the rancher, Frank Fagan, paying for the animal with a bogus check written from a Utah bank.

The lawmen started trailing Lewis in a carriage, easily keeping track of him by the description of his iron-grey horse. Lewis went through Farmington, in San Joaquin County, then crossed the Stanislaus River into Stanislaus County at about 2:00 a.m. on Saturday morning. By noon that day, Lewis had made the Tuolumne River, and he continued south through Stanislaus

County and into Merced. Steering towards Swan's Ferry on the Merced River, Lewis then turned west, making several twists and turns in hopes of losing the lawmen. Lewis spent Saturday night at a place called Dutch Corners, then started out for San Jose through the Pacheco Pass on Sunday morning. He took another detour, being tracked to Los Gatos Canyon. That route would bring him out either at Mission San Jose or at Milpitas.

Sheriff Cunningham became convinced that Lewis was trying to make his way to his partners in San Francisco. Cunningham wired all of the sheriffs in the area, then left Agent Burke to follow the trail while he went to San Francisco. Thomas had just reached San Francisco when he received word that Lewis had been arrested south of San Jose by Santa Clara County Sheriff John Adams. Having abandoned his horse at a way-stop near Gilroy, Lewis had been travelling to town with an area farmer when he was taken into custody.

Lewis was taken back to Utah by a deputy U.S. marshal. He was convicted of stealing $485 during a crooked three-card monte game, and received a six-month sentence in the Utah State Penitentiary.[6]

On returning to Stockton, Cunningham was soon turning around and heading back to San Quentin with two prisoners: James Langley, convicted of grand larceny and sentenced to two years, and Volney Cleveland, a burglar, also sentenced to two years.[7]

That Christmas, Thomas received a wonderful gift from his friend Harry Morse, who sent him a solid-silver cartridge belt buckle.[8]

In January 1875, a group of Thomas's friends, grateful for the service that he had given the citizens of California for the part he played in helping track down Tiburcio Vazquez, bought him a beautiful iron-grey horse that he had been admiring. They surprised Cunningham with their gift on January 15th, 1875. Hitching the horse across the street from the courthouse, two of his friends sent a note to Cunningham:

> "January 15, 1875—There is a crowd of suspicious looking persons on Main Street, near our business. They are in possession of fine-looking horse, which they are talking about disposing of at a price greatly below its real value. Come and investigate. Evans and O'Brien."[9]

The note found Cunningham in his office, studying some paperwork. As he left the courthouse, Thomas headed over to the group surrounding the horse and was greeted by a number of his friends. Stopping to chat with them, he asked who owned the horse that they were standing around. Taking the reins and handing them to Cunningham, J. M. Hogan, the previous owner, made a small speech. Hogan concluded by saying, "and now, sir, allow me to present him to you. Take him, and when in pursuit of the fleeing fugitive, do as you have always done—spare neither hide nor hoof."[10]

On February 19th, 1875, Sheriff Cunningham and Chief Myers attended the executions of convicted killers Phillip Cotta and Domingo Estrada in Sacramento.[11]

In early March, Sheriff Cunningham appointed a man named Charles McMurray as the deputy in charge of the jail in place of A. J. Tibbetts, who resigned his position. Tibbetts had done a very admirable job as the jailer, working hard to keep the jail in a clean and secure condition. McMurry only held the position for a few months; by early May, Alonso A. McCloud was the deputy in charge of the jail. McCloud had previously served as the jailor for

Sheriff George Webster in 1858. He continued to serve as a lawman through most of the 1880s, working as a Stockton police officer.[12]

About the same time in March, word reached the sheriff of a knifing that occurred in Stockton. The victim, Jesus Ozagarais, died of his wound on March 23rd, almost two weeks after the stabbing. The culprit, Claro Lagunda, fled after the crime and Sheriff Cunninham had been seeking information on his whereabouts.

Cuningham had picked up some clues and rode out of town towards Calaveras County on Monday, March 22nd. After being in the saddle for almost twenty-four hours straight, the sheriff found Lagunda in the San Andreas area and placed him under arrest, arriving back in Stockton on the same day that Ozagarais died.[13]

The birth of Catherine and Thomas's third daughter, Katherine Quirk Cunningham, took place on March 29th, 1875. Six days later, Thomas's joy was clouded by grief when his wife Catherine died on April 4th as a result of complications from childbirth. Only 34 years old at the time, Catherine's death came as a shock to everyone. Thomas had travelled to San Quentin to pick up some prisoners after little Katherine's birth, arriving back in Stockton on the evening of April 3rd, so he must not have been aware of Catherine's condition when he left town.[14]

Catherine's funeral took place two days later, on April 6th, at the Central Methodist Episcopal Church, where the Cunninghams worshiped. A large crowd of people attended her service and courts were adjourned that day so that all of the court's officers and attorneys could attend. The pew where the Cunninghams normally sat for Sunday church was left vacant during the funeral service and was adorned with bouquets of flowers, which was the custom at the time.[15]

Thomas must have been devastated with the unexpected death of his beloved wife, but with the constant demands of his office, he appeared to keep his mind busy with his duties. Nothing was written on the subject, but both Thomas and Catherine had family in Stockton, and relatives undoubtedly helped Thomas raise his daughters. Thomas never married again.

Two days after the funeral, Thomas was riding in a railroad car to Oroville to escort a witness back to Stockton for a trial. The following week, Cunningham sold his harness and saddle business.[16]

Sheriff Cunningham was busy that May. On May 17th, Cunningham returned three convicts from San Quentin to Stockton. One of the men, William Resley, faced trial for grand larceny. The other two, William Atkinson and C. Bragg, were witnesses in the case. Amazingly, the sheriff made the transportation of the three prisoners alone, as was most often the case in those days.[17]

On Saturday, May 22nd, 1875, a man named John D. Moore, who lived about six miles southeast of Stockton, took a shot at his wife with a rifle. The shot grazed her, then struck his four-year old daughter in the arm, inflicting a painful flesh wound. Cunningham arrested Moore for assault with intent to commit murder and lodged him in the jail.[18]

The next day, a train arrived from Visalia with a wounded man aboard. There had been an argument between the brakeman and porter on the train, during which the brakeman shot the porter. The shooting took place somewhere around Merced. Sheriff Cunningham arrested the brakeman and wired Merced County Sheriff Anthony Meany to come get his prisoner.[19]

In June, Sheriff Cunningham was handed a warrant to serve,

after an altercation led to a stabbing in Waterloo. E. Bacon and F. C. Schmidberg had been arguing over wages. During the row, Schmidberg beat Bacon over the head, Bacon responding by stabbing Schmidberg in the arm and groin. Schmidberg rode to Stockton to swear out a warrant against Bacon for assault and handed it to the sheriff for service. Cunningham rode to Waterloo the next day and arrested Bacon.[20]

That summer saw Thomas Cunningham campaigning to retain his seat.

Undersheriff Joseph M. Long
[*Laurence Valterza*]

In August 1875, Abraham Bennett resigned his position as undersheriff. Thomas chose a long-time Stockton lawman, Joseph M. Long, as his replacement. Long, a Stockton real estate and insurance broker, had served as the county assessor and deputy tax collector. He was also a notary public, and he had previously served as a deputy sheriff, undersheriff and police judge. With Long's financial and law enforcement background, he was the perfect choice for the job.[21]

Long had originally been hired as a deputy by Sheriff Thomas K. Hook on February 7th, 1865. Sheriffs C. C. Rynerson and Freeman Mills retained him as a deputy during their two-year terms in office, and Mills made him the undersheriff, a job he held until March 1870.[22]

One interesting case from Joe Long's early career happened in January 1866, when Deputy Long teamed up with Stockton Police Officer Jerome Myers to make one of the first arrests of a career criminal named William "Billy" Miner. Thanks to Old West historians and Hollywood film makers, Billy Miner's life-long criminal career would become legendary. He was the subject of the movie *The Grey Fox*, as well as a book by respected author John Boessenecker.

Miner and a partner of his named John Sinclair had stolen a couple of horses in Oakland and had ridden east into San Joaquin County, where they held up a man named Porter along the road. The bandits demanded all of Porter's money at gunpoint. Porter complied, but begged Miner and Sinclair to spare him ten dollars, telling them he had been on the way to town to buy a new pair of boots. Porter showed the robbers his worn-out boots, with his toes sticking out of the ends. Apparently moved by Porter's story, Miner and Sinclair handed him back $10 so he could buy some boots.

Officers received information that evening that Miner and Sinclair had been seen on the road leading north out of Stockton, and Deputy Long and Officer Myers headed out after them in a pouring rain. It took the officers all night to travel the fourteen miles from Stockton to Woodbridge on the muddy road. When they arrived in Woodbridge early the next morning, the officers took Miner and Sinclair by surprise as they slept. Although the two outlaws were armed with Colt revolvers and Bowie knives, they were taken into custody without incident. One of them was quoted in a local paper as having told the officers: "You fellows think you've done a smart thing, arresting us while we were asleep. If you had met us on the road and attempted to arrest us, you wouldn't have found yourselves quite so smart."[23]

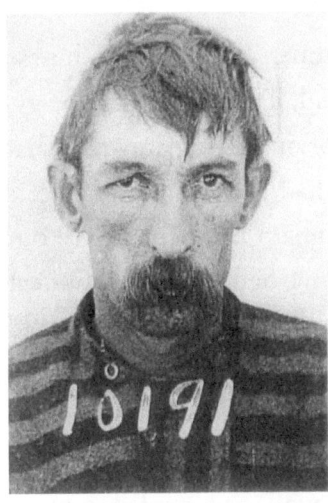

Career outlaw William Miner
[*Cunningham's mug book, SJSO collection*]

After making an unsuccessful attempt to break out of the Stockton jail, Miner and Sinclair were convicted of the Porter robbery and sent off to San Quentin. A newspaper reporter was on hand as they boarded a boat at the Stockton waterfront for the trip to San Francisco Bay:

> "They were jovial and appeared unconcerned. When the steamer moved off, they threw apples into the crowd on the wharf, and

waved their pocket handkerchiefs, as if bidding adieu to friends. A more thorough evidence of perverted nature we never saw."[24]

Joe Long made a bid for the sheriff's job in 1869, but was defeated by George H. Castle. Castle did not retain Long as a deputy when he took office on March 7th, 1870; however, Joe was elected as the Stockton police judge in May1870, serving a term of one year. After he returned to the Sheriff's Office as Thomas Cunningham's undersheriff in 1875, he held that position until his retirement under Sheriff Walter Sibley in 1911.[25]

Sheriff Cunningham was retained in office during the September elections.[26]

During the nighttime hours of October 7th, 1875, a Chinese prisoner hanged himself in the county jail. The inmate, Lin Nuey, was suspected by San Francisco police of murdering a man in that city the previous year. His description had been wired to officers around the region, and Sheriff Cunningham had kept an eye out for him and had arrested him that day. San Francisco Officer William Morehouse, who was familiar with Nuey, had traveled to Stockton the following day to identify him, but when the officer got to town, was told that Nuey had committed suicide sometime that night.[27]

One of Tiburcio Vasquez's men who had eluded capture during that long pursuit in 1874 was Isadore Padilla. Padilla drifted north and later met up with a group of other outlaws who had been robbing stagecoaches in Northern California. That group included Ramon Ruiz, Jose Maria, alias "Kokimbo;" Antone Valacca, alias "Red Antone;" Joaquin Oliveras, alias Antone Savage, an old-timer at age 65 and known as "Old Joaquin;" Mitchell Ratovich, alias "Big Mitch;" Mitchell Brown, known as "Little Mitch;" and Jose

Lenaris.

Two members of the crew were old cons who had spent at least one term at San Quentin. The leader, Ramon Ruiz, was a three-time loser. His first prison commitment was in October 1857 from Los Angeles County, where he received a one-year term for assault with a deadly weapon. He was convicted of manslaughter in Contra Costa County in May 1861, after he stabbed another man to death. That crime earned him a three-year stretch. He was next received by the prison on November 15th, 1867, on a five-and-a-half-year sentence for grand larceny out of Contra Costa County. That term expired on July 2nd, 1872. Antone Savage, "Old Joaquin," had previously been sentenced to a stretch in San Quentin from Alameda County in October 1867, for grand larceny.[28]

Stage robber Ramon Ruiz
[*Cunningham's mug book, SJSO collection*]

The bandits operated out of two hideouts, one outside of Auburn, in Placer County, and the other outside of Jackson, in Amador County. Although many other stage robberies occurred during the time that these outlaws were active, lawmen were later able to pin the following robberies on this gang:

On November 2nd, 1874, Ramon Ruiz, Big Mitch Ratovich, Little Mitch Brown, Antone "Old Joaquin" Savage and two other unknown road agents robbed the Sonora to Milton stage. At about 10:00 a.m. that morning, at a point between Salt Spring Valley and the town of Milton, in Calaveras County, the outlaws tied their horses off the road and donned their masks. Leveling their cocked revolvers and shotguns at the driver and passengers, they first stopped a stage operated by J. C. Shine. That was an up stage; Mr. Shine convinced the robbers that he was not carrying a treasure box, and the stage was allowed to drive on just as the down stage came into view.

The second stage, operated by Miller & Company, was forced to stop. One of the bandits stood in the middle of the road, one at the head of each leader horse, and one on each side of the coach. The sixth robber took the express box from the driver. The box contained express and money from Big Oak Flat and Chinese Camp. The robbers missed the box containing the Columbia and Sonora express, and the U.S. mail was left intact. The passengers were also left alone and the stage was allowed to proceed.[29]

On March 1st, 1875, Big Mitch Ratovich and Little Mitch Brown held up the Mokelumne Hill to Lodi stage, a few miles west of the small settlement of Camanche, in Calaveras County. Both bandits wore masks. The driver handed down the box as demanded and the robbers proceeded to break it open. One of them took a package, which he apparently thought contained bullion, and stuffed it into his shirt. No other valuables were touched and the stage was allowed to move along. At some point after the stage left, the bandits must have been mortified when they discovered that the package they took only contained a coal sample.[30]

The outlaws next struck on March 23rd, 1875, robbing the Sonora to Milton stage. Although only three bandits were seen that day, it was later determined that Ramon Ruiz, Big Mitch Ratovich, Little Mitch Brown and Old Joaquin Savage were involved in the holdup. The robbery occurred on the Reynold's Ferry Hill, known as Funk Hill, just inside of Calaveras County, while the stage was lumbering slowly up the grade.

Reynold's Ferry Hill had a steep grade that led from the Stanislaus River. Because of the weight of the stage and strain on the horses, stagecoach passengers were most often required to get out of the coach at the bottom of the hill and walk to the top. That is what happened on this day; most of the passengers were walking behind the stage when the masked brigands appeared, and at the point of their revolvers and a rifle, demanded the Wells Fargo box.

The driver obeyed the command, throwing down the box, and one of the robbers took it to the side of the road and broke it open with a sledge hammer. One of the passengers, believing the robbers were going to demand all of their valuables, suggested to the others that they cough up, but the bandits told them to put their valuables away. It was reported that the take from the express box was approximately $6,100.[31]

Newspapers reported that four days after the robbery, Calaveras County Sheriff Ben Thorn and his posse were ten miles behind the robbers, heading in the direction of Placerville, but the trail ran cold.[32]

The next job attributed to the band of road agents was the

August 3rd, 1875 robbery of the Laporte to Oroville stage, three miles southwest of Forbestown, in Butte County. Ramon Ruiz, Isadore Padilla, Jose "Kokimbo" Maria, "Red Antone" Valacca and one other unidentified crook were involved in the job. At about 5:00 p.m. that afternoon, while the coach ambled along, the five masked men appeared in the middle of the road. Four were armed with cocked revolvers, one with a shotgun. The stage was carrying nine passengers at the time, six men and three women. Two of the passengers rode on the top seat with the driver.

Calaveras County Sheriff Benjamin K. Thorn
[*Terry Eproson*]

The express box was located inside this coach, and it was thrown out on demand. Two of the robbers plundered the box, while the one with the shotgun and the other two covered everyone in the wagon. When they were done, the driver, F. N. Morse, asked that the bandits return the box so that the ladies could rest their feet on it. When he was ordered to drive on, Morse exclaimed, "not by a damned sight, till I get that box! You've got all out of it that is worth anything to you, now give it back!" After a little hesitation, they did so. None of the passengers was bothered, even though a woman riding on top of the coach was wearing a gold watch and chain that the robbers couldn't have missed seeing. The bandits made off with $2,300 worth of gold dust and coin from the Wells Fargo box and rode away in a cloud of dust.[33]

The gang was inactive for the next couple of months, their next job coming on October 5th, 1875. On that day, Ramon Ruiz, Isadore Padilla, Antone Valacca, Jose Maria and Jose Lenaris held up the Marysville to Downieville stage. At about 11:00 a.m. that morning, the stage rolled up to their place of concealment, located in mountains with a large pine tree next to the road and the surrounding area covered by dense undergrowth. Only four of the masked robbers showed themselves to the driver and three passengers. Three were armed with revolvers, one with a double-barreled shotgun.[34]

The express box was buried under baggage on the top of the coach and it took a little time to throw it down to the robbers. While the bandit with the shotgun stood in front of the team of horses, two others covered the coach from the sides and the fourth worked on the box with a sawed-off axe. The take was about $3,000 in coin.[35]

Marysville officer Henry McCoy was sent in pursuit of the bandits, but returned to town empty handed the following day.[36]

Seven days later, Ramon Ruiz and three other members of his gang held up the Sonora to Milton stage again, this time about eight miles outside of Milton, on the morning of October 12th. Also named in this robbery were Big Mitch Ratovich, Little Mitch

Brown, and "Old Joaquin," Antone Savage. Once again, only three of the four masked robbers made themselves known. Sam Smith, the coach driver, was reported to be one of the oldest drivers in the state and had never been held up before. He convinced the robbers that there was no Wells Fargo box on his stage, and was allowed to proceed without any further delay.[37]

The last job attributed to this gang was committed on December 1st, 1875. This time, Ramon Ruiz acted alone and did not wear a mask. He made an unsuccessful attempt at the Chinese Camp to Copperopolis stage at a point about two miles north of O'Byrnes' Ferry, outside of Jamestown, in Tuolumne County. The stage driver got a very good description of Ruiz, which he reported to authorities.[38]

James B. Hume, chief of detectives for Wells Fargo
[*Wells Fargo*]

Based on the description provided by the stage driver, Calaveras County Sheriff Ben Thorn was able to identify, locate, and arrest Ramon Ruiz. Thorn then called in Wells Fargo's chief detective, James B. Hume.[39]

One of the things that Ramon Ruiz learned while riding the trails of his life was how to become a good stool pigeon. Under close questioning by James Hume and Sheriff Thorn, in the vernacular of the day, he "peached" on his pals, giving up information on the robberies committed by the group and naming names. He also provided information on the gang's two hideouts.

Sheriff Cunningham received a wire from Hume, requesting that he meet with other lawmen in Auburn to assist in rounding up members of the robbery gang. Cunningham traveled by train to Auburn on December 21st, meeting up with Sheriff Samuel Daniels of Butte County, Placer County Sheriff James McCormick, and former Stockton Police Chief Jerome Myers, who was now working as a detective for Wells Fargo.[40]

Early the following morning, Wednesday, December 22nd, the four lawmen surrounded a cabin, located about six miles above Auburn, near a place called Doty's Ravine. Two officers went to the front and two to the back, all armed with shotguns. When the officers announced themselves, two of the bandits attempted to escape out the back but were stopped short when they came face to muzzle with the lawmen's shotguns. Two other men were arrested inside the house without incident.[41]

Those arrested were Isadore Padilla and "Red Antone" Valacca. The other two men were not wanted in the crimes. Padilla was taken to the jail in Marysville and Valacca was taken to the Oroville jail on December 23rd, while Sheriff Cunningham returned to Stockton that day on the train.[42]

That same day, Thursday, December 23rd, Sheriff Thorn and James Hume made a raid on a cabin outside of Ione, arresting Big Mitch Ratovich and Little Mitch Brown. The officers ran Jose "Kokimbo" Maria to ground the next day, in a cabin about four miles above Fiddletown.[43]

Ramon Ruiz pleaded guilty to stage robbery in Calaveras County. For turning state's evidence, he received the shortest sentence of the bunch, four years, despite having been involved in more of the robberies than any of the others. Antone Savage also pleaded guilty in Calaveras County, receiving a ten-year sentence. Mitchell Ratovich and Mitchell Brown were both convicted of robbery in Calaveras County, and both received fifteen-year sentences. Jose Maria was sentenced to five-years from Butte County; and Antone Valacca got ten years from Butte County. No mention was made of Jose Lenaris.[44]

After a trial, Isadore Padilla was sentenced to twenty years at San Quentin, but he only served about six-months of his sentence. This time he did not escape justice though; he was remanded to a higher authority when he died in prison on May, 7th 1877.[45]

5

BURGLARS, ROBBERS AND MURDERERS

In early January 1876, Sheriff Cunningham was called to the scene of a murder which occurred in a cabin along the north bank of the Stanislaus River, about twenty-four miles from Stockton. The victim had a large gash on the side of his neck. Two men were seen leaving the man's cabin about the time of his death. Cunningham arrested those two men, but nothing else was written about the case. The ride to the scene and the investigation were made more difficult by the weather; it rained steadily that day and the wind was strong and cold. The following week, the sheriff traveled to San Quentin to escort a prisoner back to Stockton who was going to be a witness in a case.[1]

Sheriff Cunningham employed some additional deputies in 1876 for his new term in office. James J. Evans had worked as a Stockton police officer and was an experienced lawman. Oscar F. Atwood would serve as a full-time deputy through the mid-1880s and would retain his deputy commission until Sheriff Cunningham left office. Atwood served as San Joaquin County's assessor in the 1890s. Alonso A. McCloud remained as the deputy in charge of the jail.[2]

In February, Sheriff Cunningham was headed back to San Quentin, this time with a convicted burglar named A. B. Stevens, who received a ten-year sentence.[3]

On July 21st, 1876, an attempted lynching happened at the jail. The subject of the crowd's ire was a confidence man, swindler and total fraud named Charles Jacobs. Jacobs marketed himself as "Professor Charles." He had a dozen aliases. Jacobs had come to the West Coast with his wife and small child, abandoning the two in San Francisco. He traveled around, selling himself as a spiritualist and medium, able to talk to the dead. He gave shows at a dollar a head. He also seduced young teen-aged girls with promises of marriage. One of the girls he enticed was the seventeen-year-old daughter of a well-respected San Joaquin County farmer.[4]

Deputy J. J. Evans
[*R. Tod Ruse*]

Jacobs met the girl during a train trip to San Jose and induced her to stay with him when they got there. Her parents became panic stricken when they didn't hear from her. The parents were able to get their daughter home with the help of authorities, but Charles Jacobs had the audacity to go to the family ranch to visit the girl. While there, the girl's father came out and inquired his name. Jacobs gave the alias that he had been using when he met the girl, and with that the father headed straight for his shotgun, while Jacobs high-tailed it back to Stockton.[5]

Sheriff Cunningham was aware of the problems Jacobs was causing and arrested him on a warrant out of San Francisco charging Jacobs with obtaining money under false pretenses. San Francisco Officer George Eastman was detailed to travel to Stockton for the prisoner. In the meantime, word had gotten around of what Jacobs had been up to with the girl and the town started filling up with angry men.[6]

Throughout the afternoon in into the evening, men came into town with suspicious looking bulges in their pockets and summary vengeance on their lips. They filled the streets in front of the jail and around the railroad depot. Someone spotted the girl's brother at the train depot, dressed in women's clothing and waiting for Jacobs and the officer, where he no doubt intended to take the law into his own hands. By six o'clock that evening, it was estimated that 300 men surrounded the jail and the numbers and intensity of the crowd increased throughout the evening. It was reported that another mob waited at the Lathrop train station in case officers were successful in getting Jacobs out of Stockton.

Sheriff Cunningham, realizing the real threat of a lynching, deputized a number of men to assist with protecting the jail, and he requested the assistance of the local militia. By 9:00 p.m. that night, 30 members of the National Guard were in place at the jail.[7]

At about 1:00 a.m. the next morning, a false alarm of fire was sounded in one corner of the city in the hopes it would lure the crowd away, but the ploy did not work. Men in the crowd were aware that the San Francisco officer intended to take Jacobs out of town, and they weren't leaving.

The fury of the crowd died down during the early morning hours, and by 3:00 a.m. the crowd had dispersed. About an hour later, Officer Eastman, handcuffed to his prisoner, hurried for the train station, surrounded by a group of heavily armed officers. Once there, Eastman and Jacobs were locked in a freight car headed for Sacramento. From there, they transferred to a train headed for Vallejo, then took a ferry to San Francisco.[8]

Jacobs pled to the charge of obtaining money under false pretenses and was sentenced to a year in jail by a San Francisco court. The parents of the girls he victimized did not prefer charges against him because they did not want their personal affairs paraded around in court.[9]

In November, Sheriff Cunningham attended the execution of Richard "Fighting Dick" Collins in Modesto. Collins was convicted of murdering an old disabled sheep herder named James Sheldon on the Stanislaus County side of the Stanislaus River at Hill's Ferry. "Fighting Dick" had a reputation as a hardened wretch and troublesome bully. He had worked as a deckhand on steamboats plying the Sacramento and San Joaquin rivers, and was known in the barrooms in all the river towns.[10]

On November 24th, 1876, Sheriff Cunningham accompanied Stanislaus County Sheriff John Rodgers in escorting Collins to the gallows, along with Santa Clara County Sheriff Nick Harris and Alameda County Sheriff Harry Morse. The gallows were the same ones used by Cunningham during the execution of John Murphy in 1873, and had also been previously used to carry out three executions in Sacramento and one in Modesto.[11]

In early January 1877, Thomas arrested two men wanted for the robbery of a Lathrop area man. Cunningham had been on the lookout for the two robbers ever since taking the report from the victim, who was able to give the sheriff a detailed description of the men, their shotguns and their wagon. Cunningham had put feelers out, and had been snooping around out in the east and northeast areas of the county without luck.

One day, Sheriff Cunningham traveled to the northwest part of the county to serve a subpoena on a witness for the grand jury. The sheriff had picked up a young boy in the area who could point out where the witness was located. When the sheriff and the lad got to Benson's Ferry, Cunningham asked the ferryman if he had seen two men with shotguns in a wagon, describing them. The ferryman said that men and an outfit matching that description had just crossed the river in the direction of New Hope, site of present-day Thornton, in northwest San Joaquin County.

After picking up the witness, Cunningham went in the direction pointed out by the ferryman, with the witness and the boy in his wagon. They came across the men and wagon that the sheriff had been searching for in New Hope. Pulling up alongside the two, Cunningham quickly came up with a strategy, telling the witness that he should buy Thomas a drink since he had traveled so far. In fact, the witness should by everyone a drink, including the two robbers. Everyone agreed and the robbers followed everyone into the tavern, leaving their shotguns in the wagon.

Once inside, Cunningham took the bartender to one side and had him go out and unload the pair's shotguns. Thomas then identified himself to the two robbers, telling them that they were under arrest. Sheriff Cunningham had the witness drive his own wagon to town, and, armed with a Winchester rifle and instructions to shoot anyone who left the sheriff's wagon, the witness followed Cunningham and his prisoners back to Stockton.[12]

Lawmen often communicated wanted information on penny postcards
[*Ray Moreno*]

The following month, on February 22nd, 1877, two inmates escaped from the jail during the night. The break was discovered the next morning when the jailer went to the cell with the prisoners' breakfast. A hole large enough for a man to fit through was cut through the six-inch thick wood plank floor. Using pocket knives, the inmates had spent a lot of time making the cuts. They had concealed their work with mattresses and blankets from their beds during the day.

The two escapees, William Clifton, charged with robbery, and Thomas McKenna, in jail for grand larceny, made a clean escape and were not heard from again, although Sheriff Cunningham spent the rest of his career looking for them. This was not the first jail escape William Clifton had been a part of; he had escaped from the Marysville jail with three other prisoners in April 1864.[13]

In September 1877, Sheriff Cunningham retained his seat, winning the election against a man named C. C. Long. The sheriff traveled to Marysville later that month to pick up a prisoner who was wanted in Stockton for assault to murder. The inmate, Edmund Woolf, had shot a saloonkeeper in Stockton on July 5th, 1877. Marysville officers had arrested Woolf after receiving a wire from Stockton Police Chief Myers. That November, Cunningham and San Francisco Police Captain Appleton Stone arrested Jose Pico, wanted on a warrant from San Joaquin County charging him with obtaining a horse and a $300 gold coin under false pretenses.[14]

On January 27th, 1878, four sheep herders were tending to a flock outside of Stockton when a quarrel started. During the argument, Antonio Frage struck one of the other herders, a man only known as Van Horn, over the head with a shovel handle. Frage fled the area and Van Horn was taken into Stockton, where he later died.

Sheriff Cunningham started trailing Frage, tracking him along the Lower Sacramento Road to Benson's Ferry on the Mokelumne River. Frage sold his dog to the ferryman for fare across the river, and headed to Walnut Grove. Cunningham learned in Walnut Grove that Frage had some family members on Andrus Island on the Sacramento River, and he started that way. The sheriff found his man with some relatives on Andrus Island, taking him into custody. Frage burst into tears upon hearing that he had killed Van Horn. The sheriff and his prisoner took a team to Courtland, where they picked up a steamer headed for Sacramento. From there, they took the train to Stockton.[15]

The *Stockton Daily Independent* ran an article on April 10th, 1878, about a museum of criminal artifacts the sheriff had put together. Titled: "Sheriff's Relics," the article read, "The sheriff's rear office, or retiring room, has recently been fitted up and put freshly in order. It contains the 'rogues' gallery'—a large collection of the criminals of this section and elsewhere in the state—a cabinet in which are preserved all manner of weapons that tell the story of many a tragedy of the past. The names of all who have been executed in this county by process of law have been neatly written, framed and hung upon the wall..."[16]

Alonzo McCloud resigned as the jailer sometime in 1878. John Ginn was hired to replace him.

A major skirmish and general insurrection broke out among Chinese laborers on Union Island on March 20th, 1878. The rioters had been part of a labor force of about 200 men employed by General Thomas Williams to built and repair levees in the Delta. Trouble started when the men were informed that 160 of them were being released, that the company could only afford to retain 40 of the men. Three Chinese foremen were thrown into the river and the Caucasian superintendent was run off the island.

Sheriff Cunningham was summoned, and he formed up a posse of deputies armed with Henry rifles and headed to the seat of the trouble. The posse spent the entire day on Union Island, arresting about 25 men in all. Warrants had been sworn out for 15 of the ringleaders and 10 more were arrested for rioting. All was quiet on the island by the time the sheriff and his posse got back into town with their prisoners at midnight.[17]

In the early morning hours of May 26th, 1878, Susan E. Bailey, the daughter of J. A. Shepard, the proprietor of the Lathrop Hotel at the Lathrop railroad depot, was awakened by a noise in her room in the hotel. She was startled to see the form of a man standing behind the door, and without creating attention, she was able to get out of her room to notify her father and two or three railroad men of the intruder.

The burglar, Michael Walsh, alias Jim Winters, soon found that he was surrounded by Mr. Shepard and the railroad workers and drew a pistol. Seeing this and fearing for her father's life, Susan jumped on Walsh just as he fired. One shot went through Mr. Shepard's clothing and a second struck Susan. The men grabbed the gun as Walsh struggled to get away, while Susan slumped to the floor with a bullet wound to the thigh. Fighting mightily, Walsh pulled out a knife and billy club, cutting a brakeman named Hulbert on the thumb, but the men were able to subdue Walsh and bind him up. Deputy Atwood came from Stockton and took Walsh to jail.

After Walsh was arrested and jailed, his true identity became known to the officers. Walsh was a hard character and long-time criminal who was wanted by Stockton police at the time of his capture for the burglary of a Stockton hotel. An ex-con, Walsh had first visited San Quentin in 1865 for burglary. He had done seven years for that conviction and shortly after he was released, he was convicted in Nevada County for burglary and sent up for another six years. He was released in 1878, shortly before he committed the Lathrop burglary and shooting.

In July, while in jail waiting for his court case to resolve, Michael Walsh attempted to dig out of his cell with a piece of spoon. Sheriff Cunningham knew Walsh's history and had been leery of him, telling the jailer to keep a close eye on him. His cell was searched one day while Walsh was out for a grand jury appearance. The spoon was located, along with a hole in the wall where plaster and wood had been dug away. Walsh had been putting the plaster dust into his slop bucket and had been saving the wood shavings. He saturated the shavings with grease that he saved from food, with the intent of starting a fire.[18]

Susan Bailey's wound was initially thought to be a flesh wound and not serious. Walsh was indicted by the grand jury in July 1878 for burglary and assault with a deadly weapon with intent to commit the murders of Susan Bailey, Mr. Shepard and Mr. Hulbert. Walsh was allowed to plead guilty to the charges, and on July 31st, 1878, he was sentenced to consecutive terms totaling eleven years. Sheriff Cunningham escorted him and another outlaw to San Quentin in early August.[19]

The following month, Sheriff Cunningham was searching for thieves after a two-horse wagon and tack were stolen from a Stockton area ranch. The thieves, two men and a woman, were last seen near Galt, heading east. The sheriff offered a $50 reward for information in the case.[20]

In late September 1878, Cunningham was invited by Nevada County Sheriff William Montgomery to act as a witness in the execution of George Butts in Nevada City. Butts had been convicted of the first-degree murder of a Forest Springs man.[21]

In November 1878, Thomas and his deputies got involved in the investigation of a series of train car burglaries. It soon became apparent to the lawmen that these crimes were being perpetrated by an organized ring of thieves.

Working with agents from the Central Pacific Railroad, the sheriff and his men arrested an old ex-convict named Hank Gossett and a man named James H. E. Johnson in Lathrop on November 12th for stealing a conductor's box from a rail car. One of the two men broke, providing information on the gang's operation. According to the informer, six men were involved in the burglaries.

The burglars' mode of operation was to steal keys to the train locks while a train was stopped at a water tank or wood pile. One or two of the crooks would enter into cars containing through-freight and choose what items looked valuable, placing their plunder in gunny sacks. Riding the car, they would throw the sacks near the next station, where one of their confederates was waiting to collect them. The stolen property would then be taken to San Francisco, where it was fenced.

The leader of the ring, James Hopkins, and another member named George Clark were arrested on November 16th, 1878, in Martinez. One of the last two burglars, a character who went by the nick-name "Pounce," was arrested out of a freight car in Sacramento, and the last member of the ring, Matt Soloman, was arrested in Carson City.[22]

The case continued into the next year. On February 8th, 1879, Sheriff Cunningham traveled to San Francisco with three warrants for the fence of the burglary operation, Abraham Lachman. Lachman operated a second-hand store, where he was known to fence stolen property.[23]

While waiting for his trial, ring member James Johnson and another inmate named John Downey, in jail on a robbery charge, escaped from the jail on the evening of March 8th, 1879. The two inmates made their move at about 7:00 p.m. that evening, as one of Johnson's pals, Matt Soloman, helped cover for them. Johnson and Downey had made a two-foot square hole through the plaster in the second-floor cupboard. They escaped through the hole and onto the roof. At the same time, Deputy Hanks, a part-time jailer, was making a round and Matt Soloman, acting as a jail trusty, diverted Hanks' attention.

Johnson and Downey made good their escape by jumping off the roof and onto an adjoining shed, but Johnson injured himself when he fell off the roof. He was captured a short time later about a half-mile from town. Downey made his way out of town and headed east. He was captured in Reno about six weeks later.[24]

On May 29th, 1879, Sheriff Cunningham assisted Sacramento County Sheriff M. M. Drew with the executions of Troy Dye and Edward Anderson, both convicted for the August 1878 murder of Sacramento County rancher Aaron Tullis. Dye was the Sacramento County public administrator at the time of the crime. Cunningham assisted in placing the rope correctly on the gallows before helping Sheriff Drew lead the condemned men to their place of death.[25]

Thomas was busy running for re-election that summer. He retained his seat in September against a man named Charles Sedgwick.[26]

At about 9:00 p.m. on the evening on August 8th, 1879, the jailer, Deputy Charles Fields, was waylaid by an inmate named Jack Welsh, in jail awaiting the action of the grand jury on a grand larceny charge. Welsh conked Fields over the head during an apparent escape attempt, leaving Fields temporarily dazed and with quite a goose egg. Deputy Fields recovered quickly enough to subdue Welsh with the help of Welsh's two cell mates.[27]

Cunningham-era deputy's badge
[*R. Tod Ruse*]

Stockton hosted former President and General of the Union Army Ulysses S. Grant at the end of September 1879. Stocktonians pulled out all the stops for the president and his wife, decorating their homes and businesses with red, white and blue flags and buntings, and honoring him with a 21-gun salute, a parade, and public reception and banquet. The children were let out of school early so that they could get in on the fun. Sheriff Cunningham took part in the festivities as a member of the Republican committee and as the foreman of Eureka Company 2.[28]

On November 22nd, 1879, Sheriff Cunningham arrested Peter Dalton, who went by the aliases of "Nick of the Woods," and "Mountain Spirit." Dalton was wanted out of Nevada County at the time for armed robbery. He was an old hand at crime and had previously been sent to prison two times. His first stretch at San Quentin was in 1860, out of Mariposa County for grand larceny. He was sent up the second time in 1866, when he was sentenced to twenty years for robbery, out of Sacramento County. That sentence was commuted to seven years, eight months by Governor Irwin. Dalton had been out for about eighteen months and was suspected of committing a number of stagecoach and highway robberies in Nevada and surrounding counties. Dalton had vowed that he would not be taken alive.

Sheriff Cunningham had received a wanted flier on Dalton from Nevada County Sheriff Montgomery and had been keeping his eye out. On Saturday, November 22nd, Thomas spotted Dalton in the Hunter Street square, on the west side of the courthouse. With other people milling around and covering his movements, Cunningham snuck up behind Dalton and stuck his Colt up against the outlaw, ordering Dalton to throw up his hands. The outlaw complied without hesitation, despite his claims. Cunningham then marched Dalton the one block to the jail at the muzzle of his revolver. Once at the jail, Dalton was searched and found to have a large Colt's Navy revolver, a Bowie knife, several files, and some silver shavings in his clothing. In the end, Dalton had been taken by Sheriff Cunningham with nary a whimper.[29]

Thomas ended up in a dispute with Sheriff Montgomery over

the posted reward money. Montgomery made a claim for the $300 reward, stating in an affidavit that he had arrested Dalton. Cunningham disputed Montgomery's claim, but there was no indication that Thomas put in for the reward money himself.[30]

Sheriff Cunningham made another of his numerous trips to San Quentin at the end of November, when he escorted three convicts to the prison. David Mathews and F. W. Shultz had received two-and-a-half year sentences for burglary, and William West was going up for five years on a burglary conviction.[31]

Thomas made his last road trip of the 1870s on December 21st, 1879, when he escorted Richard Denson to San Quentin to complete a seven-year sentence for embezzlement. Denson had been stealing from the Central Pacific Railroad, where he had worked as a freight clerk.[32]

6

THE DAILY GRIND

Sheriff Cunningham and his small force of deputies continued on with their daily grind as a new day dawned on the year 1880 and a new decade. Changes in the California Constitution took effect on January 1st, 1880, changing the way that state and local governments operated in a number of different ways. County and District courts were replaced with the Superior Court. Changes in the political code included moving state and local elections off of a two-year cycle in odd years and aligning them with national elections in even numbered years.[1]

Sheriff Cunningham made the first of his many trips to the newly opened Folsom Prison, escorting two prisoners on February 2nd, 1880. On February 12th, Undersheriff Long assisted Stockton Police Chief Orin Langmaid in arresting a man named George McCarthy on a warrant charging him with forgery.[2]

On February 19th, 1880, Sheriff Cunningham received a wire from Calaveras County deputy sheriff and Milton constable W. T. McClanahan, requesting Cunningham arrest Martin Eubanks, who was suspected of robbing a man of $140. Eubanks had left Milton on the Stockton train. The train from Milton to Stockton travelled a distance of about twenty-six miles, and Sheriff Cunningham was waiting at the depot when the train arrived. When Eubanks was searched at the jail, $120 was found hidden in one of his boots. Cunningham escorted the prisoner back to Milton on the next morning's train and turned him over to Sheriff Ben Thorn.[3]

At about 3:00 p.m. on the afternoon on Saturday, February 28th, 1880, a dramatic shooting took place right outside the front entrance to the Stockton courthouse. The victim had been walking with Undersheriff Joe Long at the time, and Sheriff Cunningham saw what happened from across the street.

John Petty had just filed some legal papers with the court and was walking outside, reading his copy of the documents and chatting with Undersheriff Long. As they went through the doors on the Main Street side of the building, both of them saw a man holding a revolver on the sidewalk. The man, Henry Parker, said something to Petty in a low voice that Long could not understand, then raised his gun and fired at Petty, striking him in the left side. As Petty was falling, Undersheriff Long, Sheriff Cunningham, and former Stockton Police Officer John Nye apprehended Parker and disarmed him of a large Colt's revolver. The hammer had been cocked back so that he could take another shot when the gun was taken from Parker's hand.[4]

While Henry Parker was being led to the jail, John Petty was taken across the street to a barber shop. He was put on a canvas cot and carried by several men to his home. There, a doctor performed surgery to remove the bullet, which had lodged next to his spine. Petty lingered until March 5th, when he passed away at about 4:00

The Daily Grind

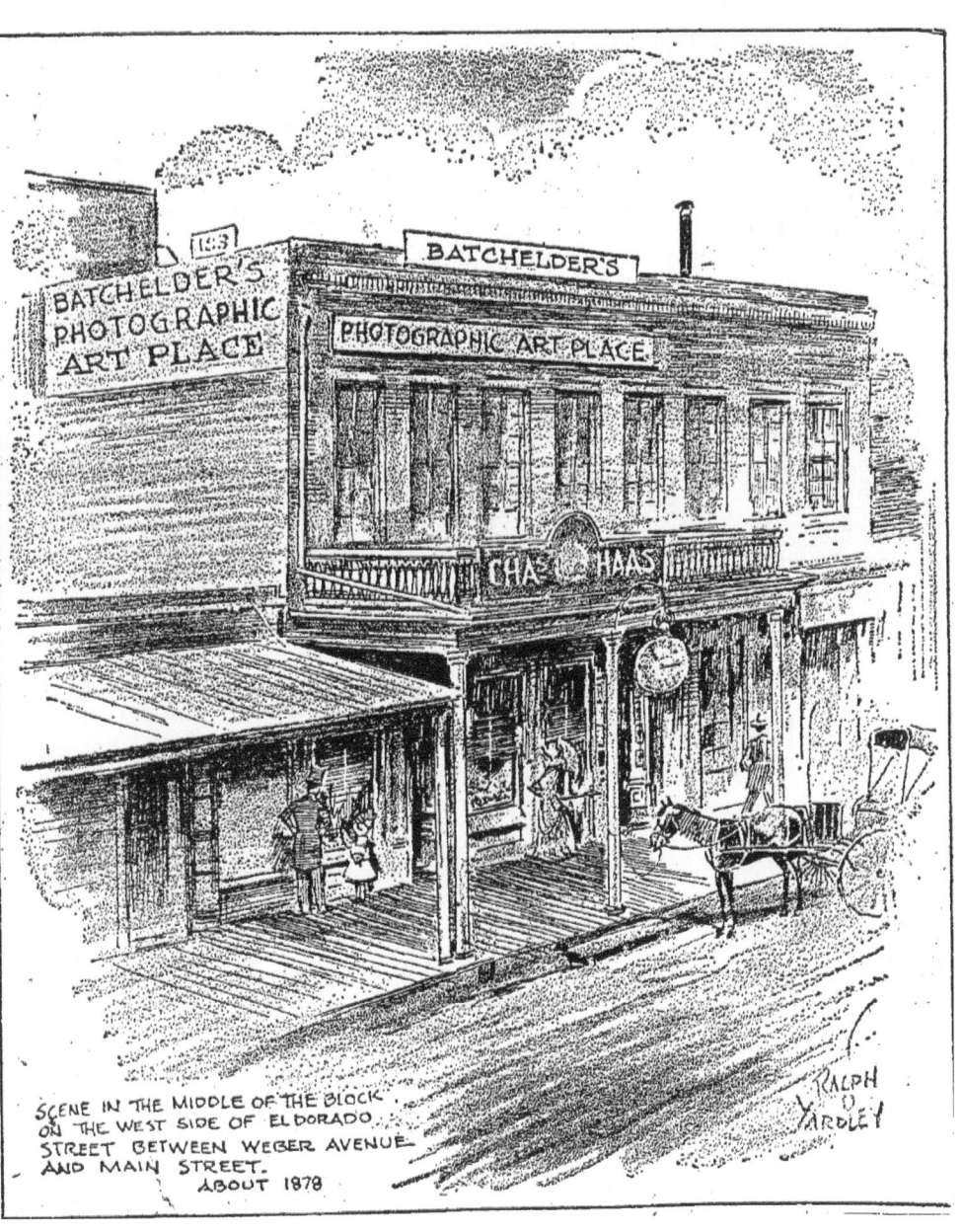

Ralph O. Yardley illustration of 1878-era Stockton
[*R. Tod Ruse*]

a.m. that morning.

It was learned that Petty and Parker had a dispute dating back several years regarding a flock of sheep. Parker had brought suit against Petty in June 1878, but had lost the case. Petty subsequently won a large judgement against Parker, and shortly before the shooting took place, Deputy Atwood had served Parker a levy against his horse, which was stabled nearby.

At his trial, Parker testified that he had known John Petty for about twelve years. Parker had been subpoenaed to testify in a case in Stockton the day of the shooting, and had gone to the Commercial Hotel, where he met a friend. He and the friend had gone into the bar when John Petty walked in. Words were exchanged, and Parker said that Petty had threatened him. Parker said that he had just been served the levy against his horse and was going to the courthouse when he saw Petty coming out the door. Petty looked as though he was going to draw his gun, so Parker shot him.

Entries in arrest ledger from Market Street Jail, 1880
[*SJSO collection*]

Testimony was taken regarding previous incidents between the two men and what had happened that morning in the saloon. Petty's character was brought into question. At the end of the trial, Henry Parker was acquitted of a murder charge.[5]

In early March, Cunningham traveled to Woodland, in Yolo County, as the foreman of Eureka Engine Company 2 to purchase a team of three iron-grey horses to pull the company's steam engine. The horses were described by the paper as very young, powerful and handsome.[6]

On March 29th, 1880, Sheriff Cunningham arrested Daniel Barton, who was wanted in Calaveras County for murder, after Cristobal Noriega and a man only known as Urbano were found shot to death near San Andreas the previous Saturday. Mid-April found Cunningham traveling to Biggs Station, in Butte County, to pick up William Waite, alias "Arizona Bill," who was wanted in Linden for battery and making threats.[7]

Thomas escorted six convicts to San Quentin on May 1st, 1880. Ah Meng was sentenced to complete three years for grand larceny; a burglar named William Cornwall went up on a two-year hitch; George McCarty, a forger, got four years; William Davis was sentenced to five years for petty theft with a prior conviction; Thomas McCarty got three years for burglary; and Frank Tomka got a free one-year view of the San Francisco Bay for burglary.[8]

During that trip to the prison, Sheriff Cunningham brought a murder suspect back to Stockton, arriving in town on the evening of May 2nd. Michael Walsh, who had been convicted in July 1878 for the burglary of the Lathrop Hotel and the attempted murders he committed at that time, had been indicted by a San Joaquin County grand jury for the murder of Susan Bailey, who had died of complications from the gunshot wound she suffered that night.

The trip back to Stockton was uneventful up to the time that the train reached town, but as they were pulling into the depot, Walsh, who was handcuffed, made a break for it. He jumped out of the car as the train was still moving and dove under the coach towards the other side. The sheriff reacted quickly, following Walsh under the train and grabbing him as they reached the opposite side. Cunningham injured his thumb, but he luckily made it without being run over.[9]

Newspapers around the country reported on Walsh's escape attempt and his re-capture. The tales of the event became more outlandish with each telling:

The *Carson Appeal* wrote: "The Sheriff was under the train like a flash, and as he grasped the robber the cars went over a trestle work 160 feet high. The robber attempted to swing free, but the Sheriff, hanging by his toes, held his prisoner by the hair for about sixty yards. The determined robber, drawing a sixteen-inch bowie knife, cut off his head, and, leaving it in the Sheriff's hands, dropped into the seething gulf below. He then swam ashore, and made his escape to the mountains, where he is roving about minus a head. The officer brought the bloody trophy to the city and claimed the reward."[10]

The *Denver Tribune* stated: "He dashed under the train, which was moving swiftly at the time, and clung to the brake beam. The Sheriff followed and a struggle ensued which lasted until the next station was reached, when the Sheriff was found to have been dangerously wounded by a formidable bowie knife which the ruffian had wielded."[11]

The *Chicago Times* wrote: "He dashed under the train, which was moving at the rate of forty miles an hour. The Sheriff followed him and a terrible struggle on the brake beam ensued. It lasted for an hour. At the end of that time assistance came, and it was found that the Sheriff had been mortally wounded by a bowie knife in the hands of the ruffian."[12]

The *New York Sun* reported: "He dashed under the train which was moving at the rate of sixty miles an hour, and mounting the brake beam, defied the Sheriff, who had followed and mounted beside him. A terrible struggle ensued, and at the next station the bodies of Sheriff and desperado were found across the beam locked in a death-grip."[13]

Sheriff Cunningham searched Walsh once they got to the jail and found a variety of lock picks and jail breaking tools in his clothing. While at San Quentin, Walsh had concealed a fine steel saw inside of a rubber comb. He sewed a variety of improvised keys into the seam of his coat for opening handcuffs and other locks. He also possessed a small glazers' knife, good for use against humans. He had $7.50 worth of gold sown into his shirt cuff and had some silver coins in his pocket.[14]

On May 6th, 1880, two men made an attempt on the Mokelumne Hill to Ione stage. The coach was moving at a good clip when the robbers made themselves known. Shots were fired by both the outlaws and Wells Fargo & Company messenger Thomas Magee. When officers reached the scene and made a search, all they found were some empty cartridges and a hat. A rancher reported that a short time after the crime, two men showed up at his house about two miles north of the scene looking for something to eat. The two told the rancher that they were prospectors. One of the men was missing a hat. The rancher provided detailed descriptions of both men to lawmen. The robbers were also suspected of committing the robbery of the San Andreas stage a little above Jenny Lind a few days before.

Sheriff Cunningham and other sheriffs in the region put out feelers, but the road agents were never caught for the crimes. James Hume collected enough information about them to identify them as Albert Hamilton, an old stage robber, and Roger O'Meara. Both fled the state after robbing the Georgetown to Placerville stage in El Dorado County on May 26th, 1880. Hamilton was never caught; Roger O'Meara was arrested in St. Louis for burglary, but was never returned to California to face charges on the stage robberies.[15]

Michael Walsh was brought before the court on May 27th, 1880, exactly two years and one day after he committed the Lathrop crimes. He was ably defended by former California State Supreme Court Justice David S. Terry, who argued that Walsh had already pled and been sentenced for the crime he was now accused of; the fact that the victim later died had no bearing. The court sided with Terry, ruling that the grand jury should never have brought an indictment. With that, Walsh was escorted back to San Quentin to serve out his original sentence.[16]

Quite a bit of excitement was created on downtown Stockton streets during the early evening hours of May 16th, 1880, when Thomas Cunningham's horse ran off while hitched to a buggy. Cunningham had left the horse and buggy on El Dorado Street near Washington when for some unknown reason the horse became spooked and took off. The horse ran furiously up El Dorado Street with the light, open buggy dancing over the uneven surface of the street. The horse made a turn at Main Street, causing the buggy to swing wide and strike a telegraph pole. Continuing up Main, the buggy bounced off several posts before crashing into a hack that was parked in the street. Although the buggy was basically left in tooth picks, the horse wasn't badly injured.[17]

The following week, Deputy Atwood escorted three convicts to San Quentin on May 23rd. Brothers Walter and Chauncey St. Clair were both sentenced to one and a half years for burglary, while John Crow was to complete a three-year sentence.[18]

It was back to San Quentin for Sheriff Cunningham on June 24th, 1880, this time with two prisoners. James McKenzie was headed to the rock for fifteen years on a robbery conviction, while George Williams was sentenced to five years for burglary.[19]

That June, Thomas's house on east Market Street was undergoing renovations, with the house being raised several feet and the lot being improved.[20]

In August 1880, Thomas was re-elected as the foreman of his fire company. Later in August, Walter and Chauncey St. Clair were returned to Stockton from San Quentin for retrial after their lawyers successfully argued that the original indictment with which they were convicted read "larcey," not "larceny." The California Supreme Court agreed with the defense attorneys, stating there was no law on the books defining "larcey."[21]

Sheriff Cunningham was called to a shooting outside of Acampo on September 26th, 1880, in northern San Joaquin County. Dennis Mullen shot James Mullen to death outside of a cabin that afternoon. The two men, who were not related, had both been drinking. Cunningham lodged Dennis Mullen in the jail that evening. He was tried for manslaughter.[22]

Local lawmen were busy dealing with thieves in the fall of 1880. In October, Sheriff Cunningham received a telegram from San Francisco Police Chief Patrick Crowley, requesting he be on the lookout for two Chinese men who had stolen two expensive bracelets. Cunningham gave the assignment to Deputy Atwood, who along with Stockton Police Chief Orrin Langmaid located one of the men. The stolen property was not located at the time.

On November 12th, 1880, Thomas travelled to San Francisco, where he arrested Richard and Mary Cornell on warrants for grand larceny from Stockton. He also brought back a horse thief named Eli Fitzgerald from San Quentin to testify against his partner in crime, O. N. Burnham. Deputy Atwood returned Fitzgerald and delivered Burnham to San Quentin two days later.[23]

San Francisco Police Chief
Patrick Crowley
[*UC Berkeley, Bancroft Library*]

Thomas was retained in office after elections held on November 2nd, 1880. There were no changes to his staff at that time.

The following month, on December 29th, 1880, a local farmer named Michael Sheridan came to the Sheriff's Office to report that he had shot and killed a man the night before who was stealing chickens from his property. Sheridan lived near the Five Mile House, in what is now the area of the intersection of Hammer Lane and Lower Sacramento Road, in Stockton. He was totally cooperative and took the sheriff and coroner back to his property to explain what had happened.

During the late evening hours of December 28th, Sheridan was returning to his house after having visited some friends at a neighbor's ranch. Sheridan had walked home, and when he got there, he noticed some of his chickens running around in his yard. He then saw that all of the chickens were missing from his coop. He grabbed his shotgun and started investigating when he stumbled across a couple of gunny sacks full of live chickens on the road. He crouched down and cocked both barrels of his gun when he heard a man approaching.

Sheridan called out to the man and told him to stop or that he would shoot, but the man kept running. The stranger reached a high-spot in the ground when Sheridan let loose with one barrel of shot, felling the man right there. Sheridan approached the man as he was drawing his last breath.

Neighbor's came to help Michael Sheridan, but there wasn't much to do. Sheridan then rode into town the next morning to report the shooting.

Sheridan was cleared by a coroner's jury as having acted in self-defense. Two days later, a judge dismissed charges against him after hearing all of the evidence.[24]

In early January 1881, Deputy Fields filed his monthly jail statistics, which gives an interesting insight into the reasons people were jailed in those days. This report recorded the arrests and bookings for the month of December 1880:

petit larceny—10
robbery—4
assault—6
vagrancy—1
grand larceny—4
burglary—4

disturbing the peace—9
manslaughter—2
assault to murder—1
battery—3
obtaining money under false pretenses—1
healthy beggars—2
run-away boys—2
prisoners en route -3
assault with a deadly weapon -1
witness—1
suspicion of petit larceny—3
embezzlement—1
suspicion of burglary—1
contempt of court—2
insane—1
soliciting—1
drunks—47
adultery—1
felony—1
misdemeanor—2
Total—116

The jailor accommodated 18 persons with lodgings and had 28 regular boarders at the time of the report.[25]

During the first week of January 1881, Jailer Fields was accused of battery by a female inmate named Carrie Johnson, alias Carrie Strauss. Described as a "woman of the town," Johnson alleged that Deputy Fields choked and gagged her by forcing a broom stick down her throat to quiet her as she was creating a ruckus in the jail.

Fields was tried by a jury in police court on January 14th, 1881. After the evidence was presented, Fields' attorney argued that the case boiled down to whether the disreputable or respectable elements of society would control the city. The jury hung, eight for acquittal and three for conviction. The twelfth juror had been dismissed during the trial because of sickness. The case was dropped against Fields after the trial and he retained his position as the jailer. A few weeks after the case was tried, the Board of Supervisors ordered that a dark cell, a cell for unruly prisoners, be constructed in the jail.[26]

The first week in February saw Cunningham on the road to San Quentin with convict David Douglass, who received a two-year sentence.[27]

On March 10th, 1881, Thomas was called to New Hope, where a Chinese laborer named Lum Bing was hacked to death in a cabin by a coworker named Ah You. Sheriff Cunningham found Ah You in southern Sacramento County and lodged him in the Stockton jail. Blood stains were found on You's clothing at the time of his arrest, and other workers identified him as being the killer. You was convicted of Bing's murder and he was sentenced to life imprisonment in San Quentin.[28]

Ah You, convicted of the murder of Lum Bing in 1881
[*Cunningham's mug book, SJSO collection*]

Thomas escorted John Keyt to San Quentin on May 25th, 1881, where Keyt was to serve three and a half years for grand larceny. In July, Cunningham was headed to Folsom with Ten Loy, to serve a ten-year sentence for burglary.[29]

Ten head of cattle were stolen from the ranch of Trahern and Dudley, west of Banta, on the night of November 26th, 1881. Sheriff Cunningham started on the case the next day, trailing the stolen cattle to Mohr's Landing, the head of navigation on the Old River, where he was compelled to end his search until the next morning. Thomas searched the hills around the landing, but not finding any clues, Cunningham returned to search the low-lying areas around the river.

Over the next several days, Thomas developed information which led him to a pasture filled with stolen cattle in Antioch, Contra Costa County. The pasture was used by Antioch butchers Landeman and Noakes.

Thomas had brought the cattle's owner, Mr. Dudley, along to identify his herd. Along with the ten head of cattle he had lost that week, Dudley identified seventeen other head that his firm had previously lost. The pasture owners claimed no knowledge of the stolen nature of the cattle found on their land and the thieves weren't identified, but the cattle owners recovered their property.[30]

In early December 1881, it was discovered that old-time road agent Billy Miner was up to his old tricks. Miner had spent a lot of time in San Quentin since San Joaquin County lawmen last had contact with him. Sentenced to three years for the Porter robbery in 1866, where Deputy Joe Long and Officer Jerome Myers had arrested him, Miner had subsequently been released on a court order discharging him two months later. He didn't stay out long; less than a month later he was back in San Quentin, serving a five-year sentence for grand larceny out of Placer County. Six-months after his release from that stretch, Miner helped rob the San Andreas to Stockton stage, where he received a thirteen-year sentence from Calaveras County in 1872.

On his release, Miner started robbing stagecoaches in California. He traveled to Colorado, where he committed another stage robbery. He was arrested after a long chase, but escaped. Miner later joined forces with an outlaw named Stanton P. Jones, and the two had drifted back to California by 1880. Once in California, Miner and Jones hooked up with two other old-time bandits, Jim Crum, an experienced stage robber in his own right, and William Miller.[31]

In late 1880, Miner, Crum, Miller and Jones formed a group with a number of other outlaws and started stealing horses over a wide region of the northern part of the state. The thieves' area of operation took in many counties. Lawmen had initially found themselves between a rock and hard ground in obtaining information about the horse thieves, but over time Sheriff Cunningham developed a lead on one of the thieves in the group named William Todhunter.[32]

Todhunter had been a troublemaker in Sacramento for several years. He had been arrested in April 1878 for drawing and exhibiting a deadly weapon and disturbing the peace. He was suspected of horse theft after he left a stolen horse at a Sacramento stable in January 1880. His story was that the horse had just wandered onto his property. He was arrested by Sacramento police for battery in September 1880.[33]

Sheriff Cunningham worked up enough evidence to secure a warrant for Todhunter's arrest and he sent the wanted information to other lawmen.

Meanwhile, Billy Miner, Jim Crum, Bill Miller and Stanton Jones staged a holdup on the Sonora to Milton stagecoach on the morning of November 7th, 1881. The bandits struck at 5:30 a.m. that morning, about ten miles outside of Sonora near the Garibaldi mine. The four were wearing masks at the time they stepped out into the road and stopped the coach.

The stage was being driven by Clark Stringham, who obeyed every command made by the bandit leader. Wells Fargo's boxes were sledged open and the contents taken. The outlaws then went through all of the passengers. One of them, John Mandorf, a Sonora merchant, lost about $550 worth of gold dust to the road agents and the loss to Wells Fargo was reported to be about $3,300 in coin and gold dust. During the holdup, Stringham told the robbers to hurry up, that he didn't want to miss the Milton train. With that, the bandit leader asked the time, and when told, shook Stringham's hand, bid him good morning, and with a wave of his hand and a cheery "ta-ta," rode off into the forest with his band.[34]

Wells Fargo detectives John Thacker (left) and Charles Aull
[*Wells Fargo*]

Word was sent out about the robbery when the stagecoach reached Milton and Sheriff Thorn was soon headed to the crime scene. He was joined by Wells Fargo's trusty detectives Charles Aull and John Thacker. Aull had served as the Stanislaus County undersheriff for Sheriff John Rodgers in the early 1870s, and had recently been a guard at San Quentin, so he was very familiar with the criminals operating in California. Thacker had been the Humboldt County, Nevada sheriff in the late 1860s and had been hired by Wells Fargo in 1875. He served as Jim Hume's right-hand man for many years.

The lawmen were joined by Sheriff Cunningham and Tuolumne County Sheriff T. M. Yancey. The officers trailed the outlaws through Stanislaus and Alameda counties to San Francisco, then back through Alameda, San Joaquin and Sacramento counties. With detailed descriptions of the robbers, after two weeks of hard work, officers determined the identities of the brigands. Sacramento police officers William Arlington and Timothy Lee joined in the investigation and manhunt.[35]

Officers traced Crum, Miner, and Miller to Yolo County, where Miller was known to have connections. Wells Fargo detectives called for the help of Yolo County Sheriff Frank M. Rahm, Yuba County Sheriff Henry L. McCoy, and Sacramento Police Officer William Arlington on Saturday, December 3rd, 1881. Together, they made a plan to go after the bandits.

On Tuesday morning, December 6th, John Thacker and sheriffs Rahm and McCoy came very suddenly upon Jim Crum, Billy Miner and Bill Miller. Crum confronted the lawmen with a shotgun but was talked into giving up. Miner and Miller escaped into nearby brush. The hunt for the two went on throughout the day, and all of the original officers in the pursuit were summoned, including Sheriff Cunningham. Thomas arrived in Yolo that evening.

The search for the outlaws continued through that night and the next day. Between 5:00 and 6:00 p.m. on the evening of Wednesday, December 7th, Agent Aull and Officer Arlington were walking along the levee on the west side of the Sacramento River, about nine miles above the settlement of Washington, when they suddenly came upon Miner and Miller. Both bad guys were heavily armed, each carrying a shotgun, two revolvers, and about 100 rounds of ammunition.

It was just growing dusk about that time, and as Miner and Miller realized that they had been discovered, they drew guns on the officers. Officer Arlington made a run for them, causing both to break for a fence and run off into the tules towards Davisville (Davis). Aull, armed with a shotgun, and Arlington, armed with a revolver, ran after the robbers. Aull let loose with several rounds of buckshot as they were running. Miller gave up after a short run, throwing up his hands, but Miner continued on with Charles Aull in pursuit. Billy Arlington took Bill Miller into custody and took him to Washington, where Arlington briefed other officers of the current pursuit.

Agent Aull gave Billy Miner a spirited chase for about a mile before the bandit threw up his hands and gave up. It was quite dark by now, and Aull procured a team and wagon to take Miner back to Washington. A horse thief named Ben Frazee was also picked up along the way. Crum, Miner, Frazee and Miller were taken to Sacramento, where their photographs were taken at Beal's photograph gallery.[36]

The old concept of "no honor among thieves" was alive and well in December of 1881, and Bill Miller started chirping like a canary, identifying all his friends and detailing their crimes. He confirmed the lawmen's suspicions that he and the others had been responsible for the numerous horse thefts around the north state.[37]

That same day, Wednesday, December 7th, 1881, William Todhunter was arrested by El Dorado County Undersheriff J. T. Ashley outside of Pino, in El Dorado County. Two days later, Thomas brought Ben Frazee and William Todhunter from Sacramento back to Stockton on the train to face charges for horse stealing in San Joaquin County.[38]

Thomas was in the saddle over the next couple of weeks with a number of other sheriffs, rounding up stolen horses and returning them to their owners. Cunningham met with Sheriff A. S. Fulkerth of Stanislaus County, Sheriff John Vogan of Amador County, Sheriff Ben Thorn of Calaveras County, Sheriff Henry McCoy of Yuba County, Sheriff Ezekiel Hall of Fresno County, Sheriff William Harkey of Sutter County, Sheriff John Boggs of Placer County, and Undersheriff A. S. McQuaid of Tuolumne County, in Modesto to start their search. With information provided by members of the Crum gang, the lawmen located about 30 horses from an area known as "The Pocket" on the San Joaquin River. A number of horses were located on a ranch in Stanislaus County owned by a man named Walden, who dealt in stolen horses and cattle. Information provided to the officers by William Todhunter led the lawmen to believe that they would be able to recover about 100 horses in all.[39]

7

TROUBLE ON THE MOQUELUMNES

In early 1882, Thomas was in Marysville visiting his friend, Yuba County Sheriff Henry McCoy, and on January 9th the two were standing on the street when they recognized a recent Folsom prison escapee named John Sansome. Sansome had been sentenced to fifteen years for the 1876 burglary of the Wells Fargo & Co office safe in Quincy. He escaped from the prison through a sewer on December 28th, 1881. He had made his way to Marysville, and was suspected of committing the burglary of the Yuba County treasurer's house a day or two before he was arrested. Sheriff Cunningham returned Sansome to prison the following day.[1]

In February, the sheriff and other San Joaquin County officers were involved in the search for murder suspect John Lentini, believed to have killed Margaret Troia outside of Galt, in Sacramento County. Sheriff Cunningham directed the search around the New Hope area, but his efforts did not produce any results.[2]

On the afternoon of Sunday, April 2nd, 1882, Thomas

responded with Eureka Engine Company 2 and the other fire units in Stockton to a large and spectacular fire at the City Mills of Sperry and Company. Volunteer firemen and about 100 citizens were able to salvage some expensive machinery, but the building was fully engulfed. The *Evening Mail* reported that during the inferno, "Chief Engineer Rolf and Sheriff Cunningham were to be found in the thickest of the engagement, the latter holding the pipe and playing into the hottest of the fire, with as much zeal as if he were pursuing a gang of horse thieves." Despite all efforts, the building was a total loss.[3]

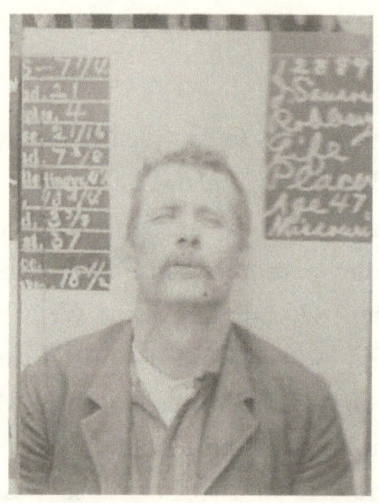

John Sansome
[*Cunningham's mug book, SJSO collection*]

Later in April 1882, Sheriff Cunningham escorted Hiram James to San Quentin to serve a five-year sentence for manslaughter. James was a Lodi resident who had been troublesome for Lodi officers for the previous couple of years. He frequented local bars and had a reputation as being a crooked card player, which created conflict for him when he played. He was fined for battery in April 1880, and in December of that year James had a dispute with a man named Shoemaker.

Shoemaker was in the middle of a card game when James interrupted him. A fight between the two ensued, James coming out on the losing end. James went for a shotgun, but a bystander took the weapon away from him before he had the chance to use it.

That fall, on the night of October 4th, 1881, James was once again in a Lodi saloon trying to get into a card game. One of the players, Frank Pygall, objected to James entering the game, calling James a crook. An argument followed and Pygall hit James. James pulled out a knife and stabbed Pygall in the stomach; Pygall ended up dying from the wound. Hiram James went to Stockton and turned himself into the sheriff the next day.[4]

The following spring, the Banta to Grayson stage was robbed by two men on the Stanislaus County side of Hill's Ferry on Saturday, April 22nd, 1882. John Coggins and Amos Morris were arrested in Stockton three days later, but the case against them didn't make any traction and they were released.[5]

In May, a stage operated by the Coast Stage Lines was held up by two highwaymen a few miles south of Soledad, in Monterey County. Eventually, lawmen developed suspects in these two robberies: Dan McCarty and John Weisenstein. McCarty was an ex-con who had been sent up for stage robbery in 1877. Warrants were issued for both outlaws.

Sheriff Cunningham got a line on Dan McCarty in early December 1882, and, along with Sacramento Police Officer William Arlington, made the arrest at the Buckeye House, thirty-six miles south-east of Sacramento, near the Amador County line.

Cunningham had planned to catch the train at the nearest station with his prisoner, but McCarty convinced Thomas that he knew he was going to prison for a long time and he had some property that he wanted to sign over to his father. Cunningham understood McCarty's situation and agreed to take him to Sacramento to meet his father. Thomas lodged McCarty in the Sacramento city jail so that Cunningham could take care of some business at the Capitol.

While in Sacramento, Sheriff Cunningham learned that McCarty's father was working on obtaining a writ of habeas corpus to free his son. Thomas hurried back to the jail in order to get McCarty out of town. To his amazement, when he got back to the Sacramento jail, he found that the officers he had left McCarty with had taken him out of the jail and were heading to Washington, in Yolo County, probably to foil the father's plans. Cunningham immediately started after them to get his prisoner back. When he overtook them, he took McCarty directly to the train station, where they left for Monterey County before anything else delayed him. McCarty ended up getting a twelve-year sentence in Folsom for the Soledad robbery.[6]

During the numerous horse and cattle theft cases Sheriff Cunningham had been involved in, he found out how difficult it was to identify the animals. In November of 1882, Thomas came up with a simple but effective way for farmers and ranchers to document individual characteristics of their animals to help remedy the situation. Called the "Cunningham device for registering stock," this small booklet had outline figures of horses and cattle, and the owners could then document ear marks, brands, colors and markings to assist them in keeping these records.[7]

In March 1883, Thomas bought three bloodhound puppies

from Texas. The pups, which cost $200, were a cross between a bloodhound and a foxhound. Cunningham was training them at the time and was hopeful they would become valuable assets for manhunts once they were grown.[8]

Two months later, in May 1883, John Lentini, suspected of the murder of Mrs. Troia in Sacramento County in February 1882, was turned in to the Tulare County sheriff in Visalia by some people who thought Lentini was having a mental breakdown. After the killing, Lentini wandered south and had been working as a sheep herder, living alone for months. Being in solitude for that amount of time began wearing on him. In a conversation with people living in the area, Lentini commented that he had killed a lady north of Stockton about fifteen months before and that officers were searching for him.

During the conversation, a bolt of lightning struck nearby and thunder clapped. With that, Lentini blurted out, "There is the sheriff in his buggy now." The neighbors, thinking that Lentini was having some sort of mental crisis, took him to Visalia. When told the story, Sheriff William Martin remembered receiving information on the Sacramento homicide and contacted Sheriff Cunningham. Thomas travelled to Visalia on the train with Mr. Troia, who readily identified Lentini. He was taken to Sacramento by Sheriff Cunningham and turned over to the Sacramento sheriff.[9]

In July 1883, Sheriff Cunningham was on the hunt for horse thieves. His first case began after two horses, five sets of harness, a saddle and a bridal were stolen from a stable in northern San Joaquin County. Thomas's journey took him through Sacramento, El Dorado and Placer counties, where he spent several days on the hunt. Along the way, Cunningham discovered that the man he was looking for was Henry Moore, who had been busy stealing property in several counties.

Moore was already in custody in the Auburn jail on a grand larceny charge when Thomas got there. Moore pleaded guilty to the charge at his arraignment, receiving a two-year sentence in San Quentin. Sheriff Cunningham then brought Moore on the train to Stockton to face his San Joaquin County charges. He received three more years there, bringing his stay in prison to five years.[10]

On July 26th, 1883, Sheriff Cunningham arrested a horse thief in Stockton who gave his name as Charles Hancock. Hancock was known to the San Francisco police under the name Charles Little. He also had an alias of Charles Wright and was an old-time horse thief.

That day, Cunningham came across Hancock trying to sell a horse and buggy outfit for much less that it was worth. Thomas pretended to be interested in buying the property, and, suspecting it was stolen, engaged Hancock in conversation, getting as much information about the crook as he could. Hancock claimed he was from Napa, but couldn't give any references when queried. He also did not know the name of the Napa County sheriff. Sheriff Cunningham arrested Hancock on suspicion of possession of stolen property and lodged him in the jail until he could figure things out.

Hancock was wanted on a San Francisco warrant at the time. He was also wanted in Oakland and in Placer County for grand larceny. The horse and property he was trying to sell in Stockton had been stolen in Sacramento. Cunningham took him to San Francisco on the train that day. Hancock ended up receiving a ten-year sentence in Folsom for the San Francisco charges.[11]

The fall months of 1883 were very busy for Stockton area

lawmen. In early September, Patrick Breen was shot and killed over a land dispute. Violence over the land in question had been long in the making. Disputes over title to a large tract of land in northeast San Joaquin County had dated back to the time before California became a part of the United States. Private individuals had been granted large ranchos throughout the state by the Mexican government in the 1840's. The Rancho Sanjon de los Moquelumnes was a 35,508-acre Mexican land grant in present-day Sacramento and San Joaquin counties, given in 1844 by Governor Manuel Micheltorena to Anastasio Chaboya.[12]

A man named Andres Pico, who had at one time been the governor of California under Mexican rule, had made claim to the Moquelumnes grant. That claim had been rejected by the United States Supreme Court on February 13th, 1865, and using a law passed by Congress on July 1st, 1862, titled "to aid in the construction of a railroad and telegraph lines from the Missouri River to the Pacific Ocean," the federal government had granted patent to sections of land in the grant to the Western Pacific Railroad, which planned to lay track from Lodi into the Mother Lode country. The railroad had subsequently sold sections of land that it didn't need to settlers, who built homes and cultivated their lands.

Because title to the Moquelumnes grant continued to be in dispute and was crawling through the courts, squatters moved into the area, built shacks or shanties, and started growing crops on land that had already been plowed, claiming they were homesteading. The squatters became known as the "Moquelemos grant settlers."[13]

In June 1883, Sheriff Cunningham had served an attachment for a crop of harvested hay, grown by a Moquelemos grant settler named W. T. Smith. Smith ignored the attachment, and when he and four of his workers started hauling the hay, Sheriff Cunningham arrested all five of them. Now, tempers between the folks with railroad title and those with grant title were at a boiling point.

During a dispute on Monday, September 3rd, Patrick Breen, a railroad title holder, was shot and killed by Samuel Markey, while four other "grant holders" stood by. All five men, Markey, Christopher Heid, D. M. Vance, George Hurlbert and Henry Beck, were arrested and thrown in jail.[14]

In the mean time, other cases continued to come into the Sheriff's Office. Two weeks later, on September 17th, Edward Murray, a Livermore stable owner, and Charles Kingsberry, who owned a farm on Robert's Island west of Stockton, were involved in an argument where Kingsberry cut Murray's throat. Kingsberry was arrested and lodged in the jail.[15]

The following day, September 18th, Sheriff Cunningham received a wire from Chicago, informing him that officers there had arrested Charles Walden, a Lodi area bookkeeper who was under grand jury indictment and wanted by the sheriff for embezzling his employer, the Grangers' Business Association of Lodi. Thomas immediately left for Chicago on the eastbound overland train.[16]

While the sheriff was gone on the Chicago trip, a Stockton man named Julius Deitrich was gunned down on the sidewalk in front of his house, as his wife and child watched in horror.

Julius' wife had been standing on the balcony of their home on the afternoon of September 21st, 1883, waiting for her husband to arrive home from work when Abraham Turcott and his two pals, Alfred Summers and J. M. Leayan, came walking down the sidewalk. Turcott made an insulting remark towards Mrs. Deitrich as they passed.

Mrs. Deitrich was relating the story to Julius when he got home, just as Turcott and his thug friends, complete strangers to the Deitrichs, came passing back by. Julius went out to the sidewalk to demand an apology from Turcott about his remark when J. M. Leayan grabbed him around the shoulders from behind, telling Julius he had better return to his house. At the same time, Turcott came in behind Julius, and drawing a revolver, reached over Leayan and shot Julius dead.

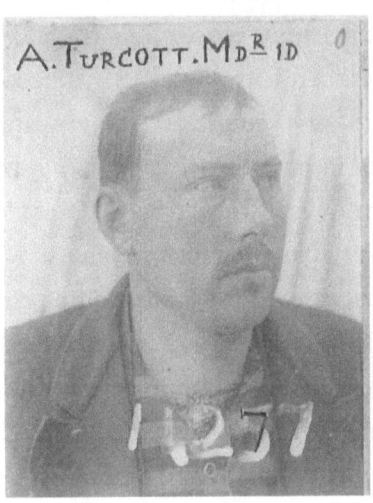

Abraham Turcott
[*Cunningham's mug book, SJSO collection*]

Stockton police officers arrested Turcott, Summers and Leayan, and walked them to jail, followed by an angry crowd who were looking to lynch them.

Julius Deitrich had been a hard-working husband and father, and Stocktonians were irate over his murder. Lynching was a real possibility. Deputies and Stockton officers had to get Turcott safely to the courthouse from the jail for his preliminary hearing on September 27th. A crowd had formed around the courthouse and the officers had to take precautions. Deputies devised a circuitous route from the jail and kept the doors to the courtroom locked, while Turcott was guarded by heavily-armed officers. He was held to answer to the murder charge after the hearing and officers were successful in returning him safely to jail.[17]

Thomas arrived back in Stockton with Charles Walden on the evening train from Chicago on October 3rd. Walden was charged with sixteen counts; fifteen counts of embezzlement and one charge of forgery, accusing him of stealing $3,500 from his former employer. On October 16th, Walden entered a plea agreement, pleading guilty to one count of forgery and two counts of embezzlement, for a thirteen-year prison sentence. The other counts against him were dismissed at that time.[18]

Sheriff Cunningham spent much of November 1883 summoning jurors, providing courtroom security, or testifying during the homicide trials for Samuel Markey and Abraham Turcott. In the middle of summoning jurors for the Markey trial, with jury selection starting on November 2nd, Thomas received a wire from James Hume on Saturday, November 3rd, requesting his assistance with a Calaveras County stagecoach robbery investigation. Cunningham arrived in Copperopolis that evening.[19]

Early on the morning of November 3rd, a lone highwayman held up the down stage from Sonora to Milton, about three miles outside of Copperopolis on the grade known as Funk Hill. Stagecoach driver Reason McConnell was nursing his coach up Funk Hill from the Reynold's Ferry on the Stanislaus River when the robbery took place. McConnell had picked up a passenger that morning, a young man named Jimmy Rolleri, who was eager to do some deer hunting. Rolleri had gotten down off of the coach at the river and was walking the brush alongside the road, well behind the coach. There were no other passengers in the stagecoach at the time.

As McConnell got close to the top of the hill, a lone road agent stepped out into the road, leveling a double-barreled shotgun at him. The robber was wearing a cloth flour sack over his head with eye holes cut in it, a derby hat, and an old and tattered duster. The highwayman ordered McConnell to unhitch the team of horses and move them away from the stage. While McConnell was doing that, the bandit inquired as to where the boy went that had been on the coach with him and McConnell told him the boy had gone off shooting.

The Wells Fargo box was bolted to the floor inside the stage and the robber attacked it with a sledge hammer, plundering its contents. The take was reported to be about $4,100 worth of gold amalgam and $500 worth of gold and silver coin. As that was going on, McConnell was able to summon Jimmy Rolleri to his location. The bandit exited the coach and was skittering off into brush just before Jimmy reached McConnell. Taking Jimmy's Henry rifle, McConnell took a couple of shots at the robber from a distance of about 100 yards. Seeing that the shots had not taken effect, Jimmy then grabbed his rifle back, took aim, and fired a shot, the bullet winging the road agent in the left hand and causing a deep crease in it. After re-hitching his team, McConnell continued on to Copperopolis, where the alarm was sounded.[20]

Calaveras County Sheriff Thorn and Tuolumne County Sheriff McQuaid were soon heading for the scene, and other lawmen were called into the area. That is when Thomas got the wire from James Hume.

A search was done of the scene and surrounding countryside and a number of items were taken for evidence. The derby hat was found, along with a package of papers, red with blood, that had been taken from the mail. A handkerchief was located, bearing a very distinctive FX07 laundry mark. The bandit's camp was located, and some more evidence was found, including a spyglass case.[21]

Sheriff Cunningham assisted the other lawmen with the search. They then spread out, questioning neighbors in the area who might have seen anyone matching the outlaw's description. Cunningham and McQuaid came across a hunter named Martin who had seen a man who was thought to be the outlaw walking out of the area. Thomas spent Sunday in Calaveras County, then returned on the train from Milton that night.[22]

Based on information provided by McConnell and Rolleri and the evidence found at the scene, suspicion immediately fell on a notorious stagecoach robber who went by the moniker of "Black Bart." Wells Fargo's James Hume was very well acquainted with Bart, who had been suspected of committing 28 other robberies against stagecoaches and their Wells Fargo treasure boxes from southern Oregon to Calaveras County over the previous eight years. Ironically, Bart's very first stagecoach robbery took place at the exact same location as this last one, at the top of Funk Hill, on July 26th, 1875.

Hume had studied Black Bart long and hard. The outlaw got his moniker after the August 3rd, 1877 robbery of a stage in Mendocino County where he left a scrap of paper on which he wrote:

"I've labored hard and long for bread,
For honor and for riches,
But on my corns too long you've tread,
You fine haired sons of bitches.
Black Bart, the Po8" [23]

Hume had long felt that Bart was living in San Francisco, and the laundry mark gave him a starting point. Hume hired former Alameda County Sheriff Harry Morse, who had since established a detective agency in the City by the Bay, to track down the origin of the laundry mark from the city's nearly 100 laundries.[24]

Sheriff Cunningham was back in Stockton on Monday, November 5th, summoning jurors for the Samuel Markey homicide trial. Jury selection for Markey, the Moquelemos land grant holder, went on through most of that week, a jury finally being impaneled on November 8th. After a jury trial, Markey was found not guilty for the slaying of Patrick Breen. Feeling he had no case against the other defendants, D. M. Vance, Henry Beck, Christopher Heid and George Hurlbert, the district attorney dropped charges against them.[25]

While Thomas was busy in Stockton, James Hume and other officers were at work tracking down Black Bart in San Francisco. Harry Morse hit pay-dirt in locating the origin of the handkerchief laundry mark, and Bart was finally run to ground on Monday, November 12th, 1883. He initially identified himself to the officers as T. Z. Spaulding, but later gave his name as Charles E. Bolton, the name by which he was known in San Francisco. The name on his birth certificate read Charles Boles. Sheriff Thorn secured a warrant for Boles for the November 3rd stage robbery. Boles maintained his innocence as officers searched his room for

Charles Boles, alias Black Bart
[SJSO collection]

evidence.²⁶

Sheriff Thorn travelled to Stockton with the witness, Mr. Martin, on Tuesday, November 13th, while Harry Morse, John Thacker and San Francisco Police Captain Appleton Stone escorted Charles Boles to Stockton on the train, arriving that afternoon. Mr. Martin identified Boles out of a large crowd of people at the train station. Sheriff Cunningham served a summons on Boles, issued in a suit brought against him by Wells Fargo to recover what he had in the way of valuables. When handed the paper, Boles said, "This don't cost anything, does it?" Cunningham replied, "Oh no, this is free." "Well, I'm taking free things now, so I'll take this," responded Boles.²⁷

Against his will, Boles, alias Black Bart, was taken to the photo studio of Stockton photographer J. Pitcher Spooner, where pictures were taken of him. While there, the officers involved in the case took the opportunity to have a group photo taken of themselves. These photos became widely published.

Bart spent the night in the Stockton jail, then was taken to Calaveras County on the Milton train by Sheriff Thorn, Harry Morse and Captain Stone on November 14th. After officers presented him with the overwhelming evidence they had gathered against him, Boles dropped all pretenses and confessed, then took the officers to where he had buried his gun and the plunder from the November 3rd robbery.

Sheriff Cunningham received a telegram the following day: "Copperopolis, November 15—To Thomas Cunningham: Black Bart throws up the sponge. We have recovered all the treasure. H. N. Morse."²⁸

Bart ended up pleading guilty to one count of robbery in front of Calaveras County Superior Court Judge Charles V. Gottschalk

The lawmen who worked on the Black Bart case.
Seated, left to right: Thomas Cunningham, Ben Thorn, Harry Morse
Standing, left to right: Appleton Stone, John Thacker
[*SJSO collection*]

on November 17th, and he was sentenced to six years in San Quentin under the name C. E. Bolton.²⁹

Trial for Abraham Turcott began on November 20th, 1883. Sheriff Cunningham made sure that security for the trial remained tight. After hearing the evidence, the jury returned a verdict of murder in the first degree. The judge sentenced Turcott to be hanged.³⁰

On December 7th, 1883, Sheriff Cunningham, along with Sacramento Police Officer Bissell, Lathrop Constable Walker and Stockton Constable James Carroll, arrested three teenage boys in Stockton for causing a train wreck. The three had cut a padlock and thrown a switch ahead of an on-coming train, causing it to ditch. The junior Jesse James's confessed to the crime, as well as confessing to stealing $190 from a train conductor's car. They were also suspected of attempting to set fire to the Standard Oil Company's warehouse in Stockton.³¹

Abraham Turcott remained in the Stockton jail, under sentence of death, while his case was being appealed. In January 1884, Deputy Fields found a two-edged dagger in Turcott's cell during a search.³²

In 1884, Thomas added William Crandall to his staff in the Sheriff's Office. Crandall had been a Stockton police officer since 1879. He joined Undersheriff Joe Long and deputies Oscar Atwood and Charles Fields.³³

On Thursday, January 31st, Sheriff Cunningham arrested Samuel Ransom near Jenny Lind, in Calaveras County, on suspicion of cattle theft. Thomas had been investigating the theft of six head of cattle from the Reynolds' ranch in eastern San Joaquin County. The cattle had been found abandoned along the road several miles from where they were taken. Ransom rolled over after his arrest and named his partner, William Breeze, a Jenny Lind butcher. Cunningham then put the irons on him, too.[34]

Twelve days later, on February 11th, 1884, Thomas was on a train, returning from Los Angeles with a prisoner named James Campbell, alias E. C. Wright, wanted for grand larceny. Campbell had skipped bail back in October of 1882 and moved to Los Angeles. He was accused of stealing wheat and hogs from the Williams ranch on Union Island.[35]

In April, the California Supreme Court affirmed the death penalty for Abraham Turcott. He was scheduled to be hanged on June 13th, 1884.[36]

Sheriff Cunningham was called to Clements on Tuesday, April 29th, 1884, to the scene of a murder. Robert Henderson was found shot to death along the railroad tracks about a half-mile outside of Clements. Cunningham learned that Henderson had been in a quarrel the night before with a man named Samuel Williams. Williams had bantered Henderson, trying to entice him into a fight, but Henderson declined. His body was found the next day.

Samuel Williams fled the area and was never caught, but Sheriff Cunningham and Sacramento County Deputy Sheriff Timothy Lee arrested Cicero Sterns on May 22nd, in the Sacramento County river town of Courtland, for being an accessory after the fact in aiding Williams to flee.[37]

On June 6th, 1884, Sheriff Cunningham received a dispatch from Governor George Stoneman, commuting the sentence of Abraham Turcott to life imprisonment. Turcott was then transferred to San Quentin prison.[38]

July found Thomas dealing with more trouble on the Moquelumnes land grant. Legal issues had continued in the courts into the 1880's over ownership of lands in the area of the original

Moquelumnes grant. A man named A. W. Bailey had recently won title over four "settlers" in federal court, but the settlers were having none of it. All four had planted wheat on four squares of property in the area formerly in question, and they were determined to harvest and sell it.

Bailey had been sued by N. W. Goodwin to recover $2,400 on a promissory note by Bailey on a separate issue, and Sheriff Cunningham placed the wheat crops from the four squares of land claimed by the settlers under attachment. Thomas appointed a local man as a sheriff's keeper to ensure the security of the crop.

The settlers claimed that they weren't going down without a fight, and they had every intention of harvesting "their" crops. They gathered other armed and angry settlers to make sure they could claim the grain unmolested.

Sheriff Cunningham had to use a cool head to prevail in this one. Blood had already been spilled over Moquelumnes land issues, and the last thing he wanted was more of it. Thomas decided that the only way to face an army was with an overwhelming army of his own, and maybe that would convince the settlers to stand-down.

Cunningham enlisted the help of Brigadier General J. A. Shepherd, commander of the National Guard units in Stockton, for help with the situation. At 4:00 a.m. on the morning of July 9th, Sheriff Cunningham left Stockton in the company of 50 members of the Stockton Guard and 42 members of the Emmet Guard, headed for the seat of the trouble.

When Sheriff Cunningham and the soldiers got to Bailey's property, they were met by forty-five armed men, but instead of showing fight, they laid down their arms, just as the sheriff had hoped. The military brass in Sacramento were not happy that the

National Guard had been used in this instance, but Cunningham had quietly taken possession of the grain, and it was processed under his orders by virtue of the writ of attachment.[39]

The Banta to Grayson stage was again held up on the morning of October 23rd, 1884, by three men. The robbery occurred about a mile and a half outside of San Joaquin City. The three road agents were lounging around a bridge as the stagecoach approached, and driver Frank Grimes had no reason to pay any particular attention to them until they pulled out guns and ordered him to halt.

Two of the outlaws were armed with double-barreled shotguns, while the other one brandished a six-shooter. Grimes handed down the Wells Fargo box on demand. There was only one passenger on the stage at the time, J. J. Sweeney, who was riding on the top seat next to the driver. One of the robbers demanded a watch and chain that Sweeney was wearing, but Sweeney refused and the outlaw didn't push the issue.

Grimes returned to San Joaquin City, where telegrams were sent to Sheriff Cunningham in Stockton and Wells Fargo headquarters in San Francisco. San Joaquin City Constable Finch and Banta Constable McCraney headed for the scene to pick up clues, while Stanislaus County Sheriff Fulkerth also headed to the area. Both Grimes and Sweeney described the robbers, who were not wearing masks, as being very unsettled and nervous, as though they were green at the business.

Sheriff Cunningham and Wells Fargo's John Thacker started out from the scene after Sheriff Fulkerth, who had already arrived and was tracking the bandits. Fulkerth trailed the outlaws to the mouth of Lone Tree Canyon in the Coast Range, on the west side of the valley about eight miles west of where the robbery occurred. The sheriff learned that the bandits had stopped at a ranch there at about noon to have a meal and then left going southbound, skirting the mountains and staying in the valley. Continuing on, Fulkerth discovered that instead of pushing on the outlaws had stopped to eat again about 3:00 p.m. that afternoon at the cabin of an old widow.

The three had stopped for a third meal about 6:00 p.m. that evening, and their horses being used up, they had ridden a short distance into a nearby canyon and had gone to sleep in a stack of hay. Sheriff Fulkerth had no problem in taking the three novice bandits into custody without any issues. Cunningham and Thacker had only been about a mile and a half behind Fulkerth by that time, and they arrived a short time later.

The three robbers, James Casey, Peter Smith and Eugene Murphy, told the officers that they were driven to rob the stage because of hunger, having been refused meals by area farmers after having walked a long way. Cunningham and Thacker brought the three to Stockton and lodged them in the jail. All three pleaded guilty at their arraignment, waived time, and were each sentenced to five-years in San Quentin.[40]

On October 15th, 1884, an ex-con named George Lane was arrested in Macville, in northern San Joaquin County, for the September 11th, 1884 robbery of the Forbestown to Oroville stage, where U.S. mail was taken. Lane had been sent up two previous times, once for grand larceny out of San Bernardino County in 1868, and another time for stage robbery out of Nevada County in 1874.

Sheriff Cunningham had received information that Lane might be somewhere in San Joaquin County, and he had put out the word. On the day of his arrest, three San Joaquin county residents, George Ringer, John Fugitt and George Manly, found Lane chopping wood near Macville. They took him into custody and brought him into Lodi, where they notified the sheriff. Thomas booked him in the jail and wired the U.S. Marshal to take Lane to San Francisco.[41]

In early November, Sheriff Cunningham telegraphed his friend, San Francisco Police Captain Appleton Stone, telling Stone that he had been re-elected to the sheriff's position. Stone also received a wire from Calaveras County Sheriff Ben Thorn that he, too, had retained his office.[42]

Thomas' middle daughter Maggie was seriously injured on November 25th, 1884, when the horse that was pulling her two-wheeled carriage became a run-way with her. Her carriage collided with a grocery wagon, throwing her violently to the ground. Knocked unconscious, Maggie suffered a dislocated shoulder and a number of cuts and bruises on her head and face. Although serious, her injuries were not life-threatening.[43]

A jury trial was being held in San Joaquin County Superior Court for accused murderer Uzza French during the first week of December 1884. French had shot a man named Peter Wells on a street in Oleta, in Amador County, on March 12th, 1884. Wells was French's brother-in-law and the two had bad blood between them. Wells had been walking down the street with his young son when he was confronted by French, who was armed with a shotgun.

Wells pleaded with French, but it was no use. French told a woman who was standing in a window behind Wells to move, also instructing two young women on the street to get out of the way, then shot Wells with 00 buckshot. Seven of the buckshot lodged in a post that Wells had moved behind, but one struck Wells in the head, killing him.

French's lawyers successfully argued for a change of venue out of Amador County, sending the trial to Stockton. French had been locked up in Sheriff Cunningham's hotel ever since.

After a trial that lasted one week, the jury found French guilty of murder in the first degree.[44]

On the morning of December 12th, 1884, the down stage from Sonora to Milton was robbed by two masked men armed with shotguns in the Salt Spring Valley area of Calaveras County. Both robbers were seen by the stage passengers without their masks at one point, and both wore heavy beards. The outlaws demanded the Wells Fargo box, which was bolted to the floor inside the coach. One bandit leaned his shotgun on the side of the stage and climbed inside to work on the treasure box, while the other one covered the driver and both passengers. During the robbery, a herder with his flock of sheep crested a nearby hill. The herder called over his shoulder that the stage was being robbed, which spooked the outlaws.[45]

The highwayman who had remained outside called to the one who was unsuccessfully hammering on the lock box inside the coach, "Lon, come on! Lon, hurry up, come on!" The stage driver was told to move along when robber number two jumped out of the stagecoach. As the coach drove away, the shotgun that had been leaning against it was run over by one of the rear wheels, causing a crease across both barrels. The robbers never made it into the strong box and the two got nothing for their efforts.[46]

That afternoon, Friday, December 12th, 1884, Sheriff Cunningham was called to the Ripon area after a Baptist preacher and school teacher named James Wells shot down a laborer named Philip Finch. Trouble arose between the two when Finch seduced Wells' sister. Finch had supposedly confronted Wells as Wells was walking home from school. Believing Finch was armed and going to shoot him, and also to uphold his family honor, Wells drew a pistol and shot Finch, killing him. Wells was later acquitted by a jury.[47]

Meanwhile, over the next week, Calaveras County Sheriff Ben Thorn and Wells Fargo's John Thacker developed some suspects in the latest stage robbery, two brothers named Albert and J. M. "Lon" Aldridge. As one might guess, the pair were greenhorns when it came to stage robbing. Lon lived on a farm about eight miles southwest of Milton, in San Joaquin County. His house was elevated on the side of a hill, with a commanding view to the east, towards Milton.

Bert Aldridge was older than Lon, and was described as a bully. He and a man named James Lynch worked together on a farm on Roberts Island, west of Stockton, but both had recently been staying with Lon and his wife and four children.

Lawmen, knowing the layout of the Aldridge property, knew that they would be spotted if they approached it from Calaveras County, so they devised a plan. Sheriff Cunningham was brought in and asked to make the arrests, coming to the Aldridge house from the west, where the outlaws didn't have a clear view.

At 1:00 a.m. on the morning of December 16th, Sheriff Cunningham, Detective John Thacker, and Stockton constables Orrin Langmaid and James Carroll left Stockton for the Aldridge place in a four-seat wagon. The Aldridges had apparently gotten wind that the law was on to them, and they had spent all night watching the road to the east, thinking that Sheriff Thorn and a posse would be coming for them from San Andreas. The Aldridges and Lynch were all sleeping when Sheriff Cunningham and his lawman friends came calling at about seven that morning.

Cunningham called each man out of the small house, one at a time. Both Aldridges, who normally wore long beards, were clean-shaven, their tan lines going to their beard lines and their faces white below that. A shotgun with bent barrels that matched perfectly with having been run over by a coach wheel and other evidence tying the Aldridges to the crime scene was located in the house.

 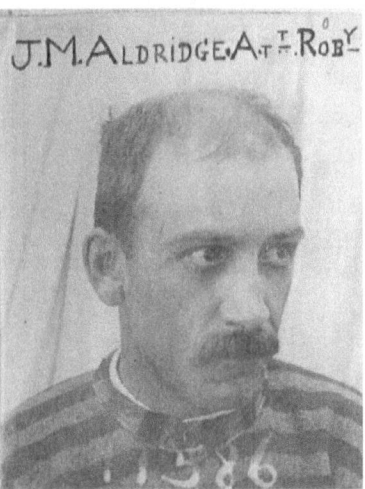

Albert Aldridge (left) and Lon Aldridge
[*Cunningham's mug book, SJSO collection*]

John Thacker sent a wire to his boss, James Hume, in San Francisco when they got the outlaws to Milton: "Have arrested three men this morning for the Milton stage robbery—Lon Aldridge, Albert Aldridge and Billy Lynch. We have them dead to rights. They are farmers, living in San Joaquin County, eight miles from here."[48]

It appears that Lynch was not actually involved in the hold up and he was not charged. Both Aldridges were convicted and each was sentenced to nine years in San Quentin.[49]

Sheriff Cunningham spoke to a newspaper reporter in December 1884, explaining that he was going to enforce gambling laws, being all too familiar with the lives that were left in ruin by the vice. Cunningham said: "Hitherto, I have not meddled in city criminal affairs; but henceforth, I shall stop gambling in this city. I know old January and I feel sympathy with him in his son's downfall through the gambling halls of Sacramento. The youth here must be protected and I am going to protect them, no matter what course the police take. I will stop all gambling that is prohibited by state laws. I will hunt gambling down as I would hunt a horse thief down."[50]

On December 30th, 1884, Deputy Fields led Uzza French into Superior Court Judge A. Van R. Patterson's courtroom for sentencing. A large crowd assembled in the courtroom to hear the verdict. Arguments by French's attorneys for a new trial took up the day, and the case was continued to the next day. After recounting the various phases of the trial and the verdict of the jury, the judge ordered French to stand up. Judge Patterson confirmed with the attorneys that there was no legal reason for judgment not to be passed, then said: "It is the sentence of the law and the judgment of this court that you be hanged." The newspaper reported: "The prisoner's eyelids fluttered and his face grew a shade paler and he resumed his seat." Deputy Fields then returned French to the jail, where he took up residence in the death cell on the second floor.[51]

8

THE SHERIFF'S LAST EXECUTION

In March 1885, Sheriff Cunningham escorted three prisoners convicted of robbery to Folsom prison. The three, William Jones, Charles Norton and Frank Moran, were each sentenced to ten years of making large granite rocks into smaller ones.[1]

The following month, Thomas and long-time Castoria Township Constable Thomas B. Walker of Lathrop were in Tulare, where they arrested two railroad men named Kelly and Kearnes on the night of April 16th. Kelly and Kearnes were accused of robbing a man of his watch and valuables at gunpoint in a railcar in Lathrop.

Cunningham and Walker worked many cases together over their careers. While they were in Tulare, Deputy Atwood arrested Albert J. Luckhardt on a wire from San Francisco Police Chief Patrick Crowley. Luckhardt, who also went by the name Lawrence, was wanted by San Francisco police for theft.[2]

Mid-August 1885 found Sheriff Cunningham on the trail of a horse thief. This ended up being another long manhunt. The case began on August 19th, after a thief named William Campbell rented a horse and buggy from the Yosemite Stables in Stockton and did not return them the next day.

Cunningham's search took him east into Calaveras County and then north into Amador County, where he located the wagon. Thomas found that Campbell had kept the horse and "borrowed" a saddle, telling the owner that he only needed it for a short ride. Instead, Campbell kept heading east. The sheriff had the wagon returned to Stockton and he kept on with his search for Campbell.

Sheriff Cunningham trailed Campbell over the Sierra Nevada mountains to Carson City, Nevada, where Campbell swapped the horse he had been riding for another one. From there, Campbell continued north into Reno, then turned west and came back onto California.

Thomas finally caught up with Campbell in Plumas County, where he had been working on a hay press. The sheriff passed through Sacramento on the train to Stockton with his prisoner on September 7. Cunningham had spent nearly three weeks in the saddle or in a buggy on this case. Campbell pleaded guilty and was sentenced to seven years in San Quentin.[3]

In December 1885, local lawmen jailed Charles Hart, alias Calhower, alias Dane, on a Grass Valley warrant for burglary. He was also wanted in Amador County for another burglary. Sheriff Cunningham wired Nevada County Sheriff George Lord in Nevada City about the arrest, adding that, "Calhower is bad enough to do most anything."[4]

In January 1886, Sheriff Cunningham delivered two prisoners to San Quentin, and while in San Francisco he attempted to serve an arrest warrant on an attorney named Kowalsky, who was under indictment in San Joaquin County for libel. Kowalsky was in trial in federal court at the time, and Thomas would have found himself in contempt of a federal judge had he enforced the warrant. When Kowalsky was notified he had a warrant, he quickly obtained a writ of habeas corpus to remain free.[5]

Sheriff Cunningham's crew of deputies changed in 1886. Charles Fields and Oscar Atwood both left the Sheriff's Office. Joseph Long remained undersheriff and William Crandall stayed as a deputy. They were joined by Thomas Benjamin, Barney Cassidy and Myron Beach, who was placed in charge of the jail.

Benjamin, Cassidy and Beach all had long careers as lawmen. Benjamin, who was Thomas's nephew, spent twenty years in the Sheriff's Office, while Cassidy spent nearly 40 years as a deputy sheriff. Myron Beach would serve as a long-time Stockton constable after leaving the Sheriff's Office.

Uzza French's case had been making its way through the appeals process since his conviction, and on March 26th, 1886, the California Supreme Court affirmed his conviction and sentence. His execution date was set for June 29th, 1886.[6]

On March 31st, 1886, deputies assumed a 24-hour death watch over Uzza French.[7]

On May 8th, 1886, Sheriff Cunningham was notified by telephone that the San Francisco police had two men in custody for the theft of a team of horses from a Stockton man. Thomas had alerted lawmen in San Francisco about the theft and asked them to keep a lookout for the horses. This was one of the earliest instances where the use of a telephone by the San Joaquin County Sheriff's Office was mentioned.[8]

May of 1886 found the sheriff on the road. He was conducting business in San Francisco on May 20th. The following week, Cunningham escorted a prisoner named William Hicks to

Sacramento to face a charge of assault with intent to commit murder after Hicks unleashed his six-shooter at someone.⁹

Sheriff Cunningham received a wire from Governor Stoneman in June, shortly before Uzza French's execution date, advising that he would not interfere in French's execution. On the appointed date of his execution, Uzza French woke up very early and dressed himself in a black suit. Father Brennan, a Catholic priest, arrived later that morning and gave French his last rites. French spent the rest of the morning eating a light breakfast, singing hymns, and reading the bible.¹⁰

The backside of the Market Street Jail is shown in the lower right side of this photograph. The gallows were erected in the enclosed yard and were accessed from the second story door.
[*Laurence Valterza*]

Shortly after noon, Undersheriff Long went to French's cell and read the death warrant to him. This was witnessed by Sheriff Cunningham, Father Brennan, and a man named Joseph Campbell. French did not show any emotion during the reading. As the sheriff and others went to leave his cell, French shook the hand of each man. He thanked Sheriff Cunningham for his kindness and added, "Do the job as quickly as possible."[11]

Sheriff Cunningham designed the gallows that was used that day, being aware of executions that had taken place around the country that had gone wrong. Without being too graphic, the design of the gallows was extremely important in insuring that the execution took place properly. Cunningham's gallows had previously been used in Sacramento and Modesto. That day, they had been freshly painted and reinforced, and the railings were draped with black and white cloth. Learning from his experience with the Murphy execution in 1873, the sheriff ordered that large screens be placed around the jail yard walls to keep people from viewing the hanging from nearby buildings.[12]

A crowd started gathering around the jail during the morning and grew to an estimated 500 people. Knowing they would be unable to view the execution, most people were interested in seeing the gallows. Sheriff Cunningham instructed his deputies to allow small groups of people in at a time and explain the history and workings of the device to them.[13]

Shortly after 1:20 p.m., after the public was escorted out of the yard and the invited witnesses granted entrance, the door from the jail's second floor opened and Father Brennan stepped out, holding a crucifix before him. French followed, leaning on Sheriff Cunningham's arm. Walking slowly down the three steps to the gallows platform, they took their places, followed by Undersheriff

Scene at Stockton Waterfront, illustrated by Ralph O. Yardley
[*R. Tod Ruse*]

Long, deputies Beach, Benjamin, Crandall and Cassidy, and the sheriffs from Amador, Placer, Santa Clara and Merced counties. These lawmen lined up along the back of the scaffold.[14]

French's arms, wrists and ankles were bound. The sheriff placed the noose around his neck and adjusted it. The black cap was placed on French's head as Father Brennan recited the Lord's Prayer, and then it was done.[15]

Several deputies and officers acted as Uzza French's pall bearers and his body was taken to St. Mary's Church on Washington Street, one block from the jail, for services. His body was interred at the Catholic Cemetery in Stockton.[16]

The rest of 1886 was taken up by routine duties for the sheriff and his men. That November, Sheriff Cunningham transported two outlaws to Folsom. Gordon Johnson was sentenced to three years for grand larceny, and J. Schuyler received a one-year sentence for second-degree burglary.[17]

Thomas started out the year of 1887 by travelling to Portland, Oregon to arrest a forger named Alexander H. Hamilton. Alexander H. had forged the name of his uncle, Alexander E. Hamilton, onto a check for $412 in Stockton on October 16th, 1886. He skipped town directly, heading for San Francisco. After blowing all of his money there, Hamilton left for greener pastures in the Northwest.

Sheriff Cunningham used a friend of Hamilton's to convey to him that there was a very nice opportunity waiting for him in Portland, but all he found when he got there was the sheriff with a nice pair of bracelets for him. He was brought back on the next steamer to San Francisco.[18]

On February 15th, 1887, Thomas passed through Sacramento on the train headed for Folsom with an unfortunate wretch named

John Lamb, sentenced to one-year for grand larceny. Lamb's story was that he worked on a farm near Stockton and one day he borrowed his bosses' horse, rode into town, and got a snoot full of Who-hit-John. He spent all his money, and the first thing he knew when he sobered up was that the saloon keeper had a bill of sale for the horse. After that, the state was in charge of his room and board for a while.[19]

In March, baseball players from Sacramento travelled to Stockton for a game. What transpired is best told by the newspaper account published in the *Sacramento Daily Record Union*:

"The Alta Baseball Club and the friends by whom they accompanied to Stockton Sunday morning, to play a return game with the Stocktons, returned home about 4 o'clock a.m. yesterday, the entire party numbering about twenty. The account they give of their reception and treatment on the Slough City does not show up a portion of the residents of that place very creditably, but if the Stocktonians can stand it the Altas certainly can. Before the train by which the latter organization were passengers had come to a full stop at Stockton, the Sacramentans who were standing on the car platforms were greeted with coarse remarks, to which they paid no attention, supposing those who uttered them were stray 'drunks' not yet recovered from their Saturday night debauch.

"After the Altas had left the train and found themselves hooted, and more bad language used towards them, they began to see that their visit was not going to be a pleasant one. On the way to their hotel and from there to Agricultural Park, where the contest was to take place, their treatment was so rude that they began to wonder whether the occupants of the Insane Asylum had not escaped and taken the town. At the ball grounds matters went from bad to worse. There was a large assemblage of spectators, including scores of ladies, and yet foul-mouthed ruffians were allowed to use an abundance of oaths and filthy epithets until finally many of the ladies went home. During the first inning, nearly all the Sacramento players came in for a share of the billingsgate, but McLaughlin was the especial target, probably because he went over there one time with the Brightons and assisted that organization to defeat the Stocktons.

"Exasperated beyond control he finally, when the side was out, laid down his gloves and mask and called to a big fellow who had been especially abusive, to step out and show how much of a man he was. The challenge showed pluck, though open to the charge of bad judgment, as the Sacramentans were a very small band compared to the rough element opposed to them, and the fight might have led to very disastrous results on both sides. As it was, the individual McLaughlin invited is said to have made haste slowly toward the front and allowed twenty or more of his companions to tear off their coats and rush ahead of him.

"Some of the Altas who were nearby closed up to McLaughlin, and the Stockton club rallied to their assistance. Some peace officers who were present endeavored to drive the would-be fighters back but made little, if any, progress. As is usual on such occasions, the spectators who had not taken part in the disturbance pressed forward to 'see the fight,' and the prospects for a very serious difficulty were exceedingly good.

"Just then Tom Cunningham, San Joaquin County's energetic and determined sheriff, appeared, and went into the matter in his vigorous way with such happy results that the turbulent element was driven back and the game went on, but at any moment, from that time to its close, there was danger of renewal of the outbreak..."[20]

On April 3rd, 1887, Hiram James was back to his old tricks at his old stomping grounds in Lodi. He was mixed up in a card game in a saloon when he had a dispute with William Harrison over one dollar. During the argument, Harrison grabbed James around the throat and choked him. James left, but returned a short time later carrying a pistol, which he leveled at Harrison. Harrison took refuge behind the bar, and during his attempt to shoot Harrison over the shoulder of a bar patron named Lemuel Dougherty, known as "New Zealand Bill," James shot Dougherty instead.

New Zealand Bill died of his wound and Hi James fled the area. Sheriff Cunningham traced James to Walnut Grove, a river town in south Sacramento County which had a large Chinese community. James was said to be an opium smoker and fluent in the Chinese language. The trail went cold there.[21]

Cunningham distributed a wanted poster for James, offering $100 for his arrest. The sheriff received word on April 10 that James had been arrested in Maxwell, in Colusa County, but when he went there to confirm the prisoner's identity, it was not James. Other reports came into the Sheriff's Office about James's location, but none panned out.[22]

Later in April 1887, Sheriff Cunningham issued a reward poster for an outlaw named Bob Scott, alias W. H. Rice, who was wanted for stealing a wagon and team of horses from a Stockton livery stable on April 14th. The horses and wagon were found in Sacramento, where Scott had left them at a stable. Scott then rented another team of horses and a wagon from another Sacramento stable, then had the team and buggy shipped to Oakland on a freight train, on which he also took passage. Sacramento police were searching for Scott at the time. Cunningham's poster related that the property from the Stockton theft had been recovered, but emphasized, "*I want the man.*" No evidence was found to indicate whether or not Scott was ever located.[23]

On April 20th, 1887, Sheriff Cunningham arrested a man who went by the name Harry Mack off the streets of Stockton for a warrant charging Mack with assaulting a Los Angeles police officer.

Los Angeles Undersheriff H. M. Mitchell sent out a wanted poster for Mack, who had jumped bail and skipped town. The description on the flier said: "Harry McDonald, alias Harry Mack, is a pimp and pug, and lives on a woman named Tillie Murphy, who left San Jose about two weeks ago to join Mack. He is about 5 feet 6; weight, 145 pounds. He is good-looking, a neat dresser, and wears knit underclothing generally. He is suspected of rolling drunks when occasion offers. He will be found around dives or houses of ill-repute, and claims to be a prize fighter, but has no marks that we know of. Please arrest and telegraph."[24]

McDonald was also wanted by San Francisco police at the time for a robbery that he committed in that city, and Cunningham turned Mack over to the San Francisco police.

That summer, on July 6th, 1887, Sheriff Cunningham was in Los Angeles, where he arrested E. F. Sutton for embezzlement. Cunningham held a warrant for Sutton, who was suspected of stealing $1,300 from a Stockton mercantile store.[25]

The following month, on August 26th, 1887, Constable Barker from Fresno County traveled to Stockton in search of a stolen wagon and harness. Given the description, Sheriff Cunningham recognized the property and suspected that the responsible parties were two men who were living in Collegeville, east of Stockton. The two, Sherman Blair and W. S. James, had recently spent time in the Stockton jail for hay theft.

Sheriff Cunningham and Constable Barker headed for Collegeville and located a treasure trove of stolen property when they got there. The officers found two wagons, four sets of harness, two saddles, and a large collection of miscellaneous items that had apparently been stolen. James and Blair were arrested and charged with grand larceny.[26]

On September 8th, 1887, lawmen arrested two horse thieves in Lathrop. The two, who gave their names as David Johnson and Daniel M. Sullivan, were initially arrested for possession of a stolen saddle. They said that they had come from Merced when they were lodged in the jail. When Sheriff Cunningham followed up with Merced officers, he learned that the horses they had been on in Lathrop were also stolen in Merced.[27]

Thomas was in Sacramento on September 21st, taking a look at the rough element of the city, in search of thieves, confidence men, gamblers and swindlers who might be visiting the annual Stockton fair, which was held the following month. The fair always drew criminals to town and Cunningham wanted to be able to recognize these folks if they turned up in his city.[28]

During his trip to Sacramento, Thomas arrested John Sansome off the streets of Elk Grove for stage robbery. Cunningham and Sheriff Henry McCoy had arrested Sansome in 1882, and Thomas recognized Sansome from a wanted poster put out by Wells Fargo for a stagecoach robbery that occurred in the area of Michigan Bluff, in Placer County. Sansome was an old-hand at crime, having been sent up the river several times.[29]

In November 1887, Sheriff Cunningham ran a confidence man named Hiram, or Herman, Kurth to ground in Salinas. Cunningham had been on the lookout for Kurth for seven or eight months, after receiving information from the San Diego Constable's Office that Kurth was wanted in that city for swindling thousands of dollars from San Diego businessmen.[30]

Kurth, a well-dressed, middle-aged man had gone to San Diego proposing to refurbish an old abandoned flouring mill. He had hired some laborers to clean up and repair the place and along the way he convinced a number of people to forward him credit in amounts from $100 to $1,000. Right when it appeared that the mill was ready to start production, Kurth skipped town.

Thomas had kept an eye out for Kurth, and when he arrived in Stockton, Cunningham wired San Diego. Kurth left Stockton, heading for Tucson, before a warrant arrived. The sheriff didn't forget about Kurth and when he showed back up in Stockton in November, Cunningham again wired San Diego for instructions. Once again, Kurth flew the coop, but Thomas kept track of him and followed him to Salinas, where he finally made the arrest.[31]

The *Mariposa Gazette* ran a story in its December 3rd, 1887 edition that documented a drunken adventure taken by some men at a local Stockton saloon:

> "Tim Hurley went down to Garwood's Ferry (on the San Joaquin River) on Saturday night last and dropped into Theodore Schultz's saloon to refresh himself after the toil and heat of the day. While there, he encountered J. B. Littlejohn, a sheep owner from Hornitos, who had a band of sheep sucking the life-blood out of Roberts Island. Whether it was concerning women, politics, or religion, the three things besides money upon which men disagree, was not learned, but the result of the encounter was a fight without seconds or bottle holders, and in entire contradiction to the rules of the London prize ring or those laid down by the gay and festive Marquis of Queensbury. During the course of the row, almost all the glasses on the counter were broken, and those friends of Littlejohn pushed Hurley into a back room. Hurley in the meantime had tapped Littlejohn on the head with a bottle and knocked him down.

Hurley's buggy was standing outside, and when he jumped into it, three men pulled him out, unharnessed the horse, and made him walk to his destination, having confiscated the entire outfit.

"Yesterday morning, Hurley visited the saloon, and having recovered the horse and buggy, demanded the harness, which was missing. Littlejohn happened to be present and drew a revolver on Hurley, to the great discomposure of the latter's mind. Hurley then started to go across the river on the ferry boat, but the boat at that time was occupied by a band of sheep belonging to Littlejohn, and the latter insisted that there was no room for him. Hurley, who was on horseback, refused to leave the ferry, and Littlejohn promptly knocked him off his horse with the blow of a club, cutting a scalp wound in his head about four inches long by one inch wide. Littlejohn continued the attack upon the prostrate man, and beat him on the arm and across the ribs, until two men who happened to be on the ferry interfered and prevented further violence.

"The wounded man complained to the authorities in this city, and Sheriff Cunningham and Constable Carroll arrested Littlejohn, who deposited $200 bail in Justice of the Peace Milner's Court. The defendant plead guilty this morning, and was let off with the fine of $20. Sheriff Cunningham and Constable Carroll also arrested two men named Childs and McIntyre on a charge of stealing Hurley's harness. They justified themselves by proving that Littlejohn took the harness and threw it into the river. They were accordingly discharged, and Littlejohn settled the matter by paying for the harness and for the costs of the court."[32]

The constable mentioned in the story was James P. Carroll, who had been a Stockton constable since 1880. His twin brother, Michael Carroll, served as a Stockton police officer. James later served as Stockton's fire chief.

In January 1888, Thomas was in San Diego, looking for a fugitive from San Joaquin County. While there, the *San Diego Union* ran an article about him:

> "...During a recent visit to this city he met many ugly customers with whom he had dealing in days past. He said he saw at least a dozen men on the street in this city who have 'done time' in San Quentin and Folsom. They are men who rank among the most desperate outlaws, and need sharp looking after. Cunningham pointed some of them out to Chief of Police Coyne, and advised him to keep an eye on them and also to look out for trouble."[33]

On April 7th, 1888, Sheriff Cunningham received notice that Hiram James, the fugitive wanted for the April 1887 killing of New Zealand Bill Dougherty, was captured in Pocatello, Idaho. Thomas quickly took the train for Sacramento, where he obtained extradition papers for James at the Capitol before traveling east.

Stockton Constable James Carroll
[*George Tinkham*]

It took Cunningham almost a week to get to Hailey, Idaho, where James was being held, and then on to Ogden, Utah, where he and his prisoner could catch the train. The sheriff was able to positively identify Hi James at that time. James had been working in the area as a railroad section hand for the previous six months. Cunningham started back to Stockton from Ogden on the westbound train on April 13th. James was ultimately convicted of manslaughter.[34]

On August 4th, 1888, shortly before 7:00 p.m. in the evening, the Sheriff's Office received a phone call from residents in a neighborhood east of Stockton who reported a double shooting. Neighbors were startled by the sound of three gunshots from the run-down shack of John Chamberlin, whose wife then came running out of the house. She ran behind a neighbor's house, all bloodied, before collapsing. She had been shot behind the right ear. She was carried to a friend's house, where a doctor examined her and ordered her to be moved to the county hospital.

Sheriff Cunningham and a deputy arrived shortly afterwards, and when they cautiously entered the Chamberlin shanty, found the body of John Chamberlin with a bullet wound in the center of his forehead.

Although grievously wounded, Mrs. Chamberlin was able to relate that her husband had asked her to go into another room to get something for him and when she returned, he shot her. She fell and rolled out the front door when he shot her a second time. She regained her feet and ran. She heard the third shot as she was running away from the house.

Mrs. Chamberlin told officers that she had been a widow with four children when Chamberlin married her the previous year. He had always been jealous without cause, constantly accusing her of being unfaithful. Chamberlin was very mean and abusive towards her. Over the previous two months, Chamberlin had been without work, and the week before the shooting he left the house, saying he was going to look for a job. He was gone several days and nights and when he returned, he accused her of having been out of the house one of those nights. Mrs. Chamberlin died the next day.[35]

In August 1888, Sheriff Cunningham was looking for swindlers who were talking San Joaquin County farmers out of their hard-earned money by offering them a very good deal on wheat seed. The con men promised victims a great future return on their investment, but all the farmers were left with was worthless paper while the swindlers got away with hundreds of dollars. Thomas was familiar with the scheme, aware that it had been used in the East.[36]

In September, Cunningham was in Sacramento, warning gamblers there not to waste their time coming to the Stockton fair the following month because he would just shut them down, arrest them, and confiscate their equipment.[37]

The following month, on Thursday, October 18th, 1888, the Sheriff's Office received notice of an escaped prisoner from the state lockup at Folsom. The convict, Andronice Sepulveda, had been allowed outside the prison grounds as an inmate trusty. Sepulveda had been serving a fifteen-year sentence for burglary and grand larceny from Monterey County, and with credits he would have been released in nine more months, after having served nine years. He was a long-time thief and burglar who had served two previous prison terms. Early Wednesday morning, Sepulveda stole two horses near the prison and was believed to be headed in a southerly direction. By Thursday, the fugitive was passing through San Joaquin County. Six miles out of Stockton, he changed horses, moving his saddle to the horse he had been leading and releasing the other one.[38]

Using a young man as his buggy driver, Sheriff Cunningham started out after Sepulveda. The sheriff tracked his man to a shallow crossing of the San Joaquin River, where Sepulveda had forded the stream and continued westward towards the Coast Range.

Thomas followed Sepulveda into the Livermore Valley, where he caught up with him just at dusk on Saturday evening, October 20th. Cunningham called out to Sepulveda to halt, but the outlaw urged his mount on. Cunningham drew his Navy Colt and shot, felling the horse out from under the fleeing convict. Immediately after firing the shot, Cunningham went to jump out of the buggy but his foot caught up in something and he fell to the ground. Sepulveda landed on his feet, ran through a hole in a nearby barbed wire fence, and fled. Thomas trailed him until it became too dark to continue.[39]

Cunningham later told newspaper reporters that he could have shot Sepulveda, but that he didn't want to kill him. He felt certain that he could have easily captured Sepulveda had he not gotten caught up and fallen.[40]

Sheriff Cunningham notified Livermore area officers of the latest developments and Alameda County Deputy Sheriff Schaffer finally caught up with the escaped convict outside of Livermore five days later.[41]

In October 1888, Sheriff Cunningham signed a petition asking Governor Robert Waterman for clemency in the case of a horse thief named Harry R. Weston. Weston had been convicted in 1885 for stealing a horse and buggy from a Stockton area rancher and was sentenced to seven years. Twenty-three years old and drunk at the time he committed the theft, Weston had never hung around the criminal class, and for those reasons Thomas felt he deserved some leniency. Governor Waterman agreed and granted the request, pardoning Weston on November 1st, 1888.[42]

Thomas retained his seat in the November election, and December 1st found him in Sacramento searching for a horse thief named Charles Harvey, who had rented a horse and buggy from a Stockton livery stable and forgotten to return it.[43]

Sheriff Cunningham added to his staff in 1889, hiring Hartman Littebrandt as an assistant jailer. Littebrandt was married to Thomas' sister Catherine, but he proved himself as a deputy.

Sheriff Cunningham and Coroner W. M. Beede were called to investigate a brutal murder in Banta on January 22nd, 1889. The scene of the crime was a Chinese laundry. A burglar had entered the business through a window during the night, and then encountering the sleeping victim, Chan Den, had bludgeoned him to death. After killing Den, the murderer then went through the victim's pockets and ransacked the whole place. The killer left few clues behind and Thomas made no traction with the investigation.[44]

On February 12th, 1889, Sacramento Police Officer R. S. Frazee was on horse patrol along the American River when he came upon three men. One of the men quickly drew a six-shooter and shot Frazee through the wrist, then the three took off into the thick underbrush along the river. The fugitives were believed to have been involved in a rash of recent Sacramento burglaries. Two days later, the San Joaquin County Sheriff's Office got a call from a railroad officer in Wallace, in Calaveras County just east of the San Joaquin County line. The railroad officer believed he had the three shooting suspects, but they resisted when he tried to arrest them.

Sheriff Cunningham and Deputy Benjamin quickly left for Wallace, arriving late on the night of the 14th. The three officers were able to take two of the three outlaws into custody without too much difficulty. The two were brothers, George and Mack Reed. The third man, an old-timer named Chandler, had fled.[45]

At about 7:45 p.m. on the evening of Friday, February 22nd, 1889, the southbound Southern Pacific passenger train from San Francisco to Los Angeles was robbed and two men were shot and killed. The crime occurred about 20 miles south of Tulare, south of a small stop called Pixley. Sheriff Cunningham joined lawmen from all over the state in searching for the culprits.

The robbery was widely covered in the newspapers. The *Los Angeles Herald* gave the following account:

> "DELANO, CAL.—February 22—A daring train robbery took place at a point about two miles south of Pixley at 8 o'clock this evening. Train No. 17 left Pixley on time, and when two miles out, two men crawled from the front of the engine, covering the fireman and engineer with revolvers and commanding a halt. When the train slowed up, one of the men still held the fireman and engineer under cover, while the other went back to the express car and exploded a bomb underneath the car to scare the messenger, and said that unless the doors of the car were opened he would explode another one.
>
> "The messenger responded when one of the robbers sprang into the car and, obtaining the keys, took the valuables in the safe. After the train halted, a brakeman by the name of Anson and a passenger, who boarded the train at Modesto, went up on one side of the car, and another brakeman and Ed Bentley, deputy constable at Delano, on the other side, to see what was the trouble. When near the express car, they were roughly ordered to halt and at the same moment a gun loaded with

buckshot was discharged by the robbers over the brakeman's shoulder, hitting the young man in the head, death resulting instantly. The parties on the other side of the car met the same reception, and Bentley was shot in the side and arm. He is probably fatally wounded. As soon as the booty was obtained the robbers hastily left, going westward..."[46]

Deputy Bentley was placed back on the train and it was backed up to Pixley, where the alarm was sounded. There was no medical help at Pixley for Bentley, so the train started south for Delano. As they approached the scene of the crime, the body of the other shooting victim, a young man named Charles Gabart, was discovered. The train was stopped and the body was recovered.[47]

The Wells Fargo express messenger sent his superintendent a message from Delano: "Train No. 17 robbed by several masked men three miles south of Pixley, at 7:45 p.m. Ordered engineer and fireman up to my car. Then placed bomb under and exploded it. In the meantime, I had put lights out and prepared for action. The shock from the bomb was very severe. When they attempted to place another bomb under me the engineer and fireman begged me to open up, as they were about to be killed if I had not obeyed, so I opened the door and was covered by two masked men and ordered out. After that they made me enter again and light up, being covered all the while. Small amount taken."[48]

Wells Fargo's superintendent, Leonard F. Rowell, was interviewed by the paper and had the following to say:

> "We regard it as the most daring train robbery that has ever taken place in this state. I wired Detective Hume, of our company, at his home across the bay last night to take the first train and get on the spot as soon as possible. He went early this morning, and every effort will be made to apprehend those fellows."[49]

Sheriff Cunningham arrived in Tulare County with other lawmen and they began their investigation. The reported take from the robbery was between $300 and $60,000. Wells Fargo remained tight-lipped about the actual take, but they offered a $1000 reward for the arrest and conviction of the outlaws, joining the Southern Pacific Railroad in offering that amount.[50]

Deputy Constable Bentley succumbed to his wounds on February 25th, 1889, re-enforcing the resolve of everybody involved in the hunt to solve the case.[51]

Thomas was still working the case in the southern San Joaquin Valley in the first week of March. On March 4th, Kern County Sheriff William Graham and his posse rode into Bakersfield with a suspect named Jesse Smith, who had been arrested at a ranch above the Liebre Hills in the Coast Range. That same day, Cunningham and his posse rode into Bakersfield with another suspect who had been picked up in the Coast Range mountains west of the San Joaquin River. Neither suspect panned out.[52]

Thomas was back in Stockton on March 11th, 1889, when he got a message from an informant he had in Kern County who told him that a couple of men whom lawmen had developed some evidence against regarding the train robbery were supposed to be leaving on a train for Arizona that night. Working quickly, Cunningham wired J. B. Hume and Southern Pacific railroad detectives with the information, then contacted Tulare and had a special train made up with officers aboard to overtake the suspects. He then left for Lathrop, where he took the southbound train at midnight. Two men were arrested in Bakersfield, but they too were not involved in the crime. Despite all of the lawmen's efforts, the outlaws remained unidentified for the time being.[53]

The March 15th, 1889, edition of the *Sacramento Daily Record*

Union ran a story about a horse theft arrest that Sheriff Cunningham made that week:

> "Saturday night two horses were stolen from Fay's ranch, near Franklin. Chief (Timothy) Lee sent out descriptions of the animals, with a request that anyone found with the stock be arrested. Unluckily for the horse thief he went to San Joaquin County, and that prince of officers, Sheriff Cunningham, soon had him in custody. He is a young man who gives the name of Frank Goodhue. He will be returned to this county to be tried for his crime."[54]

On July 2nd, 1889, Stockton Police Officer Michael Carroll arrested a forger who had been pointed out to him by a local saloon keeper. The forger had been in town a few days and had kept busy playing poker. He had passed a $50 check in town from a Salt Lake City bank. The saloon keeper became suspicious of the man and reported him to Officer Carroll.

When he was arrested, the forger gave his name as W. E. Williamson. He carried a valise with him that had all of the tools that a professional forger used in those days, including blank checks and letters of introduction, rubber stamps, different colored inks, and pens.

Working with Officer Carroll, Sheriff Cunningham telegraphed to the Salt Lake City bank. Once information about the forger started coming in, it was found that he was wanted in a number of cities across the West, including in Sacramento and Salt Lake City. Williamson used a number of aliases, including N. E Williams.[55]

Cunningham started fielding inquiries from a vast region. During the investigation, Thomas received a circular from the Wichita Clearing House Association of Wichita, Kansas. Dated

June 29th, 1889, it was addressed to bankers in Colorado, Wyoming, Montana, Utah, Nevada, Idaho, California, Oregon and Washington Territory, giving the forger's background:

> "Look out for the forger—A man calling himself N. E. Williams is now making a tour of the West, passing forged checks purporting to be certified by the banks upon which they are drawn. Within a month, eleven of these have presented at the Wichita Clearing House. They are all drawn on the Kansas National Bank, of this city, upon a pink-colored blank, like inclosed (sic), signed C. P. Newman, payable to N. E. Williams or bearer, the amount punched out with a regular needle-perforator, and certified good with a rubber stamp. The certification is signed C. P. Banks, Assisting Cashier (in some cases 'Ass't Cashier'). Sometimes, however, he has signed it as U. G. Bush, Ass't Cashier, and one as N. G. Bank, Act'g Cashier. The Kansas National Bank has no 'assistant' and no 'acting' cashier. Its cashier is Charles E. Frank...
>
> "...Please advise us by wire, if caught, and we will communicate the fact to the several banks which have been victimized."[56]

Williams or Williamson was brought before the court for his preliminary examination on July 6th, at which time he pleaded guilty. He made a "splendid speech to the court" during his sentencing, and received a three-year sentence in San Quentin.[57]

9

A HIGH-PROFILE CASE

On the morning of August 14th, 1889, a shooting took place in the Lathrop train depot restaurant that created a sensation across the country. The principals in the incident were a justice of the United States Supreme Court, a former chief justice of the California Supreme Court, a deputy United States marshal, and a former mistress of a U.S. senator and Nevada silver tycoon. The resulting criminal case demonstrated the conflict existing when state jurisdiction was exerted over a federal official in the performance of duty, and it ended in a landmark United States Supreme Court decision with Thomas Cunningham's name on it.[1]

The events that led up to that day all revolved around a divorce case known as *Sharon v. Sharon*. The involved parties were a former United States senator named William Sharon and a former paramour of his named Sarah Althea Hill, who claimed that Sharon had secretly married her and then been unfaithful to her. In truth, Hill was just one of a number of women who the senator kept for his own purposes in San Francisco. Sharon rented a room for Hill at a high-end San Francisco hotel and provided her with a $500 monthly allowance in exchange for her company.

William Tang Sharon had studied law in St. Louis and was admitted to the bar before moving to California in 1849. He settled in San Francisco the following year and traded in real estate and merchandise before moving to Virginia City, Nevada, in 1864, where he became the manager of the local branch of the Bank of California. In addition to running affairs for the bank, Sharon became involved in the silver mining and milling business, and through reportedly unscrupulous business dealings, made his fortune, becoming known as the "King of the Comstock."[2]

William Sharon
[*Library of Congress*]

Sharon's wife died in 1875, the same year he was elected to the U.S. Senate, where he served from 1875 to 1881. Living in San Francisco and hob-knobbing with San Francisco's elite at the time, Sharon was rarely in Nevada or Washington D.C. While in the

Senate, he missed 1,466 of 1,588 roll-call votes, a 92.3 percent failure record.[3]

Owning and living in San Francisco's Palace Hotel, Sharon later admitted that he had started a series of relationships with young and beautiful women, putting them up in nice hotel rooms and paying them a monthly allowance in return for their companionship and discretion. One of those women was Sarah Althea Hill.[4]

Sarah Althea was a 20-something year old mentally unstable woman and was known to have a violent temper. Born in Cape Girardeau, Missouri, the daughter of a lawyer and his wife, Sarah and her brother became orphans while they were still minors, and were raised by other family members. She had come to San Francisco with her brother in 1871 to live with relatives.[5]

Sarah Althea
[*Library of Congress*]

Because of her youth and beauty, Sarah became a socialite, easily moving about in the circles of San Francisco's movers and shakers. She stated in a subsequent court trial that she first met William Sharon in 1880, when she went to his office to seek advice about investing in the stock market. This led to intimacy between the two, and Sharon moved her to the Grand Hotel, where he visited her and made improper propositions to her, which she rejected. Sharon then made propositions of marriage, which Sarah accepted. According to her, Sharon told her that there were reasons why he could not be married by a priest. He also told her of a woman and child he had in the East, and that he was running to keep his seat in the U.S. Senate.

Hill alleged that Sharon had her write up a marriage contract that he dictated, citing California Civil Code section 75. Sarah, who was 27, and William, who was 60, both signed the document on August 25th, 1880, but there was no ceremony or honeymoon. Sharon swore Hill to secrecy about the marriage for the next two years.[6]

William and Sarah's relationship, whatever it was, lasted into the next year. Sharon contended that his relationship with Sarah became problematic. She would often go into his hotel room and office when he was out of town, searching through his papers without permission. Sometime in late 1881, Sarah agreed to receive a $7,500 payment, for which she promised not to bother Sharon anymore. Sharon ordered Sarah to vacate her room at the Grand, but she refused, at which time Sharon had the hotel manager remove the door to her room and remove all the furniture.[7]

Sarah Althea retained an attorney and fired her first salvo against William Sharon in the court of public opinion, when her attorney showed the San Francisco newspapers a piece of paper he claimed was the marriage contract. Sharon immediately denied the claim, stating that the paper was a fraud. He filed a suit against Sarah Althea in federal Circuit Court in October 1883 to compel her to acknowledge that fact. For her part, Sarah filed for divorce in the San Francisco Superior Court in late October 1883, claiming adultery on Sharon's part and seeking alimony and half of his earnings over the time they were "married." This started contentious and dueling court battles in the state and federal courts that continued on for years and provided the press with all the titillating details of the relationship that kept the public in a tizzy.[8]

Both William and Sarah hired an army of lawyers to fight their cases. One of Sarah's attorneys was a fighter in every sense of the word: David S. Terry.

David Smith Terry was a talented lawyer who had once served as the chief justice of the California Supreme Court. As quick with his fists and a knife or gun as he was with a legal argument, Terry had a reputation for resorting to violence when he was riled up.

Terry grew up in Texas and studied law in Houston, where he passed the bar. A southern Democrat, Terry came to California from Texas during the 1849 rush for gold. He eventually settled in Stockton and opened a law practice in town. Terry was elected to the California State Supreme Court during the September 4th, 1855, election.[9]

In 1856, San Francisco was overrun by criminals and crooked politicians, and a vigilante committee took it upon themselves to clean things up. In early June, Justice Terry had issued a writ of habeas corpus, ordering the Committee to release a man named William Mulligan. The Committee refused to give up the prisoner and the governor refused to intervene, so Terry traveled to San Francisco to straighten things out himself.[10]

On June 22nd, 1856, Terry was walking up Kearney Street with a group of armed men. During an altercation that followed, Terry stabbed the leader of the Vigilance Committee, Sterling A. Hopkins, in the neck. Terry took refuge, but eventually turned himself over and was held in custody of the Committee. He was kept in "Fort Gunnybags," the vigilantes' makeshift jail, until August 16, when he was released. He returned to Stockton to a hero's welcome. Despite his San Francisco difficulties, Terry was named chief justice of the California Supreme Court on September 18th, 1857.[11]

David S. Terry
[*Library of Congress*]

On September 13th, 1859, Terry, having resigned his position as chief justice the previous day, fought a duel—a real duel, with dueling pistols, seconds, a surgeon and everything—against U.S.

Senator David C. Broderick on the outskirts of San Francisco, after a disagreement between the two. Broderick was shot by Terry at the standard number of paces, and later died of his wound. Terry was found not guilty of manslaughter by a San Mateo County jury the following year.[12]

On September 21st, 1863, the editor of a San Francisco newspaper went to the San Francisco Recorder's Court to report that he had been assaulted by David Terry in his office. The editor had refused to provide Terry with the name of the author of a letter the newspaper had published that referred to Terry as a "pettifogger." Terry took exception to the editor's refusal to provide the information and struck him over the head with a rattan cane, breaking the cane in half. When the editor went to take the other half of the cane out of Terry's hand, Terry pulled a large knife out of his belt and struck the editor in the head several times with the butt of the handle.[13]

Sarah Hill won her case in the state courts, being awarded a settlement against William Sharon, along with monthly alimony, but the federal courts negated that award. During all the suits, countersuits and appeals, William Sharon died on November 13th, 1885. On William's death, Sarah produced a handwritten will that she said she found in Sharon's desk, giving her full possession of his assets. That document was deemed to be a forgery.[14]

In the meantime, Sarah Althea Hill and her attorney David Smith Terry had started a romantic relationship, and the two were married at St. Mary's Catholic Church, in Stockton, on January 7th, 1886.[15]

The final judgment regarding the Hill-Sharon case was read in Federal Circuit Court on September 3rd, 1888, by U.S. Supreme Court Justice Stephen Field, who was in California assisting with the Circuit Court calendar. A three-judge panel, consisting of Justice Field, Circuit Court Judge Lorenzo Sawyer, and District Court Judge George M. Sabin, rendered the decision. The September 4th edition of the *Daily Alta California* entertained its readers by providing an account of the fireworks that happened in court that day:

> "Promptly at 11 o'clock the judges filed into the courtroom, and everybody stood until they were seated, as is the custom when a member of the Supreme Court occupies the bench. Justice Field presided, with Judges Sawyer, Hoffman and Sabin sitting with him on the bench. At a table just in front of the Clerk's desk sat David S. Terry, accompanied by his wife, Sarah Althea Terry, and Porter Ashe. At another table, nearer the jury box, sat a number of attorneys interested in the Sharon side of the case. The courtroom was crowded with spectators, as it was known that the decision was to be rendered.
>
> "As soon as the room became quiet, Justice Field began to read the decision in a low but clear tone of voice. Mr. and Mrs. Terry leaned forward and gave the closest attention as the decision was being read. The attention of the others appeared to be divided between listening to the words of the decision as they fell from the lips of the Judge, and watching their effect on Mrs. Terry. Not the least change took place for fully a quarter of an hour, nor until a point had been reached where it became evident that the decision was going against her, Then, for the first time, Mrs. Terry began to move about in a restless manner, and her husband leaned over and spoke a few words to her, evidently to quiet her, for she once more settled down to listen attentively.
>
> "When Justice Field reached a part of the decision relating to the cancellation and destruction of the paper purporting to be a marriage contract between Sarah Althea Hill and William

Sharon, Mrs. Terry sprang to her feet and cried out in an excited manner: 'Justice Field, are you going to order me to give up that marriage contract, which is the evidence of my rights, to be cancelled?'

"Justice Field looked up from his paper, stopped and looked at her, and after carefully readjusting his glasses, said: 'Sit down, madam,' in a very quiet but determined manner. The other judges sat unmoved, and deathlike stillness pervaded the courtroom.

"In an instant the silence was broken by Mrs. Terry. 'Justice Field,' she screamed in tones of the most violent passion, 'we hear you have been bought. We want to know if it is so, and at what figure you hold yourself. It appears no one can get justice in this court unless he has a sack. We want to know what you have been paid by the Sharon people.'

Justice Stephen J. Field
[*Library of Congress*]

"'Marshal,' said Justice Field calmly, 'remove that woman from the courtroom. The Court will deal with her later.' Everything was in confusion in a moment. Mrs. Terry continued to revile the judges in the most vulgar manner, and becoming wild with rage, her voice attracted the people from numerous offices in the Appraiser's Building, who came rushing in to see what was taking place.

"Marshal Franks moved towards Mrs. Terry to obey the order of the Court, when he was confronted by David S. Terry. With an oath he exclaimed: 'No living man shall touch her.'

"With this he dealt the Marshal a blow in the face with his clenched fist that staggered him for a moment. The Marshal, however, stopped neither for Terry nor the blow, but slipping in front of him, seized Mrs. Terry and dragged her from the courtroom, leaving Terry to his deputies, who seized him and threw him back over a chair, while Mrs. Terry was hustled into the Marshal's office, struggling and screaming wildly. Terry followed her immediately, and drawing from his breast a dirk-knife, made a rush for the door of the Marshal's office, where he was opposed by Deputy Marshal Farish.

"Terry, brandishing the knife, made a dash at the deputy marshal, saying, 'You _____ ___ _____, I will cut you to pieces.' At the same moment he was grabbed by Marshal Franks, Finnegass and Detective Johnson, while Deputy Marshal Taggert, who stood just inside the counter, leveled his revolver at Terry, ready to fire in case it became absolutely necessary, and, in obedience to an order from the Marshal, Terry, finding himself covered, relinquished his grasp on the knife, which was immediately seized by another deputy, and Terry was then placed under arrest and taken into Marshal Franks' private office, where his wife was storming up and down, using the most violent language in regard to Justice Field.

"Previous to being removed from the courtroom, Mrs.

Terry had handed her satchel to Porter Ashe, saying that there was money in it. This bag, Mrs. Terry sent for, and a moment after Porter Ashe emerged from the courtroom with the identical satchel on his arm. Marshal Franks asked for it, and Ashe said he was loth (sic) to give it up, saying that he proposed to deliver it to Mrs. Terry in person. Franks again asked for it, and Ashe said he could hardly surrender it, as she dropped it during the episode in court, and it was her personal property. The Marshal told him he proposed to have it, and Ashe finally gave it up without any force being required. On being opened, it was found to contain a Colt's revolver, 41 caliber, six barrels, one chamber being empty. The weapon was put away with the knife and the bag was sent in to Mrs. Terry.

"As soon as quiet was restored in the courtroom, Justice Field resumed the reading of the decision without the least show of excitement, and without a tremor in his voice, and read continuously for over an hour. At the conclusion, the court adjourned for the usual mid-day recess, without any reference to the Terrys or their contemptuous conduct.

"A few minutes after 2 o'clock, Justice Field and Judges Sawyer and Sabin took their seats on the bench. Judge Field, without making any comments, read two orders, one committing D. S. Terry to the County Jail of Alameda County for six months, and the other sending Sarah Althea Terry to the same jail for thirty days.

"Neither Terry nor his wife was present in Court when the orders were made, but they were immediately informed of the action of the Court by the Marshal. It appeared to have a very quieting effect on both of them, and when asked what they intended to do, Terry said he supposed there was no way to get out of serving the jail time."[16]

The Terrys were taken to the Alameda County jail, where they were provided quarters in the jailer's apartment for the duration of their sentences for contempt of court. Both David and Sarah reportedly made repeated threats towards Justice Field and Judge Sawyer. David Terry filed a lawsuit against John C. Franks, U.S. Marshal for the Northern District of California, for $10,000 in damages, claiming the Marshal took him out of the courtroom by force and without reason.[17]

The events on the day of the Lathrop train depot shooting, August 14th, 1889, were extensively covered in the papers. The Stockton *Daily Independent* reported:

> "Ever since the proceedings in the case of *Sharon v. Sharon* were begun, predictions have been made that the litigation would result in tragedy. As time went on and no serious fracas occurred, the predictions were forgotten and the fear of a fatal ending to the celebrated case were dismissed. The predictions were fulfilled and the fears justified, however, by the fatal shooting of Judge David S. Terry yesterday in the dining room at Lathrop, by David Nagle (sic), a Deputy United States Marshal, who was accompanying Judge Stephen J. Field of the United States Supreme Court from Los Angeles to San Francisco. The news of the shooting was telegraphed here at once and caused the wildest excitement."[18]

An article in the *Daily Alta California* also reported the events that occurred on that day:

> "Judge David S. Terry was shot and instantly killed in the Lathrop Hotel, at Lathrop, at 7:15 o'clock this morning by Deputy United States Marshal Nagle. The shooting occurred in the presence of about sixty or seventy people, and created a scene of the wildest excitement. The cause of the shooting was the well-known quarrel existing between Judges Terry and Field,

which grew out of the latter rendering a decision adverse to Terry. As seen by numerous witnesses, Terry walked up to Judge Field in the dining room of the Lathrop Hotel and slapped him in the face, and was in the act of striking him again when Deputy United States Marshal Nagle drew a revolver and shot twice at Terry, one shot penetrating the left breast and producing instant death.

"Judge Field left Los Angeles at 1 o'clock yesterday afternoon, and was on the way to San Francisco. Judge Terry left Fresno for San Francisco early this morning, accompanied by his wife, and boarded the train upon which were Judge Field and Deputy Marshal Nagle, but both parties were ignorant of the other's presence on the train.

"One of the proprietors of the Lathrop Hotel, Fred Lincoln, was also on the train, and learned that Field and Terry were among the passengers. The train was due at Lathrop at 7:10, where it stops twenty minutes for meals. As he stepped from the train, Mr. Lincoln encountered his partner in the hotel, Mr. Stackpole, and informed him that Judges Field and Terry were on the train and would dine there, and to look out for there might be trouble.

"Judge Field came into the dining room first and took a seat at one end of the table in the centre (sic) of the room, Nagle taking the seat by his side. Scarcely had they given orders before Judge Terry entered, accompanied by his wife, and they took seats at the extreme end of another table, distant about twenty-five feet from Judge Field. At first, Terry was ignorant of Field's presence, but Field had seen Terry the minute he entered the room, and called the attention of Nagle to the fact. Mrs. Terry was the first to discover Field, and pointed him out to her husband. They exchanged words in low tones and Mrs. Terry got up and left the dining room.

"Mr. Stackpole, one of the proprietors of the hotel, was

standing in the door and observed Mrs. Terry leave and also took note of the threatening look which she cast upon Judge Field. He walked down the room to where Judge Terry sat, and addressing him, asked why his wife had left the table. 'Judge Field is here,' observed Mr. Stackpole, 'and do you think your wife would be so indiscreet as to cause trouble?'

"'Why do you ask that question?' said Terry.

"'Because I do not wish to have any trouble here,' was the answer.

"'I don't know,' said Judge Terry quietly; and then he added significantly, 'there might be trouble.'

"This alarmed Mr. Stackpole, and he walked back to the door, determined to watch Mrs. Terry when she returned.

"No sooner had Mr. Stackpole left Judge Terry than the latter arose and walked straight up to where Judge Field was sitting, and, without saying a word, slapped him in the face and then attempted to repeat the blow. Deputy Marshal Nagle, who was sitting by Judge Field, sprang to his feet, exclaiming, 'Stop; don't touch that man.' Terry paid no attention to the warning, and was just in the act of striking when Nagle fired. Terry fell heavily to the floor, and as he did so Nagle fired again. The first shot entered Terry's left breast, the second struck the floor near him, plowing up the wood and lodging in the wall.

"As the first shot was fired, Mrs. Terry had reappeared in the doorway carrying a hand traveling bag. Mr. Stackpole intercepted her, and with the aid of others took away the bag. Upon examination afterward the bag was found to contain a pistol, which was sufficient proof of Mrs. Terry's motive.

"Attracted by the report of the pistol, Mrs. Terry looked in at the door, and as she saw her husband fall, threw up her hands, and screamed wildly, 'He has killed him! He is murdered!'"[19]

The deputy United States marshal who had done the shooting

was David Butler Neagle. Neagle was a scrapper, no doubt about it. Standing 5 foot 8 and weighing in at around 145 pounds, Neagle's physical stature belied his fiery nature. In many ways, Neagle was like David Terry, only Terry stood about 6 foot 4 and weighed almost 250 pounds.[20]

Neagle spent much of his adult life chasing the various mining strikes around the West, and he had also been a saloon owner. The first shooting that Neagle was known to have been involved in was in May 1871, in Pioche, Nevada, when he shot a man named James Levy in a street fight.[21]

Neagle served as a deputy sheriff in Cochise County, Arizona in 1881. He was in Tombstone during the time of the Earp shootout near the OK Corral, and he was elected the chief of police of Tombstone in early 1882, serving in that position for two terms. While campaigning for the office, Neagle promised to rid the town of the bad element.[22]

While he was Tombstone's police chief, one of his officers was shot in the leg by a tough character who went by the name of Buckskin. Against advice, Neagle took after Buckskin alone, armed with a Winchester and two revolvers. Neagle found his man in some mountains outside of town and they had a shootout, during which Neagle shot Buckskin dead.[23]

Neagle ran for sheriff in Cochise County in the fall of 1882, but lost. The *Tombstone Epitaph* ran an editorial in their October 31st, 1882, edition, stating their view of his fitness for the job:

> "...His hasty, ungovernable temper, his inclination to harsh measures; his habit of drawing and using firearms to intimidate when unwarranted by facts, all prove him to be an unfit person to trust with...the office of sheriff..."[24]

Marshal Franks had hired David Neagle as a special deputy to protect Justice Field when he was in California riding the circuit. Franks had received a letter from W. H. H. Miller, Attorney General of the United States, directing him to provide security for Fields anytime he was in California because of the threats made to him by the Terrys. Franks deputized Neagle on June 17th, 1889. Neagle was given general instructions to stay with Justice Field at all times, and just before the trip to Los Angeles, Neagle was reminded to "be quick in his action and protect the Judge at all hazard." Franks was of the opinion that David Terry would not stop at slapping Field, but would draw a knife and use it.[25]

After the shooting in Lathrop, Field and Neagle got back on the train. Lathrop Constable Tom Walker, who was also commissioned as a deputy by Sheriff Cunningham, climbed aboard the train just before it pulled out of the station.

The *Stockton Daily Independent* reported:

"As soon as the people in and about the station realized what had occurred there was a scene of wild excitement and Judge Field and Nagle were hurried on board of their car. They at once locked the door and had the blinds pulled down so that the crowd of curious people, who surrounded the car, could not see them. Constable Walker, who had been telephoned for, boarded the train and attempted to arrest Nagle, but Judge Field remonstrated, saying that Nagle had been appointed to guard him while in this state and had only done his duty.

"The Constable feared that if he took Nagle from the train and held him to await the arrival of the up-train, some excited individual might attempt to retaliate by killing him and another murder result. He remained in the car till the train pulled out, going with it to Bantas, where he took Nagle from (the) train. A buggy was procured and the prisoner brought to the city and lodged in jail.

"From the accounts of the bystanders and eye witnesses, he was satisfied that Judge Field was not in any way implicated and he made no attempt to arrest him or search him to see if he had a weapon on him."[26]

Walker took Neagle off the train in Tracy. From there he obtained a horse and buggy and started for Stockton with his prisoner, taking back roads to avoid any crowds because word of the shooting had spread like wild fire.

"Constable Walker left Tracy with the Deputy Marshal as a prisoner at 8 o'clock yesterday morning and reached the County Jail at 10:45 o'clock, making the drive of twenty miles with one horse.

"The Constable telegraphed from Tracy that he would come to town by a round-about way to avoid crowds. He drove in San Joaquin Street and when the jail was reached, Undersheriff Long, Deputy Benjamin and several other officers were waiting inside. The door was opened before the prisoner got out of the buggy and Nagle was inside and the bolts turned before any outsiders knew he was in custody.

"The prisoner came into the jail wearing a long alpaca duster with his heavy coat laid over his wrists, which were held together by handcuffs. He endeavored to cover the 'bracelets' until inside the doors.

"As he stepped in the door in advance of the arresting officer, he said with a painful smile, 'Here's another boarder for you.'

"Deputy Sheriff Cassidy stepped forward to search the prisoner and Nagle pulled back his coat to assist the officer. Taking out his pocket knife, Nagle said: 'Here's my knife; take that.' He had about $50 in coin in his pocket and a gold watch and chain. The pistol was handed to Jailer Littebrandt by the arresting officer, and was quickly locked up in the safe."[27]

As soon as Neagle had been searched, an *Independent* reporter questioned him:

"'I would like to have your statement of the affair.'

'I am much obliged to you, but I have no statement to make,' answered the prisoner.

'Have you nothing to say?' pressed the reporter.

'No' answered Nagle. 'I am a Deputy United States Marshal and simply did my duty as an officer.'

'You are a Deputy under Marshal Franks?'

'Yes, under Mr. Franks.'

"The prisoner said nothing further and followed Deputy Sheriff Cassidy upstairs to be locked up. As the officer left him, Nagle asked that no one be permitted to see him, as he did not want to be interviewed.

"Shortly afterwards, Nagle sent for J. C. Campbell and had a long interview with him as his attorney."[28]

Sarah Althea was totally distraught and inconsolable at the death of her husband, and she stayed by his side from the Lathrop train depot until he was buried. The question was, and nobody had the answer, whether or not Sarah had removed any weapons from David's body when she rushed to his side at the train depot.[29]

While his deputies were dealing with David Neagle, Sheriff Cunningham went to San Francisco to await instructions from San Joaquin County District Attorney Avery C. White. From what he knew of the evidence, White did not believe that Neagle was justified in using deadly force, and he felt that Justice Field might be complicit. White was young and new to the office, and he took counsel from a number of attorneys, including David Terry's son, Clinton Terry, who all advised him not to take any action against Justice Field.[30]

Two gunsmiths, Van Vlear and George Ditz, Jr., were called to the jail to examine Neagle's revolver at the request of Deputy District Attorney William M. Gibson. Gibson and Neagle's attorney, J. C. Campbell, were present during the examination. The *Independent* reported:

> "The pistol was first handed to Mr. Van Vlear to examine. As he handled the murderous-looking weapon, an *Independent* reporter noticed that it was an old-fashioned, single-action Colt's six-shooter of 45 calibre (sic). It could not be fired except by pulling back the hammer, but it was evidently a trusty weapon as it showed the effects of long use by the owner. The handle was worn and chipped and the barrel and cylinder showed rust from having been carried in a hip pocket.
>
> "There were three empty chambers in the cylinder, two showing that the charges had been fired recently. The third chamber was rusty, indicating that it had been kept unloaded as a matter of safety, the hammer being kept down on the harmless chamber. The two charges used were next in rotation to the empty cylinder. The owner of the pistol evidently felt safe with five bullets in his gun.
>
> "There was a set screw missing under the barrel and directly in front of the cylinder and a ring had been attached to the underside of the muzzle of the pistol.
>
> "The gunsmiths took the number of the pistol for identification in court and were about to mark it when they noticed on the handle the letters 'T W,' which had been scratched on it by Constable Walker, so he could identify it."[31]

A Coroner's inquest was held in the Superior courtroom in Stockton. Several witnesses were called. Testimony was given that David Terry had no weapons on him when the body was examined. Constable Walker testified that he arrested David

Neagle and that his gun was found in the condition it was when it was examined by the gunsmiths. The jury returned a verdict stating that David S. Terry died as the result of a gunshot wound inflicted by David B. Neagle, on the 14th of August, 1889, in Lathrop, San Joaquin County, California.[32]

District Attorney White decided to have a warrant served against Justice Field and have him brought to Stockton under arrest. White spoke to a reporter about his decision:

> "'...I am acting solely upon the principle of duty. I have not seen Mrs. Terry nor heard from her since several hours before the Coroner's inquest. Her friends have had no influence with me nor attempted to influence me in any manner, shape or form, nor has any other party, yet I have not acted solely upon my advice, but situated as I was, I deemed it my duty to take this step.'
>
> "'...Mr. Gibson takes the position that the case against Justice Field should be investigated by a magistrate, but is not in favor of the prosecution to arrest Justice Field at present, deeming it better that he be subpoenaed as a witness, where he can be compelled to take the stand as a witness and give his testimony. That position would aid the prosecution in bringing out all the evidence, whether it be in favor of Nagle or against him, and would give the prosecution a better position in prosecuting the case."[33]

David Terry's funeral took place on August 16th, at St. John's Episcopal Church. He was buried in Stockton's Rural Cemetery.[34]

Sarah Terry swore out a complaint in front of Stockton Justice of the Peace H. V. J. Swain, who issued a warrant for Field's arrest, charging him with murder. The warrant was wired to Thomas in San Francisco. After Sheriff Cunningham received the warrant, he went to the San Francisco Superior Court to have it endorsed. After

Judge Alfred Rix consulted with San Francisco District Attorney James D. Page, San Joaquin County Deputy District Attorney Gibson, and Judge Londerback, Rix determined that the warrant was in order and endorsed it.[35]

The warrant was expected by Justice Field and his attorneys, and his release on a writ of habeas corpus had already been arranged. Sheriff Cunningham arrived at the United States Circuit Court on August 16th with the warrant in hand. Wrote the *Independent*:

> "The clock lacked a quarter of 1 when Sheriff Cunningham, accompanied by Chief of Police Crowley and Captain Lees, chief of the detective force, appeared in the building. They proceeded to Marshal Franks' office, where they were received by Marshal Franks and hurried into the marshal's office. Then their arrival was announced to Judge Field.
>
> "Sheriff Cunningham sat in consultation with Chief Crowley and Captain Lees for a few moments, when Mr. Gorham announced that if they were ready, Judge Field was. He led the way through the offices of the Circuit Court Clerk to the chambers.
>
> "Judge Field looked up as Sheriff Cunningham entered the room and rose at once. They both bowed. 'Judge Field, I have my duty to perform,' said Sheriff Cunningham, and he presented Judge Field with the warrant which had been signed by Judge Rix in the morning. Up to this time, Sheriff Cunningham had been the coolest man in the building, but just at this point he seemed to grow a tide 'bashful.' Judge Field glanced pleasantly towards him, and as he took the warrant said: 'That is right, sir. Your duty is your duty. Always do your duty.'
>
> "Judge Field glanced slightly at the document and then, with a smile, said to the Sheriff, who stood on the opposite side of the table:

'I waive the reading of the warrant, Mr. Sheriff. Now do your duty. Shall I consider myself in your custody?'

'Yes, sir,' answered the Sheriff.

"Judge Field then handed Judge Sawyer a petition for a writ of habeas corpus. The attorneys for Justice Field then went before Judge Sawyer and the writ was issued.

"After the habeas corpus writ was served on the Sheriff, it was agreed that all should go immediately into the Circuit Court, where the writ was returnable before Judge Sawyer. Justice Field went into the Court by private entrance, arm in arm with Sheriff Cunningham.

"Judge Hoffman, Judge Sabin and Judge Sawyer took seats on the bench. Justice Field took a seat in the jury box. Sheriff Cunningham, United States Marshal Franks, and District Attorney Carey sat together fronting the Court and Mr. Carey announced the object of their presence.

"United States Attorney Carey, in answer to the question put to him by Judge Sawyer, 'Have you a motion to make?' stated that he had. 'If it please the Court,' said he, 'I have to announce on behalf of Sheriff Cunningham, to whom the writ was directed, that he has the prisoner in court, and now awaits the further pleasure of the Court.'

"'Does he desire to make further return now?' asked Judge Sawyer.

United States Attorney Carey, 'Yes, sir. He desires to make a further return.'

Judge Sawyer, 'See it be made then. We can wait for it. It will not take long.'

'No, not too long.'

'Then let him proceed.'

"About two minutes afterward, the Sheriff made his return in writing. The writ was set for hearing next Thursday at 11 o'clock, and Judge Field was released on his own recognizance in the sum of $5,000."[36]

Marshal Franks and Justice Department officials in Washington stood squarely behind Deputy Neagle with their support. Attorneys from the Justice Department made up part of his defense team. Neagle's attorneys filed a petition for a writ of habeas corpus with Judge Sawyer in the U.S. Circuit Court, in San Francisco. Sawyer, who had also been the victim of threats by the Terrys, issued the writ, returnable to him. Sheriff Cunningham, who was still in San Francisco after having served the warrant on Justice Field, immediately headed back to Stockton by train, and was en route back to San Francisco with Deputy Neagle very early the next morning.[37]

The *Daily Alta California* gave its readers an update relating to Cunningham's response:

> "The injunction of secrecy in reference to the order directing Sheriff Cunningham to bring Neagle to this city were obeyed, and long before the residents of Stockton had left their couches yesterday morning, the prisoner was en route to this city on a special train. This is how the transfer was conducted:
>
> "After being served the order, Sheriff Cunningham and Charles A. Ackerman, of counsel for Neagle, departed on the afternoon train for Stockton. From Port Costa, the sheriff telephoned to District Attorney White of San Joaquin County in reference to the issuance of the order, and asked his advice as to the proper course to pursue, and as to whether he should obey the writ. Upon arriving in Stockton, a few minutes after 8 p.m., they met District Attorney White. They went to the office of ex-Congressman Budd, where consultation was held. W. E. Turner and ex-Judge J. G. Maguire were also present.
>
> "It was decided that there was no way to avoid the writ. Sheriff Cunningham objected to doing anything that would place him as a peace officer in contempt of the United States

Circuit Court. Budd expressed himself as adverse to advising any course that might cause a conflict between the Federal and State Courts. White was non-committal, and did not know what course to pursue. Then the Sheriff asserted that he proposed to take the prisoner to San Francisco and let the law take its course. It was with that understanding that the conference came to an end.

"Long before sunrise yesterday morning, Sheriff Cunningham and Mr. Ackerman had completed arrangements for the departure of Neagle. A special train, consisting of an engine and one coach, had been ordered by telephone from Lathrop and was in waiting at the Stockton depot at 4:30 a.m. Up to that hour, Neagle had not been aware that he was to be taken away. At that hour, a carriage stopped in front of Stockton's County Jail. It was quietly entered by the Sheriff, Neagle and Maguire. Mr. White was picked up at his residence, and a few minutes later the four men were aboard the special.

"Precisely at 4:45 o'clock the engine started and the run of ninety-one miles to the Oakland mole was made in less than two hours and a half. During the run only three stops were made. These were necessary in order to receive dispatches in reference to running the train. The train came by way of Livermore and the last twenty-seven miles were made in thirty minutes. The trip from Stockton to Oakland usually takes four hours, but as the special had right-of-way, its run was made in almost half that amount of time. From Oakland, Neagle and his escort took the 7:30 boat and arrived in this city by 8 o'clock. Half an hour later, Sheriff Cunningham gave Neagle temporary quarters in the City Prison.

"At 10:30 o'clock, Neagle, escorted by Sheriff Cunningham, Chief of Police Crowley and Captain Lees, left the City Prison and walked quietly down Washington street to the Appraiser's Building. In the vicinity of the Circuit Court, there was a repetition of the bustling scenes of Friday, when for the first time in the history of the Union, a Justice of the United States Supreme Court was placed under arrest."[38]

The courtroom was called to order by Marshal Franks at 11:00 a.m., when Judge Sawyer, Judge Sabin and Judge Brewer took the bench. District Attorney White and Mr. Maguire appeared on behalf of Sheriff Cunningham. Maguire argued that it was beyond the jurisdiction of the Federal Courts to take from the custody of a State official a person who had been arrested for the commission of a crime within the State's jurisdiction and against the laws of the State.

Judge Sawyer did not agree with the argument, stating that the prisoner contended that he was carrying out his duties in accordance with the laws of the United States, and therefore, the case was within the jurisdiction of the Federal Court. The case was continued, and Deputy Marshal Neagle was housed at the San Francisco County jail on a federal hold.[39]

The case against Justice Stephen Field was dismissed on August 27th, during a hearing in Circuit Court in front of Judges Sawyer and Sabin, after it was ruled that Justice Field was not implicated in the shooting.[40]

Judge Sawyer ruled on Neagle's habeas corpus case on September 16th, 1889, judging that Neagle had acted in the line of duty, in accordance with the Constitution and the laws of the United States. Neagle was ordered released from custody at that time.[41]

After the Neagle case was removed from the jurisdiction of the county, a San Joaquin County grand jury was presented the case and did not present an indictment against Neagle. Although the Field and Neagle cases were settled, lawyers from both the state and federal governments appealed all the way to the United States Supreme Court to have the issue of jurisdiction in similar cases settled once and for all.⁴²

The United States Supreme Court took up the case of Cunningham, Sheriff v. Neagle at its next session. Justice Field did not sit in on the hearing of the case and did not take a part in the decision. The majority of the Court ruled that the actions of the Circuit Court were justified, stating, in part:

> "…That Neagle was correct in the belief that, without prompt action on his part, the assault of Terry upon the Judge would have ended in the death of the latter; that, such being his well-founded belief, he was justified in taking the life of Terry, as the only means of preventing the death of the man who intended to be his victim; that in taking the life of Terry, under the circumstances, he was acting under the authority of the law of the United States, and was justified in so doing; and that he is not liable to answer in the courts of California on account of his part in that transaction.
>
> "We therefore affirm the judgment of the Circuit Court authorizing his discharge from the custody of the Sheriff of San Joaquin County."⁴³

Sarah Althea Terry never received a penny from William Sharon's estate. After David's death, she began using spiritualists in an attempt to communicate with David. She used a photograph of her late husband as a transmitter. Sarah fell deeper and deeper into mental illness, and was committed to the Stockton Insane Asylum in March 1892, living out the rest of her life there. She died on Sunday, February 14th, 1937, while in her mid-80s.⁴⁴

10

ROUTINE

In September 1889, Thomas was back to the routine duties of the job. He spent part of the month watching over the annual fair, keeping an eye out for undesirables. Local papers praised the sheriff for his diligence. The Sacramento *Daily Record Union* wrote:

> "Gamblers are greatly dissatisfied because Sheriff Cunningham will not allow them to operate illegal gambling schemes. In fact, 'skin game' gamblers and 'sure thing' fraternities are having a hard time."[1]

The Grass Valley *Morning Union* wrote:

> "Sheriff Cunningham notified L. U. Shippee of the San Joaquin Fair Association that he would be liable to punishment under the law if he permitted gambling to be conducted under the patronage of the Stockton Fair. Not even wheels are allowed to go."[2]

November proved to be an active month for the Sheriff's Office. Sheriff Cunningham wired the Sacramento chief of police on November 7th, 1889, asking his men to be on the lookout for three men who had burglarized a Stockton residence of a considerable amount of money and jewelry. The descriptions of two of the burglars matched the descriptions of a pair that had burglarized a Sacramento residence the day before. Lawmen felt that the three were probably the young rascals who had escaped from the San Francisco jail the week before. San Francisco Police Chief Patrick Crowley wrote in his description of the escapees: "They are all-around crooks, and ready for anything from petit larceny up to murder, if necessary."[3]

During the week of November 10th, 1889, a man named Martin hired a horse and buggy from a Stockton livery stable and forgot to return them. The thief drove the buggy to Lathrop, where it broke down. He traded it for a cart, and continued on to Livermore, in Alameda County.

Deputy Thomas Benjamin and Lathrop Constable Tom Walker started out after Martin. They talked to people in Livermore, who knew Martin and knew that he was from San Jose. Benjamin and Walker were in the San Jose area by Thursday, November 14th, and found that Martin had been in the Santa Clara area since getting back from Stockton. Martin had a fight with his estranged wife and had been locked up overnight by the Santa Clara constable, who was unaware that the San Joaquin officers were looking for him. Martin was released the next morning and headed for San Francisco.

Walker and Benjamin kept up their search for the stolen horse, and found that Martin had sold it to a San Jose horse auctioneer named N. D. Crossley. Crossley was interviewed by the lawmen and he told them that he had sold the animal to a friend of his for $40, but he refused to give up the name of the party who had bought it because he didn't want that man to lose out on the transaction.

Benjamin and Walker reported back to Sheriff Cunningham, who started for San Jose to follow up the case in person. Before leaving Stockton, Thomas got a message from Crossley, offering that he would return the animal for $30, Crossley's intent being that he would pay the extra $10 to his friend out of his own pocket.

The sheriff arrived in San Jose on Sunday evening, November 17th, and met with Crossley, who stuck to his proposition to return the horse for $30. Cunningham offered Crossley $15, and for some reason, Crossley took the deal. Thomas demanded a receipt. The horse was shipped back to its owner in Stockton, and the last information reported on the case was that the sheriff was headed to San Francisco to run his man to ground.[4]

On November 28th, Thomas and one of his deputies raided a cock fight outside of Stockton. The *Daily Alta California* wrote about the incident:

> "Thirty young men, including clerks, doctors, lawyers, mechanics and capitalists, some wearing fine clothes and silk hats, others plainly dressed, went out of town three miles today, to witness a cock fight. Sheriff Cunningham and a deputy appeared after two fights had been made, and consternation followed. The sports ran in all directions, but the officers corraled them, took their names, and stopped the fun. No arrests were made, but a lot of society men are in fear. The Sheriff found three roosters in a hay pile but nobody claimed them, and they were left with a keeper."[5]

The decade of the 1890s started out just as the decade of the 1880s ended for the sheriff and his deputies; there was plenty of work to go around.

On March 14th, 1890, Sheriff Cunningham received a large box containing jewelry and other plunder from a number of California burglaries, from the police in Trenton, New Jersey. The Trenton police had arrested two men named Dickerson and Roberts, the outlaws responsible for the November 7th, 1889, burglary of a Stockton home, as well as burglaries in a number of other cities. Lawmen returned the property to its rightful owners.[6]

On April 14th, 1890, Sheriff Cunningham was in Sacramento with a warrant, in search of Sacramento City Deputy Constable Frank Swift, who had been indicted by a San Joaquin County grand jury for kidnapping a married Chinese woman in Stockton a couple of weeks before. Several people from Auburn, including an Auburn constable, were also implicated in the case.[7]

Swift turned himself in to a Sacramento police station when he learned he was wanted. Sheriff Cunningham then headed for Placer County to follow up with the investigation. There, he arrested Constable H. L. Fick, returning to the Stockton jail with the disgraced Fick. Fick was already in trouble in his county for allowing a prisoner to escape from his jail.[8]

Thomas was in San Francisco on April 18th, testifying in a conspiracy to murder trial of a man named Dominico Perrazo.[9]

In June, Sheriff Cunningham arrested a thief named Emil Doro, after Doro stole a $150 diamond ring that had been entrusted to him by a widow in San Francisco. Doro pawned the ring for $20, then headed for Stockton, where Cunningham found him.[10]

Sheriff Cunningham and Lockeford Constable Charles H. Dial arrested a young farm laborer named Charles Brown in Clements on Sunday, July 20th, 1890, for the robbery of the Valley Springs to Mokelumne Hill stage, in Calaveras County, on July 14th.

Brown insisted that he was in Stockton on the day of the robbery, but the officers felt they had enough evidence against Brown to hold him. Sheriff Thorn came to Stockton to have a look at the prisoner, and found that Brown matched the description of the robber he had tracked from the scene of the crime. Brown ended up pleading guilty to the robbery charge, and was sentenced to eight years in San Quentin.[11]

In early September 1890, N. S. Harrold, a Farmington area rancher, reported that he had suffered the theft of $360 in coin and a number of pieces of silverware from his home. Harrold said that he had a Chinese servant, whom Harrold had employed for years and whom he trusted implicitly. In fact, Harrold said that when he told the servant of the theft, the servant went out into the fields and recovered some of the silverware.

When Harrold explained all of the circumstances of the theft, Thomas immediately came to suspect the servant, who was scheduled to go visit a sick cousin in San Francisco in the near future. Before leaving, the servant told Mr. Harrold that his cousin was very sick, and that he would not be returning to work. Harrold notified Sheriff Cunningham when the servant left on the train for San Francisco, and Farmington Constable Thomas Campbell, who was also a deputy for Cunningham, boarded the train with him.

When the train arrived in Stockton, Campbell and some other deputies confronted the servant, who insisted that all he had in the world was $54. When he was searched, the deputies found that he was wearing a money belt containing $374. The deputies lodged the servant in the Stockton jail.[12]

The second week of September, Sheriff Cunningham got a request from the sister of a Stockton man named William Moss, who had left Stockton with someone named Robert Kelly. Moss had inherited a large estate from his father, but had squandered most of it. Moss and Kelly had planned a trip to Europe, but the sister hadn't heard anything more after the two arrived in New York. She requested that the sheriff follow up and try to find her brother. Sheriff Cunningham sent Deputy Barney Cassidy to New York to investigate. Cassidy and New York City Detective Cosgrove located Moss, and the deputy and Moss were soon on the train headed back to Stockton.[13]

Towards the end of September, Sheriff Cunningham issued his yearly warning to thieves and gamblers to steer clear of Stockton during the annual fair, least they find themselves spending more time in town than they bargained for, specifically on Market Street in the county jail.[14]

In November, Undersheriff Long got a visit from Robert T. Scott, during one of Mr. Scott's periodic visits to the Sheriff's Office. Scott served as a sheriff's keeper, someone who was put in charge of property that was involved in litigation.

Way back in 1866, the owner of a pair of mules was served a writ of attachment by then-sheriff C. C. Rynerson. Rynerson placed the mules in the custody of Mr. Scott, who had been taking care of the surviving mule since that time. Rynerson passed the mules on to his successor in office, Freeman Mills, who passed them to his successor, George Castle, two years later, in 1870. Castle, in turn, passed the mules to Thomas Cunningham in 1872 when he took office.

One of the mules died in 1878, but the surviving mule was still going strong at about 30 years old when Mr. Scott visited the undersheriff in 1890. The *Stockton Independent* of November 14th, 1890, stated:

"Allowing the Sheriff's keeper $3 a day, which is the limit fixed by law for the pay of keepers, the surviving mule is charged with $26,280 costs. If the mule is charged with ranch fees at $2 per month, the bill against the animal struggling to outlive the courts, is $576. Adding $144 for ranch fees, chargeable against the one that grew tired of the law's delays and died, would make the bill for ranching to be collected out of the only property remaining, the lone mule, $720."[15]

Undersheriff Long made out a receipt, to which Mr. Scott attested to the fact that he still had possession of the mule, subject to the further orders of Sheriff Cunningham.[16]

Thomas added another two members to his staff in 1891, hiring A. G. "Del" Keagle and George H. Black as deputies, and bringing the total of full-time deputies on his force to six, plus the undersheriff.[17]

George Black
[*SJSO collection*]

Late in the evening on February 6th, 1891, the southbound Southern Pacific passenger train from San Francisco to Los Angeles was stopped one mile south of Alila, in Tulare County, by three masked bandits. The robbers lead the train's fireman to the express car, where a gunfight erupted between the outlaws and the express messenger. In the fusillade, the fireman was struck in the side and mortally wounded, dying the next day. Sheriff Cunningham left for Tulare County to help in the search for the bandits as soon as he received word of the robbery.

Officers found the location where the robbers had abandoned their horses, and Tulare County Sheriff Eugene Kay returned to Visalia on February 13th, saying that he believed the bandits were in the Coast Range mountains. Sheriff Cunningham returned to Stockton the same night, but he was of the opinion that the robbers were not holed up in the mountains.[18]

Eventually, Sheriff Kay and other lawmen determined that the robbery had been committed by Grat, Bob and Emmett Dalton— yes, those Daltons, the ones from Indian Territory who met their Waterloo in Coffeyville, Kansas at the hands of armed citizens during a failed double bank robbery the following year. After the Alila robbery, the three retreated to their brother Bill's ranch in the Cholame Valley, in San Luis Obispo County.[19]

During the last months of 1890, a pair of safecrackers were busy throughout California, particularly in San Francisco. Their method for entering the building and the safe was similar in each case.

A burglary and safe cracking occurred at a Sacramento book keeping business owned by A. S. Hopkins and Brothers on J Street during the nighttime hours of February 14, 1891. The crime had all the signs of being committed by the two burglars. Sheriff

Cunningham was in Sacramento the next day, and went to the business to take a look. While there, Cunningham spoke to a reporter:

> "'The same men that did this job broke open a safe in Stockton recently,' he said after he had finished his examination. 'The work is identical on the safe, and they entered the building in exactly the same manner as they did in our town. I am pretty sure I know who these men are. There are two of them, and you would be surprised at the style they put on when traveling the streets in the daytime. These men are the same fellows who blew open the safe in the Wigwam Theater in San Francisco a couple of months ago, and they are also the same chaps that emptied a safe in San Jose.
>
> "'They are, without doubt, the cleverest workers that the authorities in California have ever had to deal with—that is, in their particular line of business. What they don't know about safe-opening is not worth knowing. They can open the best safe ever made. They understand thoroughly the construction of every alleged 'patent burglar-proof' safe. Now, for instance, there is one particular safe in which the lock is always immediately back of the combination spindle. These fellows simply knock off the knob, drill through the spindle, and there they are right into the lock. With locks like the one in Hopkin's place, however, the lock is situated differently, and of course, our friends operate as they did in this case—drill about two inches to the left of the spindle and blow out the block.'"[20]

Although Sheriff Cunningham had an idea of who the burglars were, he apparently didn't have any evidence on them and he didn't name them, and the safe cracking burglaries continued through 1891.[21]

In March 1891, the legislature passed a law that took the duty of executions out of the hands of California's sheriffs and transferred them to the wardens at San Quentin and Folsom. That same month, Sheriff Cunningham and members of the Board of Supervisors traveled to Santa Cruz to inspect the new jail there, in preparation of designing and building a new jail in Stockton.[22]

Thomas and his staff moved into offices at a newly completed courthouse in April 1891. The courthouse, which was built on the same site as the first courthouse, had been under construction since 1888. County offices had been operating out of temporary quarters in a nearby downtown building during construction. With the move, Sheriff Cunningham and his deputies finally had enough office space to be able to comfortably carry out their duties.[23]

San Joaquin County's second courthouse was completed in 1891
[*R. Tod Ruse*]

On May 12th, 1891, Thomas received a letter from Sacramento Chief of Police Warren F. Drew, asking him to keep a lookout for a man named Henry Maddix, wanted for a Marysville murder. Cunningham passed on the information and description of Maddix to his deputies, and Deputy Del Keagle had Maddix in custody the following night.[24]

In June, a reporter for the *Sacramento Daily Record Union* paid a visit to the new Sheriff's Office quarters, where Sheriff Cunningham had moved his museum of criminal artifacts to the ante room outside of his office:

> "Sheriff Cunningham has in his office one of the most cheerful collections of law-breaking implements I ever saw. When I get particularly blue, I go and stand in front of it with my hat off, and muse until I am thoroughly exhilarated. The cabinet in which these treasures of the Sheriff are stored is a large one, and it is full to overflowing with all sorts of knick-knacks, bearing inscriptions which inform the spectator in a vivacious way that they have been used with effect.
>
> "The piece of glass with which Wilson cut Kennedy; the knife that killed John Griffin; the knife that killed a silversmith; the knuckles used by a San Francisco hoodlum; the knife used on Hughes; the pistol with which O. G. Langman was shot; the pistol with which Arthur McKowan killed himself; the coat of mail worn by George Cox; knots from the ropes that hung French, Martin and others; a skull dug up in the street; shotguns used by stage robbers; burglar's tools; counterfeiter's outfits, and a hundred other little bits of rare, quaint and curious criminal virtu—enough to make the most somber old sinner in the land revert lovingly to the achievements of his youth."[25]

A number of California's sheriffs gathered in San Francisco on July 18th, 1891, with the intent of forming a state sheriffs' association. The meeting was held in the office of San Francisco Sheriff Charles S. Laumeister, and included sheriffs E. D. Gibson of Los Angeles; Theodore Lacy of Orange; John H. Folks of San Diego; W. C. Conroy of Placer; C. Fox, undersheriff of San Mateo; A. J. Jennings of Santa Cruz; G. S. McKenzie of Napa; Giles E. McDougal of Santa Clara; and Eugene W. Kay of Tulare.

Sheriff John Folks of San Diego was elected chairman of the group. A committee of three, responsible for forming a permanent organization, was appointed. San Francisco Sheriff Laumeister was voted as president of the executive committee, which was charged with drafting a constitution and by-laws for the organization. Sheriff Cunningham was absent from the meeting, but was appointed to the executive committee, along with Sheriff McDougal, Sheriff McKenzie, Sheriff Gibson and Sheriff Kay. This was the beginning of the California State Sheriffs' Association, which was officially organized in 1894.[26]

Thomas spent about two weeks in August searching for a horse thief named Charles Carrillo. Carrillo stole a horse and saddle from a ranch located about eight miles north of Stockton. Cunningham circulated Carrillo's description, along with that of the stolen horse and saddle, and headed south out of town, the direction that Carrillo had last been seen.

Sheriff Cunningham tracked his man south down the valley, and several days into his hunt telegraphed back to Stockton for his saddle and bridle in preparation for a ride through rough country. Carrillo made his way through San Jose on August 15th; he was heading south at that time. He changed his course several times, but Sheriff Cunningham traced him into Salinas, in Monterey County, before he lost the trail.

On August 22nd, Cunningham received a wire from Constable

Hayden of San Lucas, in Monterey County, 56 miles southeast of Salinas, stating that he had Carrillo in custody. Thomas was back in San Jose with his prisoner on August 23rd, waiting for the next train to Stockton.[27]

On the evening of September 3rd, 1891, the southbound Southern Pacific passenger train, known as the Los Angeles Express, was stopped about one mile south of the Ceres station, in Stanislaus County, where an attempt was made on the Wells Fargo express car by two bandits. Two dynamite bombs were set off near the car when the express messenger refused to open the door.[28]

Southern Pacific detective Len Harris, a former Sacramento police officer, was on the train at the time. He jumped off and fired four rounds at the robbers. His shots missed and he was struck in the neck by return gunfire by one of the outlaws.[29]

Sheriff Cunningham, Deputy George Black, Lathrop Constable Tom Walker and his Deputy Constable Jesurum, left Lathrop at about 10:00 p.m. that night on a special train, arriving in the Ceres area within the hour.[30]

Cunningham ended up with a posse of about twelve men, and they started scouring the country west of the attempted robbery. The trail led them to the area of Newman, on the west side of the valley, but that's where the leads went cold and they came up empty-handed.[31]

Mr. J. A. Fillmore, general superintendent the Southern Pacific Railroad, was interviewed by reporters and had this to say about the robbers:

> "I do not think they can get away from us this time, for the whole country was surrounded in less than two hours after the attempted robbery. It looks to me very much like the work of the Goshen gang. They are desperate men, but Cunningham and his assistants will catch them without any doubt."[32]

The "Goshen gang" that Fillmore referred to was in relation to a train robbery that occurred on January 21st, 1890, at a railroad water stop called Goshen, in Tulare County. On that day, two armed and masked bandits boarded the engine and ordered the engineer to stop the train short of Tulare. One of the outlaws escorted the engineer and fireman back to the express car, where about $5,000 was taken from the Wells Fargo messenger. A vagrant who had been riding the train was killed by one of the robbers during the crime.[33]

The descriptions of the outlaws and the method of their operation was similar in both the Goshen and Ceres crimes, and, in fact, also matched the details of the robbery of a train near Pixley, in Tulare County, where two innocent men were killed on February 23rd, 1889.[34]

Sheriff Cunningham and the other lawmen continued on with their investigation and search through the next couple of days, not resting during that time. The *San Francisco Call* of September 6th wrote:

> "Those leading the chase are Sheriff Cunningham, Deputies Stockiard and Sell, Detectives Hume, Lawson, Packer and Smith, and although forty-eight hours have passed since the attempt at robbery, these brave men have not taken any rest, going night and day, not for the reward offered for the arrest of the villains, but to bring them to justice if possible, and rid the country of them."[35]

All of the officers in the hunt for the robbers met at the El Capitan Hotel in Merced on September 5th. Based on all of the information they had gathered up to that time, the lawmen felt that Bob and Emmett Dalton, who had been convicted of the Alila train robbery but who had escaped from the Tulare County jail and who were at large at that time, were involved in the Ceres robbery. After further discussion, the officers changed course and landed on William Dalton and Riley Dean as their suspects. Operating on that theory, officers started searching for Dalton and Dean.[36]

Thomas and his deputies returned to Stockton because Riley Dean had lived in San Joaquin County and he had contacts there. A short time after getting to town, Cunningham received word that Tulare County Sheriff Eugene Kay and one of his deputies, George Witty, had caught up with Dalton and Dean and arrested them outside of Traver, in north Tulare County.[37]

Although the officers felt they had the right men for the robbery in Dalton and Dean, both suspects were released for lack of evidence at their preliminary hearing in Modesto on September 12th. The manhunt for the real robbers and murderers in these cases ultimately proved to be one of the longest in state history.[38]

The day before Christmas 1891, Sheriff Cunningham was in New Hope, investigating the brutal robbery and beating of an elderly man who lived alone in a cabin. The victim, a man named Vincent Glenn, was tortured over a seven-hour period, from 8:00 p.m. on the evening of December 23rd until about 3:00 a.m. the next morning, by two masked robbers who were armed with pistols. It had recently been reported in a newspaper that Mr. Glenn and his brother were wealthy landowners who did not believe in banks and who buried their money instead.

The robbers demanded all of Glenn's money, but Glenn told the bandits that all he had was $80, which was in his pocket and which he produced on demand. The outlaws didn't believe the old man, insisting that he had money that was hidden somewhere. They searched his entire house and yard, but found nothing. Not satisfied, the thugs beat Glenn now and again, finally leaving him tied up and gagged. Mr. Glenn was able to attract the attention of some men on the other side of the Mokelumne River, who came over and untied him and reported the robbery.

Sheriff Cunningham spent several days in the New Hope area searching for information. He found a dark lamp that he believed was used by the robbers, but he was unable to find any trace of the bandits.[39]

The Board of State Prison Directors met at San Quentin Prison on January 16th, 1892. One of the announcements made that day was that the board had directed the warden of San Quentin to no longer provide Sheriff Cunningham, San Francisco Police Chief Crowley, or the Oakland Police Department with photographs and descriptions of the convicts entering San Quentin for their rogues' galleries. Members of the board believed that if the photographs of the convicts leaving the prison were handed around, those men would be hounded back into criminality.[40]

Sheriff Cunningham was called to Lodi on February 5th, 1892, after neighbors threatened to run a rascal named Bennett Devin out of town on a rail. Cunningham was called when it appeared the situation was going to get violent. The nature of the problem was not reported on, but Devin was so belligerent that his kids were taken from him by neighbors and placed with other people who agreed to raise them. Devin refused to leave town, and that is when things heated up. Thomas was able to mediate the situation, and Devin agreed to leave as soon as he could find a place to live for him and his wife. The neighbors were okay with the agreement, as long as Devin did it pronto, else he be tarred and feathered.[41]

Thomas arrested a thief named Phillip Huppe, alias Phillip Spiegel, on February 24th, 1892, after Huppe stole property from a number of Stockton area ranches. Huppe's room was searched, and much of the stolen property was located there, including horse harnesses and a Winchester rifle.[42]

Two days later, on February 26th, Thomas was traveling through Sacramento on the train, en route to Folsom with a prisoner named John Hoffman, who had been sentenced to two years for burglary.[43]

Thomas was working on a larceny case in early April. He had first become aware of a man named Joseph Arata and his partner, Andrew Cuneo, when he received word that the two were freely spending large amounts of money all of a sudden. A couple of days later, an elderly widow named Herlihy, who lived on a ranch outside of Lodi, reported that approximately $1,300 was missing from its hiding place on her ranch. Arata had worked as a ranch hand for Mrs. Herlihy for the previous few months, and he too was missing.

Cunningham already knew that Arata and Cuneo had headed for the foothill country east of San Joaquin County, and he wired lawmen in Calaveras and Amador counties to keep their eyes peeled. He then headed for Amador County, and when he got to Jackson, found that a constable there had received his wire and had the two in custody. Thomas returned to Stockton with the two crooks on April 8th.[44]

On June 23rd, 1892, Sheriff Cunningham and his deputies arrested Martin D. Howell on a federal counterfeiting warrant. Thomas had been working with Nicholas R. Harris, the former sheriff of Santa Clara County and now a Secret Service agent in San Francisco, trying to clean up an operation passing counterfeit coin. Howell had been passing the marked phony money in Stockton. Sheriff Cunningham had a couple of his deputies watching Howell's house, while another one tailed Howell around town until the warrant was served on him. A search warrant for his house and office was also served.⁴⁵

On July 13th, 1892, Stockton Constable James Carroll served a writ of attachment on the Carver Wild America Circus for a twenty-five-dollar rent they owed to the city baseball grounds. Eight of the circus's horses were attached, and the circus workers and cowboys were having none of it. Carroll sent for the sheriff, and Thomas was soon at the scene of the ruckus.

Circus Jack said that no officer should take a horse, and it looked for a while like the clowns might riot. The officers called their bluff, however, and Circus Jack coughed up the twenty-five bucks. Arrangements were made to satisfy the circus's other creditors, and after an hour and a half delay, Jack and his troop were on the train, headed for Sacramento.⁴⁶

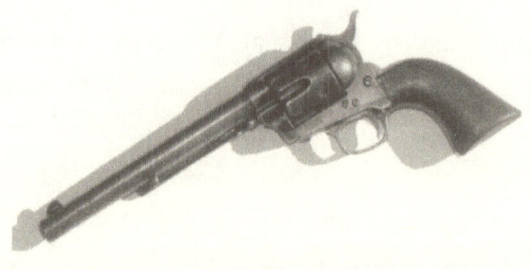

Sheriff Cunningham's 1873 Colt Frontier Six-Shooter
[*R. Tod Ruse*]

By 1892, Thomas had replaced his 1851 Colt's Navy with a more modern handgun. He chose the 1873 Colt's single-action Frontier Six-Shooter model. Cunningham's gun had a seven-and-a-half-inch barrel, and was chambered in .44-40, also known as the

.44 Winchester Center Fire round. This round was very convenient, because the Winchester rifle also had chamberings in .44-40, so the same ammunition could be used in both a handgun and rifle. This was a black powder cartridge, and made reloading the gun much easier than Thomas's percussion model revolver. Although there were more modern revolvers available at the time, the 1873 single-action model was still extremely popular and Thomas's choice was a good one. Thomas testified about his gun in an advertisement for Ditz Brothers, a local gun store:

> "July 20, 1892. Gentlemen—The Colt's Frontier single action 44 Winchester Revolver purchased from you is the most satisfactory weapon I have used. It is light on the trigger and safe and shoots accurate, and cartridges can be procured at any country store. Thomas Cunningham, Sheriff, San Joaquin County."[47]

Sheriff Cunningham carried his trusty shootin' iron with him after a southbound passenger train, The Los Angeles Express, was held up on the evening of August 3rd, 1892, near a place called Collis, in Fresno County. Cunningham was on a train headed south as soon as he got word of the robbery.

The method of operation used by the bandits in this robbery was similar to the previous train robberies. Two masked men entered the engine compartment, forcing the engineer to stop the train. The engineer and fireman were then marched back to the express car, where a demand was made for the messenger to open the door. When he refused, the outlaws set off dynamite and forced their way in, just as they had done before. The take from the Wells Fargo safe was reported to be between $30,000 and $50,000. The robbers then fled on horses.[48]

The lawmen had developed a couple of suspects since the Ceres robbery and had been keeping tabs on the two, but hadn't

The COLTS

Frontier single action Revolver is the most reliable and effective for officers' use.

For sale by

DITZ BROS.,

DEALERS IN

Fire Arms and Ammunition,

181 Main St., Stockton, Cal.

Stockton, July 20th, 1892.

Messrs. Ditz Brothers, Stockton, Cal.:

GENTLEMEN— The Colts Frontier single action 44 Winchester Revolver purchased from you is the most satisfactory weapon I have used. It is light on the trigger and safe and shoots accurate, and cartridges can be procured at any country store.

THOMAS CUNNINGHAM, Sheriff, San Joaquin County

[R. Tod Ruse]

developed any hard evidence against them. The two were a couple of friends named John Sontag and Chris Evans. Evans lived near Visalia, and after the Collis robbery, Sheriff Cunningham, Wells Fargo's Detective John Thacker and Southern Pacific Detective Bill Hickey traced the outlaws to Visalia.[49]

Southern Pacific Detective Will Smith decided to pay a visit to John Sontag's half-brother, George Contant, and try and roll him. Smith took Tulare County Deputy George Witty with him, and they talked Contant into accompanying them to the Sheriff's Office for a talk. While there, Contant made some incriminating comments, and he was lodged in the jail.

Detective Smith and Deputy Witty returned to retrieve George Contant's trunk, in which Smith felt he would find incriminating evidence. When the officers got to the cabin, they were waylaid by John Sontag and Chris Evans, who threw down on Smith and ordered him out of the house. Witty had been on the front porch, and as the two officers ran out of the yard, both outlaws opened fire, slightly wounding Will Smith but grievously wounding George Witty. Evans and Sontag then fled.[50]

The *San Francisco Call* opined, "The opinion is general that if Smith had waited the arrival of Cunningham and Thacker, the men would have easily been arrested."[51]

Tulare County Sheriff Eugene Kay deputized about 100 local men, broke them into groups, and passed out assignments. A squad of five lawmen were assigned to watch Chris Evans' house in case the robbers returned there. At about midnight on August 5th, Deputy Oscar Beaver saw movement in Evans' barn. Beaver was shot and mortally wounded when he called out to the outlaws. Evans and Sontag then fled north and east, towards the mountains. Sheriff Cunningham was within ear-shot of the Evans place and

Ralph O. Yardley illustration of the pursuit of the train robbers
[*R. Tod Ruse*]

arrived soon after the shooting occurred. Beaver died at about 2:15 p.m. the next afternoon.[52]

Cunningham, John Thacker and former Tulare County Sheriff Daniel Overall were sent east towards the Sierras. They returned to Visalia on August 6th, after having lost the trail in the area of Stokes Mountain, in eastern Tulare County. Sheriff Cunningham had to return to Stockton that night due to pressing business. Thomas told reporters that lawmen were convinced that Sontag and Evans were responsible for all of the previously unsolved valley train robberies.[53]

Why Thomas needed to return to Stockton is not known. It is known that many of the lawmen and railroad company detectives working on the case had differences of opinion, and even disputes among themselves, during the manhunt. Many of these men were motivated by the posted reward money and even bounty hunters got into the act. Maybe that was the reason Thomas didn't return to the chase. Chris Evans later commented that he and Sontag were surprised when Cunningham pulled out of the hunt so suddenly. Evans actually thought that they had killed Cunningham instead of Oscar Beaver, and only found out later that it was Beaver who they shot.[54]

The manhunt for Sontag and Evans proved to be one of the longest and most costly in state history. It took over ten months to run the pair to ground, during which time three more lawmen lost their lives and a half-dozen more were wounded at the hands of the outlaws.[55]

Sheriff Cunningham and Deputy Benjamin assisted Stockton police officers with a murder investigation during the late-night hours of October 18th, 1892. Frank Murray, a young Stockton man, staggered onto the porch of a friend's house after having been stabbed in the heart about two blocks away. Murray had previously been a boarder at the house that he ended up at and everyone there knew him.

Up on the front porch, Murray reached for some window blinds, pulling them from their brackets and causing a commotion that stirred attention in the house. The occupants came to Murray's aid and one of the men living in the house summoned police officer Henry Baker. Murray was able to say a few words. When a lodger at the house who worked with Murray asked him who had stabbed him, Murray replied, "I know all too well," before dying.[56]

Stockton Police Captain Michael Finnell took charge of the investigation, leading officers Brennis Kenyon, Henry Baker, J. H. Burnham and Charles Fields, along with Deputy Benjamin. They returned to the house where Frank Murray had died and found some boarders there that told them that two brothers, whose mother owned the house, had a grudge against Murray after Murray interfered with an assault by one of the brothers on another man. Officers found where the stabbing occurred and recovered the knife. Four men were arrested on suspicion and Sheriff Cunningham assisted in questioning them, but all four suspects were eventually released and the murder was never solved.[57]

Thomas was in Sacramento on January 22nd, 1893, with an elderly gentleman who had $1,600 stolen from him by two juveniles in November 1891. The victim, a shoe maker named Gustav Legrer, had originally had his money deposited in the bank, but for some reason had withdrawn the money and had it hidden in a boot at his house. Both boys left Stockton after the theft, one going to Denver, the other to San Francisco, where they presumably spent all the money. On his return to Stockton, the kid that had been in Denver was arrested and convicted, and got five years in the Whittier Reform School. The other kid was acquitted of the charges.[58]

Mr. Legrer had recently been told that the boys hadn't spent all of his money, but had deposited a large chunk of it in a Sacramento bank. The sheriff felt the story didn't hold water, but to satisfy Mr. Legrer, Thomas accompanied him to Sacramento to check things out. As expected, there was no trace of any such transaction, and Mr. Legrer returned to Stockton just as broke as when he had left.[59]

On March 11th, 1893, Sheriff Cunningham was pursuing Lodi Constable William J. Bailey. Bailey, who Thomas worked with on many cases, was accused of attacking a Lodi woman with evil intent. The woman reported that Bailey had initially enticed she and her husband to come to Lodi, where there was work for the husband. One day while her husband was at work, Bailey came to the woman's house while his wife was out of town. He threw her violently to the floor, with the intent to do a lot more, but she had fought hard and finally drove him out of the house. She went to the court and swore out a warrant to that effect.

The woman told her husband about Bailey's attempt four days after the attack, and the husband went looking for the constable with a gun, but Bailey was out of town at the time. That was on a Tuesday. That Thursday, Bailey returned to town and the husband was waiting for him at the train depot, intending to settle the matter once and for good.

Bailey was able to board the train before any gun smoke filled the air, and he made it to Sacramento. A warrant had been issued for William Bailey by this time, and Thomas had one of his deputies head for Sacramento to try and locate him, but the deputy found that Bailey had already left there and was headed for San Francisco. The trail went cold there.

On Sunday, March 12th, Sheriff Cunningham got word that William Bailey was in Tracy. Thomas immediately headed that way on a special engine, an unscheduled engine that was put into service specifically for Cunningham. By the time he got to Tracy, Bailey had taken a southbound freight train. The sheriff re-boarded his engine and headed south. He caught up to his man at Mendota, in Fresno County, where he took Bailey into custody.[60]

William Bailey's case was dismissed after his preliminary examination. He retained his position as constable, and he and Thomas worked on future cases together, just as they had done in the past.[61]

In March of 1893, the legislature passed a law which increased the term of office for elected county and township officials from two years to four. The new law took effect at the November general elections in 1894.[62]

Prisoners were moved into a new county jail in Stockton on March 31th, 1893. The new jail, which had been in the planning and construction phases the previous two years, was built at the northeast corner of Channel and San Joaquin streets, one block north of the courthouse. The March 12th edition of the *Los Angeles Herald* gave a detailed description of the new lock-up, which was dubbed "Cunningham's Castle" for the man who had a central role in its design and architecture:

> "This is a model jail—It will doubtless prove an example for this style of building—The structure just completed at Stockton, Cal., is something unique in the county jail line, and embraces many features that sheriffs have been endeavoring to introduce in the prisons, with poor success.

"By a novel arrangement of the cells and the passages leading to them, a prisoner can be locked up without being seen by any other prisoner, or, in fact, by anyone but officers. The cells are arranged around a semicircular wall on three tiers of ten cages each. They do not open out on the big corridor, but on little passages communicating with the corridor. This shuts off the view of a criminal, who can only see a person entering the passage communicating with his cell.

The new jail, dubbed "Cunningham's Castle," was opened in 1893
[*SJSO collection*]

"This, Sheriff Cunningham believes, will greatly facilitate the conviction of criminals, as suspected persons will always be in the dark as to whether or not their accomplices have been arrested, and will be prevented from communicating with each other by that old trick of tapping on the walls. Every sound will, by arrangement of electric wires, be communicated to the guardroom, a semicircular affair of concrete that stands off on one side of the jail, directly in front of and facing the cells.

"Special cells in a section of the building apart from that occupied by prisoners have been fitted up for the detention of witnesses. The female prisoners are to be kept in their own section, far away from the male criminals. All the cells are 6 1/2 by 9 feet in dimension and are well lighted and aired.

"The building will cost when completed $60,000. The design is two stories and basement for the front elevation, of pressed brick and sandstone trimmings. The architecture is of a composite order, being a combination of the Renaissance and what is known as the modern Queen Anne. A short flight of semicircular steps leads into a deeply recessed vestibule from which the doors open into a lobby about twelve feet wide. The hall runs diagonally across the main building to a flight of steps leading to the guardroom. Three iron doors must be passed to get this far. Once inside the guardroom, a fourth iron door closes behind the prisoner, and he is searched before passing the last iron door and across the corridor to his cell. A prisoner could never be taken out by a mob if one nervy man held the jail.

"The height of the different stories is: Basement, ten feet in the clear; first floor, thirteen feet; second floor, twelve feet, and attic ten feet. The skyline is broken by cone-topped turrets at the three street corners and by a square tower rising directly over the stairway in the center of the building, which is fifty-four feet in height to the top of the walls and seventy-five feet to the top of the pyramidal cap."[63]

With the opening of the new jail, Hartman Littebrandt was promoted to head jailer and Thomas hired Robert Hanks as a temporary assistant jailer. Hanks was a ship's carpenter by trade, but had served as the jailer for Tuolumne County Sheriff J. D. Patterson in 1859. Hanks was also a deputy for Stockton Constable William "Pony" Denig at the time Cunningham hired him, and at one time he had served as a deputy U.S. marshal.[64]

On June 2nd, 1893, Sheriff Cunningham attended a justice court hearing in Lodi, after he got word that there might be trouble. A man named Edward James was facing charges for attacking a Lodi area woman as she was driving down a country road. After pulling her out of her carriage and knocking her to the ground, James beat the woman, causing serious injuries to her head, face and body. The public was so incensed that a lynching was a real possibility.

James was being held in the county jail in Stockton, and when he was picked up by Constable William Bailey and his deputy, William "Billy" Wall, Sheriff Cunningham accompanied them back to Lodi with the prisoner.[65]

Deputy William "Billy" Wall
[*Nancy Lea Schmer, Lodi Historical Society*]

The lawmen were on edge during the preliminary hearing because tensions were running so high. When the victim took the stand, she was carrying a black satchel which she placed on her lap. Inside her bag was a loaded pistol with which she aimed to shoot Edward James. Taking no chances, Thomas had taken a seat between the witness stand and the prisoner. He also instructed the district attorney and court reporter to help shield the prisoner from the victim. It ended up being a good move, because when the victim was questioned about her injuries, she insisted on standing up to raise the veil she was wearing, and show her bruised face to the court.

The courtroom was packed, and when the victim stood up, a length of rope was thrown from the back. With that, the courtroom erupted. Sheriff Cunningham and Deputy Wall rushed James out a back door, while Constable Bailey ran for the carriage. There was a large crowd waiting outside, someone dragging a rope and the mob calling for a hanging. Crowding in on the officers and their prisoner, several men pinioned Cunningham's arms, and surged for James.

Wall stood in front of his prisoner and squared off, and when the leader of the group came after James, Wall decked him with a haymaker. Wall single-handedly kept the crowd back until Constable Bailey came up with the carriage. James was stuffed into the wagon, and the horses were spurred on to a dead run. Greatly impressed with the deputy constable, Sheriff Cunningham did not forget Billy Wall's actions that day.[66]

Two weeks later, on June 17th, 1893, Sheriff Cunningham was in San Rafael, looking to add another prisoner to his new jail. A horse thief had been operating in several counties, including San Joaquin County, and had stumped the various sheriffs when they were unable to identify him. Thomas had been keeping tabs on the descriptions provided by the sheriffs regarding horse thefts in their counties, and he was summoned to the Marin County jail in San Rafael to look at the crook. Cunningham was able to identify the prisoner as E. T. Richardson. Once he was identified, San Francisco authorities prosecuted Richardson for horse theft, and he was sentenced to three-and-a-half years in San Quentin.[67]

On September 6th, 1893, a lone highwayman stepped out into the road from behind a pile of hay and stopped a schoolmarm named Mrs. Henry Austin, about eight miles southeast of Stockton. The well-dressed robber wore a mask and pointed a pistol at Mrs. Austin's head, demanding her valuables. She denied having any money, at which time the bandit pulled the trigger, but it only clicked. He then grabbed her cape off her shoulders, and ripped a gold watch and chain from her wrist before running off.[68]

Mrs. Austin's husband was working on a harvester about a half-mile away, and she went to him to tell him what happened. Mr. Austin mounted a horse and started out after the robber, who was running down the road. When Austin got within a few feet of him, the bandit wheeled and quickly fired a shot that went through Austin's arm, near the elbow. Austin's horse jumped, dumping him to the ground. At the same time, the robber fired again, grazing Austin's face. Austin gained his feet and started running when another shot cut his suspenders in two, but it did not enter his body. The outlaw then fled on foot.[69]

Austin was brought to town and Sheriff Cunningham was notified. The sheriff and his men spent several days searching for the highwayman, but no information was found to indicate whether or not he was ever identified or arrested.[70]

That fall, on October 18th, 1893, Sheriff Cunningham

arrested Martin D. Howell on another federal warrant charging him with passing counterfeit greenbacks. A federal grand jury charged Howell with thirteen counts, including possession of the counterfeit bills and coins that he was arrested for in 1892. This was the third time the U.S. government prosecuted Howell for counterfeiting. Sheriff Cunningham accompanied Deputy U.S. Marshal Maloney in escorting Howell to San Francisco.[71]

Two weeks later, on the evening of Saturday, October 29th, 1893, Stockton Constable Jim Carroll and Deputy Constable Bob Hanks were held up by a lone highwayman on one of Stockton's streets. The man stuck what both officers thought was a pistol under their noses. The next day, Carroll and Hanks were called to the fairgrounds racetrack to deal with an emotionally disturbed man. Low and behold, it was the fella who had held them up the night before. The man was also suspected of some other area holdups.[72]

11

DEALING WITH INDUSTRIALS

On January 3rd, 1894, an erroneous report came out of Sacramento that burglars had raided the State vault in the Capitol building. Sheriff Cunningham and other sheriffs wired that they were ready to start towards Sacramento at the first request for aid, but it was quickly determined that the report was false.[1]

The first of March, Cunningham, John Thacker, and sheriff's deputies Thomas Benjamin and Joe Buzzell were on the trail of a horse thief named George Schlegel. Buzzell was a resident deputy for Sheriff Cunningham, and lived in the Banta area in south San Joaquin County. Schegel had escaped from the Whittier Reform School in Los Angeles County in late 1893 and he had come to Stockton, where he had rented a horse without returning it.

Thomas was aware that John Thacker was interested in Schlegel in relation to a train robbery that had occurred on December 23rd, 1893, at a place called Roscoe, in Los Angeles County. Thacker believed that Schlegel had escaped from the reform school shortly before the robbery. Schlegel had an unnamed companion with him when he left the school. Cunningham wired Thacker to join he and his deputies on the hunt.

The lawmen figured that if Schlegel was involved in the Roscoe train robbery, he and his partner might make an attempt on a train in the valley, so they headed south. Cunningham and his men caught up with Schlegel's partner in San Joaquin City, then took Schlegel out of bed at the town's hotel. The stolen horse was found in an adjacent stable. Schlegel was returned to Stockton and lodged in the jail, while the stolen horse was returned to its owner. Thacker determined by a postmark on a letter that Schlegel's partner was carrying that they left Whittier a month before the Roscoe robbery and they were not involved in that crime.[2]

Sheriff Cunningham annually provided police chiefs and sheriffs with a directory like this one
[*R. Tod Ruse*]

The day that the officers returned to Stockton with their prisoner, Friday, March 2nd, 1894, Deputy Benjamin assisted Calaveras County Deputy Sheriff Masterson in arresting a man named Nicolas Skipa, suspected of blowing up a boarding house in Angels Camp, in Calaveras County. The explosion, which happened on the night of February 19th, 1894, destroyed the building and rained timbers down on the boarding house's owners, Michel Magud, his wife, and their child.[3]

Later that month, Sheriff Cunningham and Deputy Benjamin returned to Stockton on March 17th, after spending most of the previous week chasing some thieves. The objects of the pursuit were William Murphy, Charles Anderson and Lee Winters, who were wanted for having stolen a large amount of property from a rancher named Charles Swift and his neighbors.

Swift had employed one of the thieves and the other two had been working as wood choppers in the area when Swift noticed three men in a spring wagon rounding up a number of his hogs. The men ended up killing one of the porkers and took it to a neighbor's house on Monday, March 12th. Swift went to Stockton and swore out a warrant for Murphy, Anderson and Winters, who got wind that a warrant was out for them. They decamped the area at about 2:00 a.m. the next morning, taking a number of saddles, bridles, farm tools, chickens and other property, and headed east.[4]

Thomas and Deputy Benjamin took up the outlaws' trail later Tuesday morning, following them through Stanislaus, Calaveras, Mariposa and Tuolumne counties, before backtracking into Mariposa County again and catching up to the three near Coulterville. Although the trio were armed with shotguns and had been riding good mounts, they did not resist when confronted by Cunningham and Benjamin.[5]

In April, Thomas escorted James Crowley on the train to Folsom, where he had been sentenced to twenty years. Sheriff Cunningham later escorted William Kenney to San Quentin, where he had been sentenced to do a four-year stretch.[6]

In 1894, the United States was in the second year of an economic depression. An Ohio businessman named Jacob Coxey formulated a plan to have unemployed laborers from all over the nation march on Washington to protest the unemployment caused by a stock market panic in 1893, and to petition Congress to create government jobs through public works projects. Informally known as "Coxey's Army," Coxey himself called the loose-knit organization "The Army of the Commonwealth in Christ." Groups were formed all over the country under a military-type structure, with "generals," "colonels" and "captains" leading the marches. A number of these groups were organized in California cities, including San Francisco, Oakland and Stockton.[7]

Many of the men who joined these groups were militants, while many others were just looking for free passage back East to get home to their families. These men initially had the public's sympathy, and donations were made to the groups to help with their travel to Washington. But trouble makers began causing problems in many parts of the country, especially out West. Newspapers covered the happenings in different cities. The *San Francisco Call* covered many of the stories:

> "Reports of a disquieting nature were received today by Attorney General Richard Olney respecting the lawless acts of various 'armies' of Coxeyites in the West in seizing trains and interfering with mails. The Attorney General counseled with the Secretary of War, and it was decided to adopt a line of policy pursued last week in dealing with these cases. While general instructions had

been sent to the military commanders in the troubled districts to give all lawful assistance necessary to the United States courts in repressing these outrages, it was felt proper to send specific instructions today to General Otis at Vancouver Barracks and to General Brooke, commanding the Department of the Platte, to take active steps to hold off the marauders in these districts, acting, of course, as auxiliary to the United States marshals.

"General Schofield has received a telegram from the United States Marshal at Montpellier, Idaho, stating that a gang of Coxeyites have seized the property of the Union Pacific at that point, with the intention of holding it until transportation is furnished them. The Marshal said he and his men are guarding the railroad property and ask to be relieved by United States troops."[8]

Two companies of Stockton men, totaling 100, arrived in Sacramento in mid-April, awaiting instructions from the head of the San Francisco group, led by a man named "General" John Barker:

> "SACRAMENTO, April 17—Stockton's two companies, the second regiment of the Industrial Army, are still here, under the promise of General Barker that definite orders will be given them by noon tomorrow. The city has been feeding Stockton's 100 men today, but how they are going to get away is the question. It cost Sacramento $600 to get rid of the Oakland regiment, but if they are to keep coming in large bodies she will have to shut down or go into insolvency."[9]

More of the Industrials invaded Sacramento and stayed in the area for a month, using up any good will that the people had for them in the beginning and wearing their patience to the breaking point. Newspaper reporters talked to members of the group to determine their intentions. The *Chico Weekly Enterprise* wrote:

"Colonel Inman and many of his officers of the Industrials at Sacramento were always candid enough to admit that they cared more to go to their homes in the East than they did for Washington or Coxey. Barker's officers assert, however, that they have the fixed purpose in view of reaching Washington as soon as they can get there.

"It is doubtful, nevertheless, whether a majority of the Barker Army do not have the object in mind of reaching their homes, without respect to the Coxey movement... Out of ten men interviewed at the park yesterday, four said they were going to Washington to force the Government to give them work. The six others said they had friends and homes in the East, and would leave the Army at the point nearest their homes."[10]

One reporter interviewed a local man who had offered work to a number of Industrials:

"'Well.' said W. D. Lawton yesterday, 'I am done trying to do anything for these men who are masquerading about the country under the guise of unfortunates who want but cannot obtain work.

"'Yesterday I sent James McCoy out to Barker's camp of self-styled Industrials to offer employment to from eighty to one hundred men at $1 a day, exclusive of their board and lodging, but the offer was refused.

"'The Olive Company, with which I am connected, has 2,000 cords of wood to be cut and removed at once in order to prepare the ground for cultivation, and we thought it a grand opportunity to give these men work.

"'And what do you think was Colonel Barker's reply? Why, he said the offer could not be accepted—that they did not want to interfere with the local labor market! How is that for a lot of men who are claiming that all they want is an opportunity to earn an honest living?'

"It was not the first time Lawton had tried to coax some of the Industrials to work. Several days ago, he went out to Sutter's Fort, where Carpenter's army was encamped, and offered to employ the whole outfit in cutting wood at $1.75 per cord, but they would not accept the offer."[11]

By mid-May, Barker and his men had completely worn out their welcome in Sacramento and they finally decided to leave:

"The Barker Army of idle men left Sutterville on Saturday morning, marching in the direction of Stockton. They were led by Mrs. Anne Smith, who rode at their head. The $250 voted them by the city trustees was paid over, and they are to get $250 more, contributed by the local banks, when they get to Stockton. For these sums, they promised to go away and keep away from Sacramento. They arrived at Elk Grove about 4 o'clock, and left there yesterday morning about 9 o'clock."[12]

Aware that a large group of men was headed towards San Joaquin County, Sheriff Cunningham formulated a plan of action. A formidable group of officers met the Barker Army of 340 men at the county line on May 13th and stayed with them. Thomas was not going to have a repeat of what happened in Sacramento:

"Lodi, May 14—The Industrial Army passed through here at 12:20 this morning amid pouring rain, presenting a most forlorn and dejected appearance. Sheriff Cunningham and a force of deputies, together with Constables Bailey and Wall, met the crowd near the county line. General Barker and Mrs. Smith were in charge, and as soon as the officers made their appearance, these officers (Barker and Smith) hastened to explain that none of the members of the army were implicated in the thefts and horse stealing at Elk Grove, but that the crimes were committed by followers who sought to make the army responsible.

"Nevertheless, the Sheriff remained with the column while it marched to Woodbridge, where the residents provided food for the mid-day meal. The march was then resumed to Lodi, where the army will be quartered in stalls at the race track for today and tonight. As there were two attempted burglaries here early this morning and as many hard-looking characters are straggling on behind the column, cashier Cogswell of the Lodi Bank put on the time lock for twenty hours and will transact no business until the army is gone.

"Supervisor Ennis sent to Stockton for a supply of stale bread and the army will be given supper and breakfast before resuming the march to Stockton. Extra officers will be on duty tonight."[13]

Sheriff Cunningham and the local officers kept a tight rein on the group all the way to Stockton.

"STOCKTON, May 15—Colonel Barker's army of the unemployed, accompanied by Mrs. Anne Smith, arrived here this afternoon, 340 strong, and went into camp on the old baseball grounds, which were selected by Sheriff Cunningham and Chief of Police (Samuel) Henry. Provisions were supplied by local officers, and the men were made comfortable for the night.

"The commanders agreed with the Sheriff and Chief to leave in the morning, and they will be taken away on a barge, which will be sent out under sealed orders, probably down the river to some convenient landing near San Francisco. The men say they are going East, but the officers have nothing to say in that regard."[14]

The plan worked to perfection. The men were loaded on a barge the following morning and were returned to San Francisco. Any negative impacts to the citizens of San Joaquin County were

Coxey's followers departing Stockton by barge
[R. Tod Ruse]

minimized and their stay was short, thanks to Sheriff Cunningham and local lawmen.[15]

The June 7th, 1894 edition of the *Sacramento Daily Record-Union* printed an article detailing a slick arrest that Thomas made of a bicycle thief:

> "J. Helmore, alias John Hughes, is a pretty 'slick' individual, but he was outclassed yesterday, and the result is he is now behind the bars.
>
> "A few days ago, word was received by the police that a valuable bicycle had been stolen from the courthouse at Stockton, and the officers were on the lookout for it. Yesterday, officers Talbot and Higgins saw a bicycle in Zamansky's pawnbroker's store, and on inquiry learned that a man had borrowed $5 on the machine, pending its sale for $30.
>
> "Talbot and Higgins made up their minds to keep an eye on the wheel. During the day, Talbot met Sheriff Cunningham of Stockton and told him of it. Cunningham went to Zamansky's,

where he was fortunate enough to run up against Helmore, who had called to say that he had made a sale of the machine for $30. Cunningham said that he would like the wheel himself and would give him $32.50 for it. Helmore accepted the offer, and was requested to write out a bill of sale. He asked the purchaser's name, and when the latter said it was T. Cunningham, the fellow did not even blink. If he had ever heard of San Joaquin's veteran Sheriff and terror of evil-doers, he did not betray his emotions, for he coolly handed over the bill of sale and accepted the coin.

"'Yes, I am T. Cunningham,' said the portly Stockton official, as he folded up the paper and put it in his pocket, 'and I am Sheriff of San Joaquin County. I want that money back again, and I want you also, for stealing the machine from Stockton.'"[16]

The article went on to say that Helmore had a claim check on him that led officers to recover some property that Helmore had stolen from a train car at the Sacramento depot. The manufacturers of the bicycle had an outstanding $50 reward for the recovery of any of their bicycles, and Sheriff Cunningham paid officers Talbot and Higgins their halves of the reward, which he intended to collect from the company.

In June 1894, a nation-wide strike of Pullman train passenger car employees was in full-swing. The strike stranded Sheriff Cunningham, who was in Oakland, returning to Stockton from San Francisco. Thomas was extremely anxious to get back home on pressing business, and the Southern Pacific made up a special train to get him back home.[17]

Thomas was in need of another deputy in September 1894. He didn't have to look far; he hired Lodi Deputy Constable Billy Wall, swearing him in on September 13th. Billy would not disappoint.[18]

In October 1894, Sheriff Cunningham and his deputies were

searching for a missing person. The young man, Monte Graham, was from Monterey. His family hadn't seen him since October 2nd, when he told them that he was going to San Francisco on a two-week vacation. The family reported him missing to the San Francisco police.

Not finding the young man in San Francisco, officers there put out a be-on-the-lookout for him in mid-October. Sheriff Cunningham and his deputies were familiar with Graham, because he had ended up in their jail as a lodger on October 13th. He was on the verge of delirium tremens and was kept in the Stockton lockup for three days, until he felt better. He didn't have any money on him when he left the jail, but said he intended to travel to Sacramento.

Sheriff Cunningham coordinated with San Francisco detective John Seymour, and Stockton lawmen kept up their search. Finally, on October 29th, Cunningham and Stockton Detective Michael Carroll found Graham working on a Stockton area ranch, where he had been working with horses since being released from jail. Graham told the officers that he was embarrassed to face his relatives and friends. He didn't realize that his unexplained absence had created so much anguish for his family. Thomas sent Detective Seymour a wire, stating that "Monty" had been run to earth. The San Francisco detective was then able to deliver the good news to Graham's mother.[19]

That November, Thomas retained his office, this time for a four-year term. This was the last time he ran for sheriff. He added to his staff and hired Isaac H. Robinson as a deputy, mostly to work as a clerk in the office, maintaining all of the criminal records. Robinson had previously served as a Stockton police officer and chief of police. Thomas also made Robert Hanks the permanent assistant jailer.[20]

On February 28th, 1895, Sheriff Cunningham arrested Charles Ward, ex-superintendent of the San Joaquin County Hospital, on a warrant charging bribery, after Ward was indicted by the grand jury. Ward was accused of bribing James Brown, the chairman of the San Joaquin County Board of Supervisors, to accept the bid of a certain architect for the design of a new county hospital building. Ward was ultimately found guilty and was sentenced to ten years in San Quentin.[21]

Just after midnight on the morning of March 3rd, 1895, two men attempted to rob the Overland Express, train number 3, a few miles east of Sacramento at a place called the Ben Ali Switch. Shortly after leaving the outskirts of the city, the conductor noticed two men on top of one of the cars who seemed to be putting on some clothing. The conductor figured the two were hobos and thought nothing of them putting on clothes because it was chilly outside.

A few minutes later, as the train pulled into the Ben Ali wayside station, the two men scrambled over the coal in the tender car and jumped into the cab, stuffing the barrels of their two revolvers into the faces of the fireman and engineer. The bandits, each described as being about 5 feet 10 inches tall and dressed in linen dusters, white slouch hats and white masks, ordered the engineer to stop the train under threat of his life.

The outlaws ordered the fireman to go back and uncouple the express car from the rest of the train, and they followed him out of the engine. As soon as they were gone, the engineer set the airbrakes and fled the engine, hiding in the darkness behind a nearby fence. With the air brakes set, the fireman could not disengage the coupling on the express car. Hearing an approaching train and frustrated in their efforts, one of the robbers struck the fireman over the head with his revolver, causing a deep scalp wound, and both hightailed it out of there.[22]

Sacramento County Sheriff Frank T. Johnson and Placer County Sheriff W. C. Conroy started out after the robbers with their posses. The trail led the officers back towards Sacramento, where it was lost in some hard-pan dirt. Sheriff Cunningham was called, and he traveled to Sacramento to assist with the search.[23]

Later that night, two men matching the descriptions of the train robbers entered a Sacramento saloon, robbing the barkeep and all of the patrons. The *San Francisco Call* gave an account of what happened:

> "SACRAMENTO, March 3—Police circles were electrified by a telephone message that reached headquarters at 10:40 o'clock tonight, carrying the news that the train robbers had entered Scheld's Brewery, robbed the till, held up the customers, and then fled in the direction of the upper Stockton road at a full gallop. Sheriff Cunningham of Stockton, who is in town working on the train robbery, was notified, and now is speeding after the fugitives. Cunningham has earned a great reputation as a thief taker.
>
> "The robbery tonight was effected with peculiar boldness. L. D. Windmiller, the barkeeper at the brewery, which is situated at Twenty-eighth and M streets, on the eastern boundaries of the city, was playing cards with Henry Dean, George Lemaister and Charles Nelson.
>
> "About 10:30 o'clock they heard a cart drive up. Then two men of medium height, dressed exactly as were the train robbers—in long dusters and with black-cloth masks—stepped into the room.
>
> "'Don't move or you are dead men,' was their orders. Then

one advanced to the till, while the other held the men at the table under cover. The victims did not move, but a big dog started for the intruders.

"'The man with the gun ordered, 'Hold that dog or I'll shoot.' The dog was seized and quieted. The robber at the till got $13. Then he approached the table and made the men stand up, when he went through their pockets one by one, carefully slapping the outsides to see that nothing was overlooked. From Dean the searcher took $4. Lemaister lost $3. Windmiller, the barkeeper, had only 85 cents, while Nelson lost only a rule.

"As soon as the men had accomplished the object of their visit, they backed toward the door, still keeping their revolvers ready for use. Then, with a warning against pursuit, they jumped into a cart that was standing outside and started on a furious gallop in the direction of the upper Stockton road. As soon as he recovered from his fright, Windmiller ran to the telephone and called up the police station. Sheriff Johnson was informed at once, and started Cunningham in pursuit..."[24]

Despite the efforts of the lawmen, the outlaws' trail went cold for the moment.

Five days later, a little after 10:00 p.m. on the night of March 8th, 1895, robbers hit another train, this time about four miles north of Stockton at a place called Castle Switch. One of the robbers stepped out next to the track at the switch, while another climbed over the tender and dropped into the engine. The train's engineer later gave a newspaper reporter a blow-by-blow:

"'The man had some dark knitted substance over his head for a mask,' said Mr. Ingle, 'with holes cut in it for his eyes. A second man climbed over the tender a moment later. They told me to stop the train, and then they made the fireman and myself get out and uncouple the express car. After that, they walked up to the engine and one of the robbers said, 'Now you go ahead, we've got a gang up here and we want you to go up to them.'

"'When we had gone some distance with the express car, he made me stop. The train was about a quarter of a mile back and the robbers seemed to fear no danger from that quarter.

"'They made me and the fireman get out and walk to the express car. Then they ordered Messenger House to open the car. This he did, taking a shot at the robbers and then retreating to the back of the car. They tried to get the express messenger to come out. He refused and threatened to shoot them if they came to the door.

"'After parleying for several minutes, they gave me a dynamite stick and told me to light it and throw it into the car. I got out some matches and tried to light the fuse, but every time the wind blew my matches out.

"'While I was trying to get the fuse lit, I was talking to the messenger, trying to get him to come out and telling him he was a fool to run the risk of getting blown to pieces and having the rest of us blown up too. He said there was no use of their coming in as there was nothing in the car.

"'The men threatened again to blow the car to pieces with dynamite if it was not opened, and the express messenger then complied with their demands. The men got inside, taking us with them, and ransacked the car. All the money was in the big safe and they did not try to open it. They got nothing whatsoever. After satisfying themselves that there was nothing of value outside of the safe and that [it] had been securely locked, they jumped out of the car and went ahead to the engine again, taking us with them. Reaching the engine, the men uncoupled it from the train, and firing some shots in the direction of the passenger cars to scare the occupants, I suppose, pulled the throttle and started toward Lodi.'"[25]

The statement that the robbers got nothing whatsoever wasn't strictly true; one of the outlaws took the express messenger's six-gun and shotgun.[26]

Word of the robbery was wired to Stockton and Lodi. The engine, minus any occupants, slowly rolled into Lodi a short time later and an engineer from another train jumped aboard and stopped it. It had a stick of dynamite sitting on the seat in the cab.

Sheriff Cunningham was still in Sacramento investigating the March 3rd robbery, so deputies Ike Robinson and George Black, along with Stockton police officers Mike Carroll and J. H. Burnham, started for the scene of the crime. The express train was held there until officers could investigate and interview any passengers, and then it was taken to Lodi.

A vagrant had been stealing a ride on the train when the robbers boarded it, and they warned him to keep his mouth shut, which he did. After the robbery, he told a train man that he had come face to face with one of the robbers while on top of the baggage cars. He was the only witness that would have been able to actually identify the bandit, but the vagrant, who had been let off the train at Lodi, swung back aboard it when it started for Sacramento and disappeared before officers had a chance to talk to him.[27]

As soon as word of the robbery reached Sacramento, sheriffs Cunningham and Johnson, along with a posse of officers armed with double-barreled shotguns, obtained a light engine and headed for the crime scene.

The *San Francisco Call* of March 10th gave an update on the status of the case:

"LODI, March 9—There have been many detectives in town today, but up to the present time little that is new relative to the train robbery has developed. At daybreak, Sheriff Cunningham and deputies Wall, Black and others were early on the trail, and on the first train from Sacramento Detectives Gard, Hume, Ahern and Snyder came here, and taking rigs, scoured the surrounding country.

"Cunningham and Wall found a place two miles from Lodi where a buckboard, with 1-1/8-inch tires and 4 feet 9-3/4 inches between the wheels, had been tied for some time, and traced the vehicle to Cherokee Lane, going toward Stockton, where it was followed by Cunningham and others.

"Another posse going north found a nest of four tramps, who said that early this morning three men in a buckboard coming from Lodi had asked the road to Sacramento. Gard, Hume, and other officers at once followed the trail north, while the other officers, dividing into two posses, remained in the tules to search for the robbers toward Stockton."[28]

The "Gard" that the article was talking about was George E. Gard, Chief of Detectives for the Southern Pacific Railroad. Gard was a long-time lawman, having served as one of Los Angeles' first police officers. He had also been a deputy sheriff in Los Angeles, and at one time served as both the chief of police of Los Angeles and as the Los Angeles County sheriff at different times. He was appointed the U.S. Marshal of the Southern District of California by President Benjamin Harrison in 1890. After his term of marshal was up, Gard was hired as a detective by the Southern Pacific Railroad.[29]

Despite the best efforts of the lawmen, the bandits seemingly disappeared into thin air.

One week later, in mid-March 1895, a saloon near the Cliff House in San Francisco was robbed by two men. Then, on Saturday, March 16, the Ingleside House in San Francisco was robbed and a man named Cornelius Stagg was shot and killed.

Based on the descriptions of the robbers and the way the crimes were committed, Sheriff Cunningham believed the robbers were the same ones that had robbed the trains at Ben Ali and Castle Switch. Cunningham traveled to San Francisco, where he worked with his friend Isaiah W. Lees, Captain of Detectives of the San Francisco Police Department, as reported in the *San Francisco Call*:

> "Sheriff Cunningham of Stockton came to this city on March 19, three days after the murder of Stagg. He had been on the trail of the two robbers who held up the eastbound Overland Express train on March 3 at Ben Ali, a wayside station near Sacramento. Their descriptions corresponded exactly with the robbers who operated at the Cliff House and at the Ingleside House.
>
> "The Sheriff remained here for four days and took a hand in searching for the Stagg murderers, believing that if they were found, the two (would be) train robbers. He was very much chagrined when the object of his visit was published, and bluntly said that there was no use of looking longer for them here, as they would have left the city."[30]

San Francisco Police Captain
Isaiah Lees
[*SFPD collection*]

The robbers struck again during the early morning hours of March 30th, 1895, this time stopping the northbound Oregon Express, train number 15, at a place called Reed's Station, seven miles south of Marysville. During the robbery, Tehama County Sheriff John J. Bogard, who was returning to Red Bluff as a passenger on the train, was shot and killed, along with one of the robbers.

The method of operation of the outlaws was similar to what they had done during the attacks on the two other trains earlier in the month. One outlaw jumped into the cab from the tender, and then the fireman and engineer were marched back to the express car, being joined by a second robber.

The robbers gained entry into the express car, but finding no valuables and not being able to open the safe, they forced the train men to escort them to the passenger cars, where one of them went through all of the passengers.

Sheriff Bogard had been in his bunk in the sleeping car, and was alerted to the robbery by the porter. Bogard grabbed his gun and engaged one of the outlaws as soon as he entered the car the robber was in. During the exchange of gunfire, Bogard killed that bandit, but the second robber came into the car behind him, shooting the sheriff in the back and killing him instantly. The second outlaw then fled.[31]

Both bandits had been wearing coveralls, and when the dead robber was searched it was found that he was wearing a bicycler's outfit underneath. He was also carrying the revolver stolen from the express messenger during the Castle Switch robbery.[32]

Officers in Marysville got busy trying to identify the fugitive. One of the lawmen found a bicycle not far from Reed's, and through investigation, it was found that the bicycle, along with a second one, had been rented in San Francisco. On March 31st, Sheriff Cunningham, along with George Gard and John Thacker, left Marysville, headed for San Francisco. By April 1st, officers had established the identities of the bandits was one Oscar S. Browning, alias Brown, alias Sam McGuire, who was killed during the robbery, and Henry "Harry" Williams, alias Jack Brady, alias John McGuire, the current fugitive. Both were ex-cons.

The lawmen found where the two had been living in San Francisco, and in searching their rooms, found their trunks, in which were located pictures of them on their bicycles. Various sightings of Williams were reported to the officers, none of which panned out, and he remained elusive for the time being. But with some of California's best lawmen, including Thomas Cunningham, Isaiah Lees, James Hume, George Gard and John Thacker, among others searching for him, it would only be a matter of time before Harry Williams was run to ground.[33]

A few days later, on April 4th, 1895, Sheriff Cunningham was on a train returning from Los Angeles with a prisoner named Thomas Durham, wanted in Stockton on a warrant charging forgery. The following week, on April 9th, Cunningham was on the train to Folsom, where he deposited James Crowley for a twenty-year sentence. Shortly after that, Thomas was headed to San Quentin with William Kenney, who was to serve a four-year term.[34]

On April 21st, Thomas was on a steam ship, heading for Portland, Oregon to pickup three bunko artists. The three, John R. Green, Clinton R. Smith and John T. Gray, were accused of scamming a Lodi area farmer out of $2,000, in return for a box of rocks.[35]

In May 1895, the other shoe finally dropped in the County

Hospital scandal, when Sheriff Cunningham arrested James E. Brown, chairman of the Board of Supervisors, for accepting a bribe. Brown had been indicted by the grand jury on the charge, and Thomas arrested Brown out of his office on a warrant on May 8th. Brown was bailed out of jail and was ultimately acquitted of the charge after two separate jury trials.[36]

The *Stockton Record* reported on the June 1895 grand jury report. Regarding the Sheriff's Office, the article included a paragraph about Sheriff Cunningham:

> "The cash book of this officer shows that he has been at an enormous personal expense in his endeavors to secure the arrest of criminals guilty of heinous crimes committed in this and adjoining counties, and that during the great railroad strike he was daily incurring heavy expenses in his efforts to preserve the peace and dignity of this particular county, for which he has not and will not ask remuneration."[37]

A month later, on July 23rd, 1895, Thomas was named as the guardian for a young boy named Parker J. Wilson in the will of Thomas' old friend, the late Parker D. Wilson, which was filed with the county clerk that afternoon. The court later officially named Thomas as the boy's guardian. Although surprised at being named the boy's guardian, he was honored and took his duties very seriously. Parker was about fourteen years old at the time.[38]

Harry Williams was finally found and arrested by a Sacramento sheriff's posse on July 26th, 1895, hiding under a bridge in the Sacramento River area of southwest Sacramento County. After the Reed's robbery and murder of Sheriff Bogard, Williams had fled to the hills of Shasta County, where he stayed out of sight. He was wounded while engaged in a shootout with Shasta County deputies

George Martin and Mart Bowers at Clear Creek on June 19th. He hadn't been seen from that time until Sacramento County Sheriff Johnson received a reported sighting of him near Courtland on July 25th.[39]

When Williams was arrested, a Wells Fargo messenger's shotgun, number 84, was found in his knapsack. The shotgun had been taken during the Castle Switch train robbery north of Stockton on March 8th. Williams, who was going by the name Brady at the time, denied involvement in any of the crimes he was accused of, and bragged how he had outsmarted officers during his time on the lamb.[40]

Sheriff Cunningham visited Williams in the Sacramento County jail the following day, and his visit was documented in the *San Francisco Call*:

> "...he was visited by Sheriff Cunningham of Stockton. Brady recognized him immediately.
>
> 'Hello, Sheriff,' he said, extending his hand. 'How are you?'
>
> 'Do you know me?' queried the veteran thief-taker.
>
> 'Certainly, I do,' answered Brady, 'and I've met you twice during the period you all have been hunting me. Once on the San Francisco ferry boat, where you looked me right in the face and made me think I was a goner sure. The other time was seated in a buggy in front of the Yosemite Hotel in Stockton, and you came up, and looking me straight in the face, asked me where I was going, and I told you I was going to drive a commercial traveler to a station a few miles from Stockton. Remember?' queried Brady. 'Oh, no one would know me by the description and pictures that were in the hands of the officers, and it was the knowledge of this fact that made me so reckless in traveling around the country. I was only recognized by one person, and that was a fellow I had worked with near Biggs Station. He gave me away.'"[41]

Cunningham did recall seeing Williams one time in Stockton during a chance encounter, but it had happened almost two years before the train robberies, while Williams was working at a Stockton livery stable. Williams had started out one night to drive a man to Lathrop. Williams was bundled up against the cold air that night, and Thomas asked him where he was going.[42]

Williams was tried and convicted of Sheriff Bogard's murder, and was sentenced to life in Folsom Prison. He was paroled in 1914.[43]

The July 27th, 1895, edition of the *Stockton Record* included an article about a false bank alarm received by the Sheriff's Office:

"Ready for Bank Robbers, but the alarm was a false one—Thomas Cunningham and his deputies were prepared, however, mistake or no mistake—an error caused by an awkward janitor.

"Bank robbers didn't make a descent on the First National Bank yesterday, but if the bandit Brady had suddenly pushed his gun into the cashier's face at the institution and some one of the other bank officials had notified the Sheriff's Office, there would not have been much more activity about the place than there was.

"It all happened about 3 o'clock. Sheriff Tom Cunningham, like Chief Rolf of the Fire Department, has the system about his office down to perfection and many little contrivances about the place are calculated to add to the efficiency of his department. One of these is a system of private alarms from all the banks. When the alarm goes off and the number of designating a bank drops, something is supposed to be wrong at that place. The First National and Stockton Savings banks, being in the Yosemite Theater building, they are commanded, to use the military term, from the windows of Sheriff Cunningham's office on the east side of the courthouse. A fleeing robber on San

Joaquin Street could be picked off very nicely with a rifle from this point.

"When the alarm came in, Sheriff Cunningham did not wait for particulars, but sending Deputy Tom Black (sic) on the run for the bank, he went over to the private arsenal in the Office, and taking down a very trusty gun, he moved over to the window and awaited developments.

"The advance of the deputy on the bank was followed by several policemen, and in a few seconds, they emerged from the place covered—not with gore—but with guns.

"It appears the janitor, in cleaning up the bank, had shoved a box up against the alarm button and went on sweeping all unconscious of the excitement his mistake was making. He was in turn alarmed himself at the sight of the officers.

"Explanations followed, Sheriff Cunningham put up his gun, and had almost forgotten all about the incident an hour after it happened."[44]

On August 1st, 1895, Sheriff Cunningham received a telegram from San Jose police, requesting he arrest and hold two men wanted for grand larceny. Information was that the two were making their way to Stockton in a road wagon. Cunningham forwarded the information to Deputy Joe Buzzell, who worked at the San Joaquin River bridge at the Mossdale crossing. Buzzell took the two into custody at about noon. The outlaws offered no resistance and acted surprised at their arrest.[45]

A couple of weeks later, on August 17th, Thomas returned to Stockton, after taking his ward Parker to the military academy in Belmont, in San Mateo County.[46]

Cunningham was in San Francisco on October 25th, 1895, where he and San Francisco Detective Thomas Gibson arrested a man named J. W. Rockwell at his home on Bridge Street, on a warrant charging Rockwell with the theft of sheep from a Stockton rancher in 1893. Rockwell had bought a flock of sheep from the rancher, paying him with a draft from what he purported was a San Francisco business. When payment didn't come through, the rancher followed up and found that the address for the San Francisco business office was really a saloon. Rockwell was tried, convicted and sentenced to fourteen years in prison.[47]

Thomas was called to the scene of a murder on November 26th, 1895, along the Mokelumne River, north of Lodi. A rancher named N. A. Knight had found some blood on straw on his farm. Looking further, Knight found a hat, a roll of blankets, and a sailor's bag with blood on them. Several papers in the property were in the name Peter Soderberg. Knight went to Lodi and reported his finding to Constable H. B. Coleman, who returned with Knight to his ranch. The two then started searching the area, and found the victim's decomposed body about 100 feet away, along the riverbank. No other clues were found and nothing more was written about the case.[48]

12

DEATH OF A DEPUTY

Thanksgiving Day of 1895 would become one of the darkest days in the history of the San Joaquin County Sheriff's Office. You see, that evening Sheriff Cunningham lost one of his deputies to gunfire.

The day had started out uneventfully. People all over the country were staying home to relax and join family and friends to celebrate the holiday, November 28th, 1895. It was a good day to stay indoors and gather around the fireplace because it was cold outside and a threat of rain was in the air.

That morning, Henry Tison Sr. and three of his sons loaded their wagon in preparation for a hunting trip. Henry lived with his wife and six of their seven children at the corner of Monroe and Fremont streets in Stockton, where they had lived for several years. Tison and his second oldest son, eighteen-year-old Henry Jr., had recently returned from a year-long trip to Oregon, where they had purchased some land. They intended on making a two or three-week hunting trip into the Coastal Range mountains and then return to Oregon.[1]

Henry Sr., known as "Old Man Tison," Henry. Jr., and two of the younger Tison boys, Julius and Moses, loaded up their wagon and headed south on the French Camp Road. Henry Jr. later spoke to a newspaper reporter and told him of their journey:

> "'We started out Thursday to go to the Coast Range on a hunting trip. Father had been drinking heavily for some time, and we wanted to sober him up and break up the effects of his spree. Towards evening we concluded to find someplace to camp. We met a contractor who had been doing some work for Grant Brothers, the railroad builders. We knew the man slightly, though I can't remember his name, and stopped in the road to talk for awhile. He said he was going to turn into a field close by for the night, and we asked him if there was any place nearby where we could camp. He replied that we could camp almost anywhere in the neighborhood. After driving on for awhile we saw a nice place near some trees to put up for the night and decided to camp. Father made a fire and started to cook supper. The fire was made at the foot of a big tree, for there was quite a hole in the ground at the root of the tree. We did not think that the tree would catch fire, or we would have laid the fire somewhere else. After working for some time, we found that we could not get at the fire on the inside, and that it was impossible to extinguish it. Father then said to let the tree burn and if there were any damages to pay, we would settle with the owner. After finding that we could do nothing with the fire we all lay down to sleep. I think father and one of my brothers was asleep when we heard a rig drive up.'"[2]

The Tisons had set up camp on the McLaughlin ranch, about two miles south of the San Joaquin River drawbridge at Mossdale, on the road between Stockton and Tracy. The field was being used as pastureland by the McCormick Brothers, a meat packing company out of Stockton.

Henry Jr.'s statement about hearing a rig drive up contradicted a later statement by the elder Tison, and was also in conflict with the fact that two men on horses had actually come through the gate. The horses that the Tisons heard were ridden by John Staiger and Ed Sweem, ranch hands for the McCormick Brothers. The two cowboys were just returning from Stockton, where they had celebrated Thanksgiving at the home of one of their bosses. It was raining as they rode through the gate and onto the ranch. It was then that they saw the Tisons camped out and the tree burning.

Ed Sweem was later interviewed by a reporter for the *Stockton Independent*, and gave this account:

> "'Staiger and I live in a tent on the ranch about seventy-five yards north of the gate. This morning about 9 o'clock we went to Stockton. At that time there was no one camped on the ranch. We got back about 9 o'clock tonight and as we reached the gate, we saw a big fire not far beyond it inside the field. We rode up to it and saw that an oak tree had been set fire by some campers who were lying under their wagon close to it. There was an old man, a grown young fellow, and his two sons. We rode up to them and said:
>
> 'You will have to put that fire out.'
>
> 'We can't do it,' said the old man.
>
> 'But you will have to do it,' Staiger said.
>
> 'Look here, you sons-of-bitches,' exclaimed the old man, 'we won't put that fire out and you fellows want to get away from here damned quick!'"[3]

Sweem told the reporter that the old man backed up his words at the point of a revolver, and threatened to shoot them if they didn't leave. The cowboys turned around and headed for the San Joaquin River bridge to contact Deputy Joe Buzzell. Henry Tison Jr. later gave this account of the first encounter with the ranch hands:

> "'There were two men, and one of them called to us. Father answered, and then they came nearer. One of them wanted to know what right we had to come into the field and set fire to other people's property. Father told him we did not fire the tree intentionally, and that we had done our best to put the fire out but could not. The man was very abusive. I don't know who he was, but we supposed from the way he talked that he owned the place. Father then said he would try again to put the fire out, and would pay what damages there were if he could not and the tree burned down. The man said that he would give us two minutes to put the fire out or he would make us do it. Father was very nervous and unstrung from drinking, and wasn't going to be ordered about like that. The man said, 'If that fire is not out in fifteen minutes, I will be back with a Winchester and make you put it out.'
>
> "'The men went away, and we set to work again to try and extinguish the blaze. We worked hard. We had to pack the water up a ten-foot bank. It was wet and slippery, and we tumbled down and got wet and muddy. The fire had run up the inside of the tree and out onto a large hollow limb. This burned off and fell, striking my little brother on the head and stunning him. Then we concluded again it was no use to try further, and quit. Father was afraid the men might come back when we were asleep and shoot us. He was not afraid to meet the men face to face, but didn't want to have any crowd come back with them and take a shot at us when we could not defend ourselves. He thought that the men might do this, for the one who talked so much said he was coming back with a Winchester. Father took

my rifle and placed it against the wagon where he could get it easily.'"[4]

Joseph Buzzell, one of Sheriff Cunningham's resident deputies, was working at his job as a watchman at the drawbridge at the Mossdale crossing of the San Joaquin River. The son of a pioneering San Joaquin County family, Joe lived with his wife Mary and their two children in Banta. The ranch hands had seen Buzzell at the bridge with the night watchman, E. L. Remington, when they had crossed a short time before.

Deputy Joseph Buzzell
[*SJSO collection*]

On returning to the bridge, Staiger and Sweem told Joe of their encounter at the McLaughlin ranch. Buzzell, in turn, telephoned Sheriff Cunningham in Stockton for instructions. Fearing violence because of the report made by Staiger and Sweem, Thomas told his deputy to be very careful and not attempt to eject the campers, but to try and persuade them to be on their way.

After speaking with the sheriff, Joe strapped on his revolver, pulled on his raincoat and hat, and stepped out into the rain, starting out towards the McLaughlin ranch on horseback with Sweem and Staiger. Not having been a party to the first confrontation and having to act solely on the information provided by the two cowboys, Joe Buzzell didn't know quite what to expect when they arrived at the ranch.[5]

As is normal in these types of events, accounts varied as to what happened next, depending on who the witness was. As best can be determined through witness statements and evidence at the scene, the following occurred:

When Deputy Buzzell and the cowboys reached the ranch, Buzzell got off his horse and walked up to Henry Tison Sr. He identified himself as a deputy sheriff and ordered the Tisons to put out the fire in the tree and move off of the private property. Words were exchanged, the senior Tison telling Deputy Buzzell that if he wanted the fire out, he could do it himself. According to everyone present, when Tison refused to put the fire out and leave, Deputy Buzzell attempted to grab hold of him. Tison moved back to his wagon and grabbed his Winchester rifle, raising it towards Buzzell. Seeing the immediate threat to his life, Deputy Buzzell drew his revolver and ordered Tison to drop his gun, but Tison wouldn't listen.

Buzzell shouted, "Here, put down that gun, I am an officer!"

"Well, so am I," Tison replied, as he continued to raise his gun.

At the same time the boys shouted out, "Don't shoot, Pa!"[6]

The investigation revealed that Deputy Buzzell probably shot first. Sweem thought that Buzzell had fired two shots. One of his rounds struck a wooden post by where Tison was standing. It was thought that the other bullet had struck Tison. Tison returned fire, striking Deputy Buzzell twice. The lawman died where he fell.

When the gunfight commenced, the Tison boys grabbed their pistols and joined their father, shooting at the cowboys. Sweem shot back with his Winchester, but Staiger, being unarmed, hightailed it out of there. Sweem fired a few more shots, then turned and headed for the road. He met Staiger at the road and it was agreed that Staiger would remain at that position and watch for any movements by the campers, while Sweem went for help. Sweem's horse collapsed twice during the wild run to the bridge, but he spurred the animal on. It was later determined that his horse had been shot.[7]

It was about 10:00 p.m. when Sweem reached Mossdale. E. L. Remington, the bridge-tender, telephoned Sheriff Cunningham in Stockton and informed him of the shooting. The sheriff immediately formed a posse and headed out for the bridge. He was accompanied by deputies Ike Robinson, George Black and Billy Wall, as well as Stockton constables Myron Beach and James Carroll, and Stockton Police Officer Walter Walker, who was Joe Buzzell's brother-in-law. The sheriff and his men arrived at the scene of the shooting at about 12:30 a.m. on November 29th. They found John Staiger next to the road, and he reported seeing no movement from the camp.[8]

Deputy Buzzell's body was found lying about six feet away from the camper's wagon. His horse was nearby, suffering from a gunshot wound to the knee. The lawmen shot the horse to put it out of its misery. Staiger's horse had also been shot and was lying dead nearby. The campers' wagon and all of their effects were still there, but they were gone and their horses were missing. The officers started a search of the area. They located Tison's rifle in the tall grass and underbrush not far away, but Deputy Buzzell's revolver could not be found and the officers felt that the killers had taken it with them. The Tisons' horses were located nearby in the brush.

Officers were placed on all of the roads and bridges leading out of the area. Word was sent to Stockton for the coroner. A deputy was also sent back to pick up the sheriff's bloodhounds. Sheriff Cunningham went to the Mossdale bridge and took over the telephone, providing officers throughout the area with the information on the suspects which had been given by the ranch hands. It was suspected that the killers were from Stockton, and the sheriff phoned officers there with a description of the suspects and their outfit. The lawmen who had stayed in Stockton immediately began to work on the case, with Stockton police detective Oscar Marshall heading up that portion of the investigation. Officers from all over the west side of San Joaquin County continued their search throughout the night, but found no trace of the fugitives.[9]

Joseph's brother Willard lived in Stockton and had stepped into the Turner Saloon at about midnight to get something to eat when he heard about the shooting. In shock and dismay, he hurriedly grabbed a conveyance and headed to the scene to lend whatever help he could.

A search of the scene and surrounding area was commenced at daylight with the bloodhounds, but the rain, which had continued throughout the night, had obliterated any trace of the fugitive's tracks. The banks of the San Joaquin River were heavily covered with a thick growth of willow and wild thickets, making the search very difficult. Sheriff Cunningham described the country that the Tisons fled into as being so dense with underbrush that a man could hide within five hundred feet of the campsite and totally avoid detection.[10]

Early in the morning on Friday, November 29th, a citizen phoned the Stockton police station and gave officers a clue to work on. The man told of the outfit which left the Tisons' house on Thanksgiving morning. Officers at the crime scene had determined that the wagon left behind was painted green, and had yellow wheels. This fit the description given by the citizen. The Stockton officers traced the route the Tisons had taken and learned that they had gone south out of town on the French Camp Road, which correlated with all of the other information.[11]

That same morning, officers at the scene had been contacted by a man named Julius Opper. Opper was the contractor that Henry Tison Jr. later described meeting on the road. Opper's story was that on Thanksgiving afternoon he met Tison and his sons, though he did not know them by name, as they left the county road and turned into the pasture where they found a place to camp. He thought of joining them, but looking at the sky and seeing that it was going to rain, continued to another ranch farther down the road. He first heard of the shooting that morning. He declared that he would be able to positively identify the people he had seen.[12]

Mary Buzzell was not told of her husband's tragic death until later that morning. She had gotten up early and prepared breakfast for Joe as usual, and was just finishing up when officers arrived and notified her. She was overcome with shock and grief at the news. Left alone to fend for herself and her two small children, Mary mustered the strength to accompany her husband's body to Stockton on the noon train.

By noon, officers were certain that the Tisons were their suspects. Officers were posted around their house in Stockton.

Deputy Ike Robinson and Deputy Constable Jim Sullivan brought the Tison's outfit back to town, accompanied by Julius Opper, who had been detained as a witness. There was a general feeling among the officers that the Tisons would soon be in custody.

Buzzell's body was brought to the mortuary of Lang and Ball in Stockton, where an autopsy was performed by doctors Clark, Snedigar and Bently at 1:30 p.m. that afternoon. The doctors determined that Deputy Buzzell had been shot once in the head and once in the chest. They stated that either wound would have been fatal in-and-of itself.

The Tison boys reached home sometime that night, having traveled all day. They evidently reached their house without alerting the officers, and had secured a buggy in which they were about to leave when they were arrested by Deputy Sheriff Barney Cassidy and police officers Michael Finnell and J. H. Burnham. Although the boys said they were on the way to turn themselves in, the officers were of the opinion that the boys had planned to return and retrieve their father. Upon arriving at the jail, the three boys were either unwilling or unable to tell the officers where their father was.

A reporter for the *Evening Mail* did a jailhouse interview with Henry Tison Jr. the following morning. The reporter found the young Tison's manner "open and frank." The reporter wrote: "His story was told without hesitancy, and is without doubt a truthful narrative of the killing of Buzzell and the wounding of Old Man Tison."[13]

Henry Jr. told the reporter of their planned hunt, of the events that occurred on Thanksgiving Day, and of the first encounter with the cowboys. He then spoke of the shooting and its aftermath, saying:

"'After the men had gone, we began to think what was best to do. Father said the best thing to do was to catch our horses and go back to Stockton and tell what had happened. We did not know then that the man was killed. My brothers and father went out to look for the horses, while I put the things back into the wagon. When I stepped around the tongue, I saw the man lying on the ground, and found that he was dead. Presently the others came back and said that the horses were gone. We supposed that the men had driven them off. When Father found the man dead, he didn't know what to do. He was half crazy with nervousness from the effects of drink and the excitement. We urged him to go back with us, but he said he did not know what to do. He thought he would strike out alone and might go to Stockton and might not. He took his rifle and left. We then started to walk in, but could not find the McDougald bridge. After tramping about until midnight, we came near the railroad track. A man was walking the tracks with a rifle under his arm. I called to him, and found it was Father. We all walked on together, thinking we could cross the railroad bridge without being seen. We did not want to be arrested, but wanted to give ourselves up in Stockton. When we got to the bridge my little brother said he saw some men patrolling it. We then ran back to try to make the McDougald bridge again. We walked and walked, going through the brush. Somehow, we got away from the river and lost our bearings. It was very dark and storming. Finally, we struck a heavily wooded spot with plenty of brush about, and decided to lie down until morning. When morning came Father could not get up. I forgot to tell you he was wounded. The ball went across his stomach, but I do not think it went very deep. He is rather fleshy, and I think the ball went around the fat on his stomach. I had to lift him to his feet, for he was stiff and weak. I begged him to come on with us, but he said he could not. He told us the best thing for us would be to come to

Stockton and give ourselves up, and let him lie where he was until he was able to walk. I took the Winchester from him, and my brother gave him a thirty-eight-caliber revolver. We gave him what money we had, one of us $1.00 and the other $1.30. He promised to go to some farmhouse as soon as he was able, and get something to eat. Then we left him and came to Stockton.'"[14]

Although the next statement made by Henry Jr. contradicted what he had just told the reporter, he said the boys had paid a fisherman twenty-five cents to get them across the San Joaquin River. They followed the levee until they came to a slaughterhouse on the French Camp Road, following it in to town. The newspaper reporter was so enamored with Henry Jr. that after hearing his version of the incident, wrote: "The full particulars of the shooting of Deputy Buzzell are now in. They show that Buzzell, Sweem and Staiger stood up the party of campers near the San Joaquin bridge last Thursday night about as Arizona cowboys might be expected to stand up a 'tenderfoot', and order him to dance at the muzzle of their revolvers for amusement sake. If the story told by Henry Tison, son of Buzzell's slayer, is true, it is very likely not only that the campers will be discharged as having acted in self-defense, but that Sweem and Staiger will be confined behind iron bars on a charge of assault to murder." Other papers followed suit. The newspapermen were not the only ones who took the boys story to heart.[15]

The papers had reported on the Tisons' lot in life, the fact that while the elder Tison and his son Henry had been in Oregon, Mrs. Tison, left at home with five children, had been compelled to seek aid from the Board of Associated Charities in order to keep the wolf from the door. Public sentiment rested squarely in the Tisons' corner. People felt the boys were very forthcoming and honest in their account of the tragedy, and looked upon Sweem and Staiger with skepticism. Although Sheriff Cunningham and other lawmen were convinced that Tison had murdered Deputy Buzzell, many people felt that Tison and his sons were not hurting anything by camping out on the plains, and that Deputy Buzzell had no right to demand that they move.[16]

The case was followed closely in the papers. Days passed, but nothing was heard of the elder Tison. Speculation about where he might be varied widely. Everyone had an opinion. All sorts of theories were advanced as to his whereabouts. Some thought he was still lying in a lonely spot in the brush, suffering from the wound in his stomach which prevented him from moving around. Others thought him mortally wounded. One theory was that he had committed suicide. Another was that he had been devoured by wild hogs. Many officers felt that Tison had either sneaked into town with his sons, or was just outside of town. They felt certain that the boys would not have abandoned their father had he been wounded.

Joseph Buzzell's funeral was held on Sunday, December 1st, at 2:00 p.m. that afternoon at the Lang and Ball funeral home. The services were conducted by the Reverend Sink of the Congregational Church. During the service, he stated that the spectacle of a man risking his life in the performance of his duties was one that should demand the respect of all law-abiding citizens. The minister also spoke of the obligation of every person to observe the laws of the country and respect the officers whose duty it is to enforce them. The funeral was largely attended, and many people from the Tracy area came to pay their respects to the dead officer.[17]

The coroner's inquest was held on Tuesday, December 3rd,

and was attended by a large crowd of curious spectators. The three Tison boys testified, each corroborating the others. Sweem and Staiger also testified, and it was reported that it was plain that those present believed the boys' story over the statements of the ranch hands. From the questions put forward by the jurors it was very evident their sympathies were with the Tisons. Mr. McCormick, Sweem and Staiger's boss, testified that the two had spent Thanksgiving Day at his house, and although they drank alcoholic beverages that day, they were perfectly sober when they left his house.

The jury did not agree on a verdict, nine of the jurors returning a verdict declaring Tison's act was justifiable while the other three returned a verdict to the effect that Deputy Buzzell was killed by Tison.

After the inquest the Tison boys, who had been in custody since their arrests, were set free. They made statements to the press that they were going out in search of their father, but they never left town. The boys said that their father was still in the brush where they had left him, and that he was now dead. The peculiar actions of the boys fired speculation among the officers and others that the elder Tison was either in Stockton or not far from it, and that the family was in touch with him. Although the boys claimed not to know where their father was, they didn't seem to be worrying much about it.[18]

Sheriff Cunningham offered a $250 reward for Tison—$100 for information leading to his arrest, and another $150 for his conviction for murdering Deputy Buzzell. Tison was known to have ties in San Francisco and the sheriff felt he may have made his way there. Cunningham solicited the help of his old friend Isaiah Lees in helping to search for the killer.

The sheriff, when questioned about his opinion as to Tison's fate, replied:

"'Well, to tell you the truth, I believe that Tison is living and furthermore that he is not in the wilds, but has sought some civilized center where he is now concealed. To my mind the facts in the case show this. In the first place, Tison did not take any guns with him. His object in this would, of course, be to avoid attracting any particular attention. Then, you know, he asked the boys for what money they had, according to their statement. The old man said he might want to get something to eat or buy some whiskey. This shows that Tison had in his mind a plan of getting away. I do not believe that the boys would have left him had he been in the condition he was described by them. One of the boys surely would have stayed with him. He knew that they had nothing to fear, even were there any evidence against them. He took the brunt of the killing upon himself by becoming a fugitive in the eyes of the law. I am satisfied Tison is alive and I offered the reward because of that opinion.'"[19]

Sheriff Cunningham and the other officers firmly believed that Deputy Buzzell's killing was unjustified, and felt that Tison was the aggressor.

On Sunday, December 8th, the Sheriff's Office received a telegram from authorities in Knights Landing, in Yolo County along the Sacramento River north of the city of Sacramento, advising that they had arrested a man thought to be Henry C. Tison, Sr. If Tison had been trying to make his way northward towards Oregon, it would have made sense for him to make his way up the course of the Sacramento River, which would have put him in the area. The man fit the description of Tison, even having a scar from a bullet wound on his temple. Tison had been wounded several times during the Civil War and had a similar scar. Deputy

Tom Benjamin left on the 1:00 p.m. train that afternoon with a man who knew Tison on sight.

The Tison boys were convinced that the prisoner in Knights Landing was not their father, reaffirming the officers' feelings that the boys knew of their father's actual whereabouts. On arriving in Knights Landing, Deputy Benjamin wired back that the man in custody there was not Tison.[20]

It had now been nearly a week and a half since the killing, and there was still no word on the killer. It would be nearly two more weeks before the search would end.

Merced County Deputy Sheriff Wegener was the foreman on a ranch located about six miles north of Merced. Deputy Wegener had received the information Sheriff Cunningham had put out and was alerted when a man, looking ill and frail, showed up at the ranch in search of work. The man, who identified himself as John Baker, fit the description of the suspect, but Deputy Wegener wanted to be sure of his suspicions so he decided to watch him. Wegener gave the man a job to keep him in the area, then went to the Sheriff's Office in Merced to have another look at the flier sent by Sheriff Cunningham which listed the suspect's information. Once he did that, Wegener was more convinced than ever that he had the right man.

Wegener gained the man's confidence and told him that he had some work for him to do in town. Once they got to Merced, Wegener confronted the man, telling him that his true identity was known. Henry Tison readily admitted who he was. He told the deputy that he had "been within aces of giving up" several times.[21]

Deputy Wegener brought Tison to Stockton on the afternoon train on Thursday, December 19th. A large crowd gathered at the station to await the arrival. Sheriff Cunningham, Deputy Cassidy, and Constable Maurice Byrnes were at the station to receive the prisoner. A man who knew Tison was brought along to identify him. As the train pulled into the station, the curious crowd surged around the steps to get a glimpse of Tison. After being satisfied that they had their man, the officers quickly escorted him to an awaiting hack and were promptly driven to the county jail. Sheriff Cunningham paid Deputy Wegener the $100 he had offered for Tison's capture.[22]

As soon as they reached the jail, Dr. Clark examined and treated Tison's wound. He described the wound, saying that the bullet struck Tison on the front wall of the abdomen, to the right of the median line, and ranged downward across the abdomen, coming out on the other side about an inch lower that where it entered and making a wound four inches long.[23]

After being treated, Tison granted an interview with a reporter for the *Evening Mail*. He wore a grizzled beard of a few week's growth and was dressed in the same clothes he wore on the night of the shooting, the hole made by Deputy Buzzell's bullet showing in his shirt. Tison told of the hunting trip, of his decision to put up that night, of opening a gate and entering onto the ranch property. He told of camping out there, of building a fire, and of the confrontation with the cowboys. Speaking about the shooting, Tison said he had seen some men come up on horseback:

> "'One of them jumped off his horse and came over to where I was standing. He asked, 'What the hell are you doing there?' I told him we had come into the field to camp. He asked what authority we had to do so, and I told him we had none. 'What are you doing with that gun?' he asked. I told him I had it for my protection. 'I am an officer,' he said; 'put that gun down,' at the same time reaching for me with his left hand and pulling his

pistol. I jumped back as he did this and began backing away. As I did so he shot, the ball striking me in the stomach. I then jerked my gun up, and as he fired again, I shot by the flash of his pistol. I shot at him as fast as I could work the lever. I called to the boys that I was shot, and they began firing. There were a number of shots fired then, I don't know how many. One of the men on horseback was firing.'"[24]

Tison spoke about his journey after splitting up with the boys. He told how he made his way south, working through the country until he reached a town called Volta, in Merced County. He sold his pistol for $2.50 there, then went another five miles to Los Banos. After staying there for a while, he crossed over the river to the eastside, going to Merced. He remained there for about five days, and then found work with Deputy Wegener.[25]

Henry Tison Sr.
[*Cunningham's mug book, SJSO collection*]

Tison told Sheriff Cunningham that after the shooting, one of his boys had thrown Deputy Buzzell's revolver away in the bushes. Stockton Constable James Carroll went back out to the scene with Henry Jr., and after about an hour's search, found the weapon in a clump of bushes. The gun had two empty shell casings in it, and was rusted from the elements.[26]

The preliminary hearing for Henry Tison took place in Justice Parker's court on Tuesday, December 24th. No new information was discovered, and Tison was held over for trial on a charge of murder. Public sentiment leaned heavily towards Tison, and the case continued to receive extensive coverage in all of the local papers.[27]

The trial commenced on January 7th, 1896, at 10:00 a.m. before Superior Court Judge James Budd. The *Evening Mail* reported:

> "The prosecutor was exceedingly fair in his statement of the case, and did not say that he would attempt to prove that Tison fired first, but merely that Buzzell was killed while performing his duties as a deputy sheriff; neither did he state that a verdict of guilty would be asked for, but merely that the jurors would be asked to render a verdict as the testimony adduced would warrant."[28]

Doctors Bentley and Snedigar, the autopsy surgeons, testified for the prosecution, as did John Staiger and Ed Sweem. Staiger related his account of waking the Tisons from their sleep and ordering them to put out the fire in the tree.

"'I said this was a hell of a way to do, to set a man's tree afire,'" the witness testified. "Then the old man reached for his gun and told us he had enough of me. I ran for the wagon.'"

"The crowd tittered so audibly at the herder's tale of fear that the bailiff had to rap for order," reported the *Mail*.[29]

Dr. Clark and the Tison boys testified for the defense. Then Henry Tison Sr. took the stand and told his story. After his testimony, both Constable Carroll and Deputy District Attorney DeVries, who was prosecuting the case, commented that Tison had made the best witness they had ever seen on the stand.

The case was sent to the jury without closing arguments by either counsel. Judge Budd was very brief in his instructions to the jury, but at the conclusion of his remarks told the jury that an officer had no more of a right than anyone else to unlawfully approach a citizen.[30]

The jury was given the case at the end of the second day of trial. It was out a mere eight minutes, and promptly returned a not guilty verdict. There was a roar from the crowd in the courtroom upon the reading of the verdict, which was quickly suppressed by the bailiff.[31]

Deputy Buzzell was buried under a large oak tree in an unmarked grave in the Stockton Rural Cemetery, and was all but forgotten by everyone except his family, friends, and fellow officers.

13

EMBEZZLERS, STICK-UP MEN AND THUGS

In January 1896, the San Joaquin County Board of Supervisors voted 3-2 in favor of amending the county licensing ordinance and reducing the taxes on bookmaking parlors and pool rooms from $15 a day to $75 a month. Sheriff Cunningham had actively fought against any tax reductions.[1]

On March 9th, 1896, the former head cook at the County Hospital in French Camp, Walter Mackay, went to the hospital with a revolver and evil intentions. Mackay had been fired the previous month, and had been replaced by a man named Bernard Cook. Mackay had initially greeted cook Cook with a handshake, but then pulled out his gun and shot Cook. Other employees responded to the gunshot, and several men, including the head nurse, overpowered Mackay and got the revolver way from him.

Patients at the hospital and county poorhouse were very fond of Cook, and threatened to lynch Mackay, but Sheriff Cunningham arrived in time to prevent that from happening. Cook survived, but ended up being paralyzed from the waist down.[2]

A few months later, the May 7th, 1896, edition of the *San Luis Obispo Morning Tribune* carried a story about an arrest that Sheriff Cunningham and San Luis Obispo Sheriff S. D. Ballou made of an embezzlement suspect from Stockton:

> "Sheriff Cunningham of San Joaquin County, left yesterday on the morning train, having in charge E. C. Neilson, who is wanted in Stockton to answer to the charge of embezzlement.
>
> "The veteran sheriff of San Joaquin County has been here for several days doing some quiet detective work, attempting to locate his man. He was aware of the fact that Neilson was somewhere in this part of the county.
>
> "Neilson left Stockton about the 29th of February, and ever since then Sheriff Cunningham has been exerting every effort to effect his capture. About a week ago, Cunningham chanced to be in the post office at Stockton when one of the citizens came in to get his mail. The man stopped to read a letter within a few feet of the officer, who recognized the handwriting as that of Neilson, and a close scrutiny of the envelope revealed the postmark of Port Harford. Here was a clew and Cunningham decided to follow up and visit this county.
>
> "In company with Sheriff Ballou, he went to Port Harford. A search about the beach and the Hotel Marre, and an interview with Mr. Gagliardo failed to disclose any clew which would lead Cunningham to think that his man was anywhere in the vicinity of the Port. Finally, the officers walked out on the wharf and entered the freight office. As they stepped inside, Sheriff Cunningham espied a man at the counter talking to the agent, whose features struck him as being much similar to those of Neilson, and so he remarked to Sheriff Ballou. The latter took a hasty glance at the suspect and remarked in a whisper, 'That's your man, Cunningham.'

"At the same time the man, who had aroused the suspicions of the officer, started in the direction of the hotel. Cunningham followed him and made the arrest. The moment the stranger spoke, his voice was recognized by Cunningham and his identity was no longer a secret.

"Sheriff Cunningham told a *Tribune* representative the following story regarding his prisoner at the Southern Pacific depot yesterday morning:

"'I have known E. C. Neilson for a number of years. He came to Stockton in 1869, while I was running a harness shop. He was a Dane, just recently from the old country, and it was from me that he learned to speak English. For a number of years past he has been head bookkeeper for Buell and Company, a large firm of Stockton.

"'It seems that for a number of years past, he has been manipulating the accounts of his employers so as to embezzle large sums of money at different times. When I left Stockton, the expert had not yet finished his work on the books, but had discovered a shortage amounting to nearly $8,000. Neilson has always been one of the most highly respected citizens of Stockton, and not one of his fellow citizens would have suspected him in the least of any criminal action. He is very prominent in I.O.O.F. circles. He has three married daughters residing in Stockton. I think Neilson is about 53 years of age.'"[3]

The article went on to say that Neilson had come to the Port Harford area on March 17th, and had been frequently checking in with the agent at the freight depot, apparently expecting a package.

Sheriff Cunningham and Stockton area officers were looking for a San Francisco murder suspect in mid-May of 1896. Captain Lees was confident that Joseph E. Blanther, a deserter from the Austrian Army, was responsible for robbing and killing a San Francisco woman named Philopena Langfeld in her Geary Street home on Friday, May 15th, 1896. Blanther's description and image appeared in newspapers, and a salesman named Rothschild, who worked in a Stockton clothing store, notified Cunningham that he had sold some overalls to a man who looked just like the murderer described in the papers on Tuesday, May 19th.[4]

The man who Rothschild waited on had a bicycle with him, and Rothschild was a bicycle enthusiast himself, so when the conversation turned to bicycles, some of what the man told Rothschild did not ring true. The stranger, who was dressed in similar clothing to what was described in the papers, did not appear to have ridden the distance he had claimed to, based on the condition of his clothing. Then too, the man didn't have any luggage or parcels strapped to his bike, as would someone who was riding a long way. The man with the German or Austrian accent told Rothschild he was heading for Oakland. The salesman sought out Sheriff Cunningham shortly after the stranger left his store, giving Thomas a description of the man, and saying that he was about the same height as Thomas, that being 5 feet, 11 ½ inches tall. Sheriff Cunningham alerted all local officers, as well as the officers in Sacramento, believing the stranger would go that direction.[5]

The following day, a farmer who lived east of Stockton reported to Cunningham that at about 10:00 that morning, he was hailed along the road by a man riding a bicycle. The man looked just like the published pictures of Blanther. The stranger asked the farmer the way to Milton, but he didn't wait around for an answer. At the time, the bicycle rider was making his way towards Linden, not Milton.

Sheriff Cunningham immediately telephoned the Milton constable and provided a description, then he and his deputies

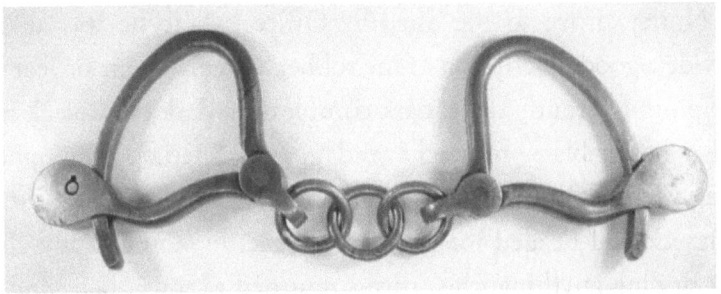

Handcuffs like these, made by Adams and patented in 1862, were commonly used by lawmen during Sheriff Cunningham's day
[R. Tod Ruse]

fanned out in the area that the bicycle rider had been spotted by the farmer, but they didn't find anything. Blanther ended up getting arrested in Meridan, Texas in November 1897, where he committed suicide while an inmate in the jail there.[6]

On Saturday afternoon, June 6th, 1896, a young man named Oliver Nutley was driving into Stockton along the French Camp Road when he came upon a well-dressed man on the side of the road. Thinking the man might want a ride, Nutley reined up his horse, but instead, the man stepped up and grabbed the reins, saying, "I want your money!" The stylish highwayman then pulled out a six-shooter and pointed it at Nutley, at the same time letting go of the reins and grabbing Nutley by the coat collar. Lifting Oliver out of his cart by his collar, the outlaw then went through every pocket, but only came up with 25 cents. Nutley had actually been carrying a considerable amount of money at the time in a purse in an outer pocket, but when the bandit ripped the pocket, the purse slipped around into the lining of the coat. After the outlaw was done with Oliver, he ordered him to drive on, with the threat, "If I hear any more of this, I will blow your brains out."[7]

Nutley drove to the Sheriff's Office, where he was able to provide a good description of the robber as being about six feet tall, 200 pounds, stoutly built, dark complexion, dark eyes, black hair, and a heavy black mustache and goatee. Sheriff Cunningham, along with deputies Billy Wall and George Black, and Constable James Carroll headed for the crime scene, looking for any clues. Not finding anything, the officers returned to town, believing the outlaw had gone into Stockton. It appears the robber was never caught for this crime.[8]

Later that year, the *Hanford Journal* ran a short article, which, true or not, was good for a chuckle:

> "The veteran Sheriff Cunningham of Stockton says that when a train or stage is held up, the proper course to pursue is to wire the officers at Visalia and ask if any citizens are missing. That's tough on old Mamma Tulare."[9]

In October 1896, Amador County Sheriff U. S. Gregory requested Thomas' assistance with a case involving the theft of gold amalgam from an Amador County mining company. The suspected thief was a man named John Hammond. Hammond's travels had been watched, and when he made for Fresno to visit a sister-in-law, Sheriff Cunningham followed him there. Believing that Hammond might try to send some of the amalgam from Fresno, Cunningham had already alerted the express company to delay any shipments until he arrived in town.

Hammond's sister-in-law attempted to send amalgam to a smelter on March 6th, and Cunningham wired Sheriff Gregory to have a warrant issued for Hammond. He was immediately arrested by the sheriffs, and he confessed to the crime and cleared his sister-in-law.[10]

On December 17th, 1896, Sheriff Cunningham got a request

from Sheriff A. H. Roth, of Adams County, Illinois, requesting Cunningham arrest an embezzlement suspect named James Shepherd, who was supposed to be living with a brother in the Lodi area. Knowing the legal requirements for such an arrest, Thomas had telegraphed Roth, explaining the necessary information and requesting Roth provide what was needed.

Two days later, the information was received and a warrant was issued for Shepherd. Thomas sent George Black and Billy Wall out to serve the warrant, and on their way, the deputies met O'Neal Township Constable H. B. Coleman of Lodi, who told them that Shepherd was dead. Disregarding the requirements of the law, Sheriff Roth had apparently wired Coleman and requested that he go out and arrest Shepherd. When Coleman and the Lodi justice of the peace contacted Shepherd, he was working in a field. Protesting his innocence, Shepherd asked the officers if he could change clothes, and they let him go into the house. He grabbed a gun instead, and backed the officers off of the property, then took a fatal dose of strychnine.

Leg irons like these were used in the late 1800s
[*R. Tod Ruse*]

The *San Francisco Call* said, "...Sheriff Cunningham is the maddest man in San Joaquin County at what he declares to have been the bungling work of the Lodi constable and the Illinois sheriff, by which Shepherd was given the opportunity to commit suicide."[11]

During that same week, Sheriff Cunningham arrested a horse thief named Harry Bryant, in Berenda, in Madera County. Bryant stole a horse and buggy from the Reynolds and Turner stables in Stockton. He ended up pleading guilty, and he was sentenced to two-and-a-half years in San Quentin.[12]

At about 7:00 p.m. on the evening of January 6th, 1897, Sheriff Cunningham received a call from Lockeford, informing him of a robbery and assault on the proprietor of the Chinese laundry in the town. The victim, Ah Goon, was threatened and attacked by three Chinese ruffians, known as highbinders. They stole $5 from Goon, missing another $100 he had concealed in his clothing. After striking Goon over the head and badly injuring him, the three jumped into a wagon and headed out in the direction of Stockton.[13]

The sheriff sent deputies Black and Wall out to intercept the bandits. The deputies located their men near the junction of Waterloo Road and Cherokee Lane, and took them into custody. The outlaws' wagon had broken down at that location, and Black and Wall summoned Stockton's patrol wagon to fetch their prisoners to jail.[14]

In early January 1897, several attempts were made to wreck passenger trains in the Ripon area. On the night of January 11th, two different switches were thrown open in an attempt to derail trains, but neither attempt was successful. Dent Township Constable Joseph Johnson of Ripon started investigating, and

Sheriff Cunningham was notified and started for the scene, but no traction was made on the cases at the time.[15]

Thomas was in San Francisco on January 30th, 1897, searching for Harry M. Earl, a young man wanted by the Tacoma, Washington police for embezzlement. Earl had been in Stockton for a time after the crime was committed, and Cunningham was familiar with him. When he was made aware of the Tacoma warrant for Earl, Thomas started looking around Stockton and found that the thief had left for San Francisco. That Saturday night, Sheriff Cunningham and San Francisco Police Officer Robert Graham located their man and lodged him into the city jail, holding him for Tacoma.[16]

A double murder occurred in New Hope on the evening of February 2nd, 1897, the victims being two respected members of the community. The slayer was a local store and saloon owner named Charles F. Kleupfer.

Kleupfer had been sitting in his saloon that afternoon, playing poker with Archie Morris and John Gould. After some disagreements, Morris and Gould left and headed to another saloon across the road. They took seats, and started a conversation with Charles Dodge and Alexander Borland, who were sitting at a table.

Kleupfer, who was drunk, had followed Morris and Gould, and started making trouble with them. In an effort to calm the situation, Dodge and Borland got up and led Kleupfer out of the place, but as they reached the door, Kleupfer spun around with a gun in his hand and fired four shots. Borland fell dead in his tracks, shot in the head, while Dodge ran to the back of the room before collapsing. He died without uttering a word.[17]

Both Dodge and Borland were well-known and respected in

the New Hope area. Witnesses said that they had used a minimum of force while escorting Kleupfel out of the saloon. After the shooting, Kleupfel returned to his store, where Union Township Constable Andrew A. McCulloch took him into custody. Sheriff Cunningham was called, and he and Deputy Wall made the twenty-mile trip to New Hope over muddy roads.[18]

In March 1897, newspapers were reporting that Thomas was seeking presidential appointment for the position of United States Marshal for the Northern District of California, to replace the outgoing Barry Baldwin. Cunningham's name continued to be mentioned for the job throughout the summer months and into the fall, but, being that this was a political appointment, it ultimately came down to politics and an ex-state senator from Tuolumne County named John H. Shine was eventually given the job.[19]

Charles Kleupfer was found hanging in his cell in the Stockton jail on the morning of April 6th, 1897, by his cellmate. Kleupfel had written letters to his brother, to his attorney, to head jailer Tom Benjamin, and to the coroner.[20]

On April 14th, 1897, George Jones, the constable in Lodi and also a resident deputy sheriff, was arresting William Loomis for being drunk and disorderly when Loomis, assisted by one of his sons, started resisting arrest and assaulting Jones. The constable had been called by business owners when Loomis was creating a ruckus. While escorting Loomis to the Lodi jail, they were intercepted by Loomis' son, Boyd Loomis, who urged his father to resist. The old man struck Constable Jones in the head, while Boyd came around behind the lawman with a knife.[21]

During the struggle, Jones pulled out his revolver and struck the elder Loomis over the head, but apparently not hard enough, because Loomis kept up the fight. Jones' gun went off, striking William in the chest. Boyd fled, but later turned himself in. William Loomis died a few hours later. The shooting was deemed justifiable.[22]

On the same day as Constable Jones was dealing with his struggles, a young man walked into the Sheriff's Office saying that he had committed a crime in St. Louis and that he was tired of running and wanted to turn himself in. None of the deputies were familiar with the man, but they got to work and sent out wires making inquiries as to any wants. The following day, Sheriff Cunningham received a wire from the superintendent of the American Express Company, saying that the man he had in custody was wanted in St. Louis for embezzling from the company while he was an employee.[23]

The following week, on April 23th, 1897, Sheriff Cunningham and his deputies were once again dealing with an army of about 250 unemployed men who took over a freight train in Lodi, demanding to be taken east and refusing to get off. The group was being led by someone named Leffingwell, who was quite contrary. Deputy Wall went to Lodi to try to get the men off the train, but he made no headway with the group. After being delayed all day, the bosses at the Southern Pacific Company ordered the train to be returned to Stockton.[24]

The men initially refused to get off the train once they got back to Stockton, but they were eventually persuaded by Sheriff Cunningham and the other officers to take up camp down by the riverfront. The men spent the night in a camp there. Provisions were solicited, and the group was fed breakfast. Then, just like in 1894, the men were loaded onto a barge and sent down the river to San Francisco. Thomas later submitted a bill to the Board of Supervisors for $170 worth of expenses he had incurred in dealing with the situation. The Board delayed the decision until that December, and then refused to pay the bill.[25]

The *San Francisco Call* ran a story about an arrest that Thomas and Billy Wall made in May 1897:

> "STOCKTON, CAL., May 24—Sheriff Cunningham and Deputy Wall went into the country near French Camp yesterday and arrested a young man by the name of Love, who is wanted at Fruitvale for obtaining money under false pretenses. Love says there is some mistake. He was taken away this afternoon by an officer from Oakland."[26]

At the end of May 1897, citizens in the eastern part of Stockton were being held up by a lone gunman. The proprietors of two roadhouses were the first victims on May 26th, then the bandit hit the streets, holding up people as they walked down the sidewalk. The robberies continued the following night. The *Stockton Record* gave an account of one of the stick-ups:

> "Frank Rossi is the bartender in Bertola's saloon on Weber Avenue, and he lives on the corner of Fremont and East streets. He was going home at about 10:30 last night when he was accosted by a masked man near his place of residence. The stranger shoved a pistol in Rossi's face and told him to yield. Rossi gave up his watch and $12.50 in coin, and he was ordered to move on. He was very much frightened, and when asked to give a description of the highwayman, said that the only thing he could see was the muzzle of the pistol barrel staring at him."[27]

The story was the same with the other victims. The only picture of the bandit that emerged was that he was tall and thin, and he wore a dirty white slouch hat. In all, five separate people on the streets fell victim to the bandit over a two-night period. The newspaper article continued:

"Sheriff Cunningham led the forces. He was seconded by his deputies, Wall and Black, constables Carroll and Beach, Chief of Police Kingsbury, and Officer Kenyon. They spread over the northern and eastern part of the city and walked about, hoping to be stood up or catch sight of a suspicious looking character. Constables Howe and Hersom of O'Neal Township were also on the lookout. Officer Craig was on watch, and the Superintendent of Streets Bidwell delegated himself as a citizen official and was out rambling the highways with a shotgun, ready to hold up the robber on first sight.

"The hours passed away until 1 o'clock this morning, when a pistol shot was heard. To some of the officers, it sounded in the southwestern part of the city, and to others farther east. A break was made for the supposed spot, but met with no results. Early in the morning the man-hunters came in, leaving the highwayman at large."[28]

The following morning, a young man named A. L. Paynter went to the police station, which was located in the courthouse, and gave a highly improbable story of having been held up the previous night by a man wielding a wagon wheel spoke in one hand and a pistol in the other. The officers paid little attention to the tale. The newspapers followed the lawmen's movements closely all day and into the night:

"All day yesterday, the officers were busy laying their plans to capture the great unknown, should he attempt his operations again. It was naturally supposed that the man would appear in another part of the city, if at all, but the officers would take no chances on that. At about 8 o'clock, the scene in front of the police office looked as if a Sheriff's posse was about to start on the trail of a Sontag or Evans, or a Dunham.

"Sheriff Cunningham was at the center of the group comprising a number of policemen, his deputy sheriffs and all the constables of Stockton and O'Neal townships, and even jailer Bob Hanks. The manhunters were deputies Wall and Black, Chief of Police Kingsbury, Captain Simpson, officers Carroll, Craig, Kenyon and Marshall, constables Carroll, McCann, Beach, Vinelli, Howe and Hersom. Sheriff Cunningham remained in his office till a late hour to respond to any call.

"It was a case of now you see them and now you don't. The crowd was there and then it was dissipated like mist before the sun, and all that could be seen of the posse was a stray officer here and there in various parts of the town by some belated pedestrian. The city and outskirts were covered completely. Some drove about the outside districts, while others patrolled the more thickly populated portions, all hoping to be stood up. Once in a while one officer would meet another and swap stories, but that was all. No highwayman made his appearance, and the only echoes of his presence were the improbable stories of Paynter and the unknown man who said he was stopped on Weber Avenue. It was 3 or 4 o'clock this morning before the officers finally sought their beds."[29]

Despite all of the lawmen's efforts, the outlaw was never located.

In July 1897, Sheriff Cunningham was up before the Board of Supervisors, seeking a change in the allowance he was given to feed prisoners in the county jail. At the time, the sheriff was allowed 12 ½ cents per prisoner, per meal. That amount worked out fine when there were more than twenty-five inmates, but it wasn't enough when there were less. Cunningham proposed that he be allowed 15 cents per prisoner when there were twenty-five prisoners or less. The majority of the Board agreed with Thomas, and the allowance was changed.[30]

14

THE TRAIN WRECKERS

During the late evening hours of September 4th, 1897, a northbound Southern Pacific train chugged to a stop about three miles north of the Ripon station, at a place called Morano Switch, in southern San Joaquin County. Someone had piled railroad ties across the tracks and set them ablaze in an attempt to stop the train. It was fortunate that this was a slow-moving freight rather than a passenger train traveling at full speed and the engineer had no trouble in stopping short of the obstruction.

The engineer and fireman clambered off the engine and walked towards the flaming wall blocking the tracks as the brakeman cautiously climbed down from the caboose. The train crew fully anticipated that robbers would rush them, and the brakeman obtained a pistol from the express messenger before continuing to the front of the train.[1]

The air was still that night, the only sounds being the occasional chugging of the huge steam engine and the chirping of crickets. The railroad men looked around and noticed that all that surrounded them were wide-open spaces that stretched into the darkness. Stumped, the men got to work clearing the ties off the tracks. The train then continued on to the Lathrop station, where a call was made to the Sheriff's Office in Stockton, notifying officials of the incident.

Investigating deputies found shoe tracks at the scene leading into a nearby field and showing that one of the suspects wore long, sharp-pointed shoes. Lawmen also found one other piece of evidence at the scene, one which would later prove invaluable to the prosecution. A piece of cloth from a duster, measuring about eight inches long and one inch wide, was found clinging to a barbed wire fence opposite the switch and along the trail of the footprints leading into the field. For Sheriff Cunningham and his deputies, the crime would mark the start of a long manhunt.[2]

The lawmen got their first break in the case within twenty-four hours of the crime, after one of the suspects told a man named George Cook of their scheme, wanting him to assist them with a second attempt on the train. Cook, not wanting any part of the conspiracy, went straight to the sheriff.

The two principal suspects were very familiar to Cunningham and his men. George Williams and George Schlegel had met each other while incarcerated in reform school several years before and had been close confidants ever since. Williams grew up in the Banta area, near Tracy, and was thoroughly familiar with the terrain of southern San Joaquin County.[3]

On April 20th, 1892, Williams had walked into the Southern Pacific's Banta station and held up the agent at the point of a six-shooter. Although the take didn't amount to much, George collected up all of the cash in sight. After spending the night in Ripon, he fled towards the Sierra Nevada foothills. Sheriff

Cunningham was quickly on his trail since the railroad agent easily identified Williams as a young man who lived in the local area. The sheriff caught up with Williams in Sonora and brought him back to Stockton for trial. George was readily convicted, but because of his youth, he was sentenced to a two-year stretch in the Whittier Reform School in Los Angeles County. Deputy Del Keagle transported the prisoner, and later recalled how during the entire trip, Williams talked of someday wrecking a train and robbing the passengers.[4]

George Williams
[*Cunningham's mug book, SJSO collection*]

George Schlegel was a hard-case who hailed from Los Angeles. His first arrest came in 1892, when Los Angeles Detective Miles Bowler slapped the irons on him at a place called Three-Mile House, on the San Fernando Road. Schlegel was wanted for grand larceny and initially resisted when approached by Detective Bowler, reaching for his pocket. Bowler threatened to shoot him on the spot if he made another move. After placing the cuffs on, the officer found a loaded .38 Colt's revolver in Schlegel's pocket. Schlegel was convicted and sent to the Whittier Reform School, where he met George Williams. The two hit it off right away. Schlegel was only there a mere three weeks before he escaped, but he and Williams kept in touch and came to San Joaquin County together after Williams was released.[5]

After serving his stint, George Williams immediately returned to his stomping grounds around the Tracy area. He was an intelligent young man and began experimenting with explosives in an attempt at inventing a smokeless version of gunpowder. Williams eventually won a patent for his gunpowder and secured investors to finance his enterprise.[6]

George Schlegel, in the meantime, wasted no time in keeping the sheriff and his men busy. As documented in a previous chapter, Schlegel walked into R. S. Johnson's livery stable and rented a horse shortly after arriving in Stockton. As Schlegel rode away, Mr. Johnson called after him to look out that the horse did not run away with him. Schlegel smirked to himself that the stable man was the one who should look out!

Schlegel armed himself before riding out of town, never intending to return the rented horse. After the sheriff's men took a report from Mr. Johnson, they headed for George Williams' place in search of Schlegel. The deputies felt that Schlegel would have headed there, but when they checked they could not find him and Williams was not cooperative. Deputies finally caught up with Schlegel in San Joaquin City after a three-day chase.[7]

Veteran Wells Fargo detective John Thacker later recalled the arrest. Looking at a sawed-off Smith and Wesson revolver which hung in Sheriff Cunningham's museum, Thacker related that

Schlegel was a suspect in a train robbery in Roscoe, Los Angeles County, at the time. Thacker was with Sheriff Cunningham and Deputy Thomas Benjamin when they arrested him:

> "'I was with them when they got to him that time. We found him in San Joaquin City. Benjamin ran his hand under the pillow the first thing and got that pistol. He had it before Schlegel had time to do anything.'"[8]

It was later learned that George Schlegel was not involved in the Roscoe train robbery, but he was convicted for horse stealing and was sentenced to San Quentin for three years. In the meantime, George Williams was living life large. He was living with a woman and was blowing all of the money he could get his hands on towards his mistress. He wasn't working, but was supposedly carrying out experiments with his gunpowder. The money he received from shareholders in his gunpowder company went right through his hands. He had interested a lot of people in his scheme and had succeeded in getting a considerable amount of money from them in small sums at different times. He rented an office, but his normal office hours were between one and three in the morning. He never appeared during normal business hours because creditors "disturbed his peace." Because of these business practices, Williams found himself deep in debt.[9]

George Schlegel was paroled in late 1896, and just as before, he partnered up with George Williams as soon as he got out. They both took up residence in southern San Joaquin County, living between Tracy and Lathrop, but they spent much of their time in Stockton. Williams then started making a lot of trips into south San Joaquin County in the spring and summer of 1897, ostensibly to keep up his gunpowder experiments, but more likely to plan out the intended train robbery.

George Schlegel
[*Cunningham's mug book, SJSO collection*]

After receiving the information about the attempted train robbery from George Cook on September 5th, 1897, Sheriff Cunningham put a tail on Williams and Schlegel, who were staying in rooms nine and ten at the Vermont lodging house in Stockton at the time. The two partners left town on Wednesday, September 8th, and when they did not return, the sheriff and his men felt certain that another attempt at a train robbery would be made. Cunningham accompanied deputies George Black and Billy Wall on the southbound train out of Stockton that evening. The officers felt that the bandits might have a comrade on the train to signal ahead. Thinking that his presence on the train might cause too much curiosity, Cunningham got off at the Lathrop station. He sent his deputies on with the train in case it encountered any trouble down the line.[10]

At about 9:00 p.m. that night, Southern Pacific train Number 17, dubbed the Los Angeles Express, neared the Morano Switch.

From about a mile north of that location, the engineer saw a large fire burning on the tracks. The train robbers had stacked about a dozen ties across the tracks from a nearby pile. They placed a large amount of straw under the ties, then ran a fuse from there to an adjacent field. They set a match to the fuse and by the time the train approached the switch, the pile was fully ablaze.

Billy Wall had been riding in the cab with the engineer, while George Black rode in one of the cars. As the train chugged to a stop about thirty yards short of the burning obstruction, both deputies jumped off the train to investigate. No sooner had their feet hit the ground than the train came under gunfire. Several hobos were hitching rides on top of a baggage car and one of them was hit in the thigh by one of the shots. Several other rounds hit the side of the train, but nobody else was hurt. The passengers were in a panic, thinking they were about to be robbed or attacked. Muzzle flashes were seen off to the west, but as soon as the firing stopped the culprits disappeared into the darkness. Wall and Black returned fire and started out in the direction of the shots, but soon returned to the train as it was impossible for them to pick up the trail in the darkness. When word of the attack on the train reached Sheriff Cunningham at the Lathrop station, he borrowed a shotgun and started out for the crime scene. The lawmen took up the search at daylight, scouring the bottom land to the San Joaquin River. The elements were working against them, however, because a strong wind had come up about midnight and obliterated any tracks that may have been left in the sandy fields and roads.[11]

Williams and Schlegel wasted no time in getting to the river, and made their way to Modesto, where they read in the newspapers that they were wanted for the crime. From there, they returned to the wild country along the San Joaquin, an area that Williams was familiar with and which afforded them the ability to elude capture. On September 9th, the two held up a wood chopper in the area of San Joaquin City, carrying off all of his provisions. At that time they were well armed, having a shotgun, two Winchester rifles, and a large supply of ammunition. From all appearances Williams and Schlegel likened themselves to Sontag and Evans, the two notorious train robbers from the Tulare area who had shot it out with lawmen and eluded capture for several months, four years earlier.

Nothing more was heard of the two until the evening of September 12th, when a man named Ed Margin and his wife reported that two men had attempted to stop their buggy about nine o'clock that night in the area of the Mossdale bridge at the San Joaquin River, on the road between Tracy and Stockton. Margin said that he was a distance north of the drawbridge when he noticed two men standing behind a tall fence alongside the road. As he got close, the two jumped the fence and started for his buggy. They were slowed up when one of them fell while coming over the fence. This delay allowed Margin to lay whip to his horse and outdistance the two. Though Margin and his wife had not gotten a good look at the men, authorities were convinced they were Williams and Schlegel.[12]

Sheriff Cunningham and his deputies were keeping pressure on the fugitives, diligently searching the riverbanks and surrounding areas. The desperados' shoe prints were located during the search and it was determined that Williams' left shoe had three nail holes in the heel, which left a distinctive imprint in the damp sand and made it easy for the officers to follow.

Cunningham returned to Stockton for a few hours on Monday morning, September 13th. While at the office, he received a telegram advising that two men with rifles were seen in the vicinity of Newman, in neighboring Stanislaus County. The sheriff headed out that afternoon, meeting Wells Fargo detective John Thacker at the Lathrop train station. The two met with Stanislaus County Sheriff R. B. Purvis and a posse in Modesto. The lawmen then set out for the Crows Landing area with horses, again searching the wilderness areas around the San Joaquin River.

Cunningham and Thacker had been traveling in a buggy, and the sheriff was aware that the posse might have been spotted by

Cunningham with some of his deputies who served during this period. Left to right: Joe Long, Sheriff Cunningham, Billy Wall, unknown, and George Black.
[*R. Tod Ruse*]

Williams and Schlegel. Near nightfall on September 14th, they traded their surrey for a ranch wagon, hoping to throw the fugitives off guard by the ploy. That night, the posse arrived at a ranch which was close to the river near the town of Newman, owned by a family named Jorgenson. Shortly after arriving there, the posse got some very interesting information from the seven-year-old Jorgenson boy. The little lad told the officers that he had seen two armed men near their ranch the night before. This was welcome news, and it strengthened Cunningham's belief that Williams and Schlegel were in the area.

Armed with the Jorgenson boy's information, the officers were convinced they were very near their prey. The lawmen camped on the front porch of the Jorgenson ranch house that night. Fearing that Williams and Schlegel might attempt to steal their wagon in the middle of the night, Sheriff Cunningham ordered the nut on one of the wagon wheels be removed, just in case.

The sheriff and his men were up and on the road at 3:00 a.m. the next morning. In a short time, they came across the unmistakable track of Williams' left shoe. Later that morning, while they were on the trail, Mr. Jorgenson alerted the officers and told them that he had just seen two men run from a haystack on his property and head towards the brush. Sheriff Cunningham held a quick meeting with the others, telling Thacker to take one of the possemen and follow their trail, while he and the others would try to head them off and keep them from making it back to the overgrown banks of the river.[13]

After seven days and nights on the run, Williams and Schlegel would find themselves in chains in a very short time. Detective Thacker later explained how the arrests were made:

"'It was in an alfalfa field that we ran them down. Williams was about twenty-feet ahead, while Schlegel was lagging behind, being unable to keep pace with Williams on account of his sore foot. (Schlegel had injured his foot while on the run and it became infected.) When I got within range of them, I called to them to throw up their hands. Williams looked up, and, seeing me, threw down his gun. He carried a shotgun. Schlegel still held his weapon, a Winchester rifle. I had my rifle leveled on them. I told Williams to come to me. He draggled along, reluctantly. I had the top hand, and I was going to play it. Schlegel showed more fight. He dropped the butt of the rifle to the ground, but still held the barrel. When Williams threw down his gun, Schlegel picked it up and held it in the same position as he held the rifle, only in the other hand. I told him to throw down those guns, but he still held them. Of course, I had a bead on him and had the drop, because I could kill him before he could raise either gun to fire. He then walked down a ditch, and only the upper part of his breast was then in sight. I thought, 'What's the matter with that damned fool; does he want me to kill him?' I again commanded him to throw down the arms, threatening to shoot if he did not do so at once. He then dropped both guns, and walked toward me. After coming five or six feet, he hesitated, turned and picked up both guns again. I did not want to shoot him, but it looked now as though I would have to. I was all alone. Young Newsome was in the buggy, and Cunningham could not get a sight on Schlegel from his position. He heard me call to him to throw down the guns, and Tom came up through the alfalfa as fast as he could. He was buttoned up in a heavy coat, and when he came up the sweat was standing out in beads as big as marbles. Before he came up, however, Schlegel stood both guns against a barb-wire fence, and walked toward me. I told him to throw his pistol away, and he did, throwing his coat back in the meantime to show he had no more weapons. Both men had been running. Their faces were all flushed, and they were winded. As soon as we ironed them, they called for water.'"[14]

Sheriff Cunningham learned from Williams and Schlegel that he had come close to them several times during the hunt; once on Sunday night, September 12th, when they were hiding behind a barn which the posse passed by, and once the next night about 11:00 p.m., as the two watched the lawmen pass by their hiding place.

Cunningham and Thacker arrived in Stockton with their prisoners on the afternoon train. George Williams had been very entertaining during the trip, telling a reporter at the Lathrop station that he and Schlegel had endeavored to escape capture by making hot-air balloons out of tents. The *Evening Mail* reported that "the story was swallowed, to the amusement of the train robbers as well as the officers." Authorities could finally relax when they heard the heavy metal doors of the county jail clank shut behind the two ex-cons.[15]

Although there was stronger evidence against Williams and Schlegel for attempted train robbery, both were charged with two counts of the more serious crime of attempted train wrecking, a capitol offense in California at the time.

The judge heard damning evidence against the defendants during their preliminary hearing. George Cook testified about his conversation with Williams, in which Williams outlined the September 4th attempt on the train and his determination to repeat the attempts until he was successful. Another witness testified to loaning Williams a duster, which was torn when returned. The tear matched perfectly with the piece of cloth that was recovered on the fence at Morano Switch that day after the first attempt. After hearing the evidence, the judge bound both Williams and Schlegel over for trial.

After the preliminary hearing, the handwriting was on the wall for George Williams. He knew his chances of being acquitted in a trial were between slim and none. Williams knew that if he were able to avoid the gallows, he would be wearing stripes for a long, long time. This began wearing on him, and he offered to turn state's evidence against his former comrade-in-arms in order to save himself. The district attorney was having none of it, and Williams went to trial on the charges on October 18th, 1897. After listening to the evidence for two days, the jury spent less than an hour in deliberations before returning guilty verdicts on the two charges of placing an obstruction on a railroad with the intent of derailing a train. Because of his young age and the impression he had on the jury, they voted that Williams should receive life imprisonment rather than the death penalty.[16]

The trial for George Schlegel was scheduled to begin on the afternoon of October 21st. Seeing what had happened to his partner and apparently hoping for a chance at having his sentence commuted at some point in time, Schlegel chose to plead guilty just as his trial was getting under way. A jury was required by law to fix punishment, and so a jury was impaneled to pass judgment. Just as the Williams jury had done the day before, the twelve men deciding his fate voted for life imprisonment for George Schlegel.[17]

George Williams, always the schemer, spoke with a reporter shortly after his trial. He explained that he was convinced that the foreman of the jury would sign a petition he was circulating for a commutation of his life sentence. Williams told the reporter:

> "You see, I had the sympathy of the jury, inasmuch as they fixed the punishment at life imprisonment instead of hanging. If it

were possible, that jury would sentence me to from one to five years. I was figuring on serving three years and two months, which would let me out in 1900 sometime. Then I could commence the twentieth-century with a new lease on life."[18]

Williams continued his campaign to be pardoned while serving time at San Quentin, and in 1911, with the help of San Joaquin County Sheriff William Riecks, a childhood friend of his, Williams was pardoned and released from prison.[19]

15

END OF AN ERA

In mid-September 1897, Sheriff Cunningham and Stockton Chief of Police John Gall wrote to San Francisco detectives E. M. Egan and Raymond Silvey, as well as Oakland Police Detective Denny Holland, requesting they assist officers in Stockton during the annual fair. In addition, Cunningham added Mark Smith to his staff of full-time deputies. Smith joined Undersheriff Joe Long, and deputies Isaac Robinson, George Black, Barney Cassidy, William Wall, Robert Hanks and Tom Benjamin.[1]

The *San Francisco Call* wrote an article in about the shortcomings of California's two prisons, in which the reporter spoke with Thomas and Wells Fargo's James Hume:

> "Sheriff Cunningham of Stockton and Detective Hume of the Wells Fargo system say they can see the handiwork of the graduates of California penitentiaries in many of the more recent crimes, such as robbery, burglary and stage-robbing."[2]

In early December 1897, Sheriff Cunningham and Alameda County Sheriff Clifford White were on the trail of a horse thief.

The December 11th, 1897 edition of the *Livermore Herald* gave the details of the search:

> "Sheriff Tom Cunningham of San Joaquin County spent yesterday in this county trailing a horse thief. The fellow started from Stockton Thursday evening with a phaeton, driving a buck skin horse and leading another, which he took from a ranch and made off with it in this direction. He was seen passing Livermore Saturday and Haywards yesterday.
>
> "Sheriff White spent the day yesterday with the veteran officer, and yesterday morning they found that the man they wanted had backtracked and was in Contra Costa County. Last night at eight o'clock, Constable Fitzgerald received a telegram from Sheriff Cunningham, stating that the thief had been captured and the property recovered."[3]

On January 4th, 1898, Thomas received an invitation to attend the execution of Theodore Durrant, who was convicted of raping and murdering young women in the belfry of the San Francisco church he attended. Cunningham had apparently softened over time, and the old lawman politely declined the invitation, telling a reporter he did not like seeing a man hanged.[4]

The Sheriff's Office received a wire from the San Francisco police on March 11th, 1898, requesting they be on the lookout for Charles Dunne, who was suspected of shooting a man in a San Francisco saloon during the early morning hours that day. San Francisco officers believed that Dunne would be headed towards Stockton, because he had contacts in the valley.

Deputies George Black and Billy Wall, along with Stockton Constable James Carroll and Stockton police officers Mathew Diarmid, Walter Walker and John Craig were detailed to the railroad depot to watch for Dunne. The officers positioned

Sheriff Cunningham and his deputies in 1898.
Thomas was known to remark that this was his favorite picture.
Left to right: George Black, Joe Long, Billy Wall, Sheriff Cunningham, Mark Smith, Tom Benjamin, Barney Cassidy, and Bob Hanks.
[*R. Tod Ruse*]

themselves on both sides of the train as the 1:08 pulled in, and Billy Wall and George Black boarded before the train came to a stop. Dunne saw the lawmen and attempted to flee the car, but he was in the deputies' clutches before he could say Bob's your uncle. The presence of the officers had drawn a crowd, but they worked together to quickly secure Dunne and lodge him in the jail.[5]

Sheriff Cunningham was very busy during the last week of March 1898. Burglars had been active in the southern part of San Joaquin County, as well as in Stanislaus County. Thomas worked with Stanislaus Sheriff R. B. Purvis and Castoria Township Constable George Shepherd of Lathrop in trying to track down the burglars. Then, later that week, Cunningham spent four days in Mariposa County, assisting with the hunt for two train robbers who had held up a train near Goshen, in Tulare County, at a place called Cross Creek. The robbers, Cliff Regan, a long-time outlaw, and Walter Low, were later run to ground after a long manhunt.[6]

Thomas returned to Stockton on April 1st from Merced with a wagon load of stolen property and a burglar named Jack Breen in tow. Breen was a local Stockton thug who hung around the waterfront with other hard-cases. Breen was also indicted by the grand jury later in April for the January 1898 arson fire at the Farmers' Union warehouses in Stockton.[7]

In April 1898, the United States declared war after Spain invaded Cuba, a mere 90 miles from U.S. shores. Fearing that Spain's end goal was United States soil, Americans throughout the country heeded the call to arms.

In California, the Presidio at San Francisco became the base of operations for the Pacific forces. In May, Sheriff Cunningham sent a letter to all of California's sheriffs, suggesting they each raise a company of 100 volunteers to defend the state. These volunteers would be mounted and could assist the sheriffs as posse members, or in the defense of their counties against invaders, should it become necessary. Cunningham called his volunteers the Rangers.[8]

In San Joaquin County, Sheriff Cunningham's Ranger unit never got close to the 100 members that he originally envisioned, and they largely became a ceremonial unit, riding in parades and at events. Maybe feeling a little nostalgic for some of his old manhunts after the group rode in Stockton's Fourth of July parade, Thomas said he was game to lead his group of Rangers on a ride through the Coast Range mountains to San Jose, for the September 9th California Admissions Day celebration. That ride never materialized.[9]

In August 1898, Thomas declined his party's nomination for re-election to the sheriff's position at the local Republican convention. In recognition for his long service, Cunningham's fellow delegates gave him three cheers, and presented him with the following proclamation:

> "Whereas, Thomas Cunningham has, during his twenty-six years of service as Sheriff of San Joaquin County, won the approbation, not only of this community, but of the State at large, by an unparalleled record of efficient and tactful administration of the duties of his office, unswerved by personal and political considerations, and
>
> Whereas, He has for reasons of his own, declined to be a candidate for re-election to this very important office; therefore, be it
>
> *Resolved*, that this convention, with deference to public opinion and in justice to itself, cannot allow this opportunity to pass without a public and formal expression of its appreciation of the high natural qualities of this man, as well as his acquired business habits, which would render any other sort of record

impossible.

Resolved, that if in the future any public trust should be confined to him, we feel sure that we are only expressing the convictions of all in saying that the result of such trust would almost necessarily be equally satisfactory."[10]

On September 1st, 1898, Sheriff Cunningham donated his collection of museum pieces to the people of San Joaquin County, naming the Board of Supervisors as trustees. The museum collection had grown over the years to include guns, knives, sandbags and slungshots, a saw blade concealed in a comb, a piece of armor known as a "coat of mail," brass knuckles, counterfeit bills and coins, and the handkerchief used by Black Bart, with its unique FX07 laundry mark.[11]

Sheriff Cunningham at his desk, with his museum in the foreground
[*R. Tod Ruse*]

On September 10th, 1898, Sheriff Cunningham sent Billy Wall and George Black over to the California Navigation and Improvement Company with an arrest warrant for E. H. Wilber, true name Charles H. Cadwallader. Cadwallader was wanted for embezzling $75,000 from a Union City, Indiana, bank.[12]

Sheriff Cunningham received word from Sheriff Simmons of Randolph County, Indiana, on September 15th, saying he was in Sacramento with requisition papers for Cadwallader. After his arrest, Cadwallader's lawyers worked to obtain a writ of habeas corpus for him, but in the meantime, Sheriff Simmons served Sheriff Cunningham with extradition papers, and, handcuffing himself to his prisoner, Simmons left for the railroad depot.

Cadwallader's attorneys stayed busy, trying everything they could to keep him in the state of California. At each town where the train made stops, officers with court papers tried their best to talk Simmons out of his prisoner, but to no avail. Cadwallader's attorneys were successful in obtaining a writ of habeas corpus in Sacramento. By that time, the sheriff and his prisoner were approaching the last stop in California, at Truckee.

The local constable and several other officers met the train and served the paper on Sheriff Simmons. Showing one heck of a lot of spunk, the sheriff took the summons, but, still cuffed to his prisoner and with his revolver laying over his knee and ready for action, he told the lawmen that any attempt to take his prisoner off the train would be met with bloodshed. Apparently, the officers believed him, because the train continued on its trek eastward with the sheriff and his prisoner aboard.[13]

On November 24th, 1898, Sheriff Cunningham treated the prisoners in the county jail to a Thanksgiving turkey dinner and all the trimmings, as had been his tradition.[14]

On December 6th, 1898, the San Joaquin County Board of Supervisors voted to purchase Sheriff Cunningham's collection of criminal records and photographs for $5,000. There had been a lot of talk about the value of the collection before it was bought by the county and before the vote was taken, the *Stockton Record* ran an editorial about the advisability of such a purchase, which read, in part:

> "...Let us see how the rogues' gallery affects crime and its commission in this county. For twenty-six years, Sheriff Cunningham has been accumulating the photographs and records of men who offend against the peace and dignity of the State of California. To bring it down to this year: In this, the closing term of District Attorney Nutter, sixteen criminals have been sent to the penitentiaries without a trial. To say without a trial does not impute unfairness. To the criminal, whose very existence implies dishonesty, an oath in court is but a breath of wind. To deny the offense is his first charge. To him, there is no compunction of conscience in the mental operation. Here is where the rogues' gallery steps in as a factor in modern criminology.

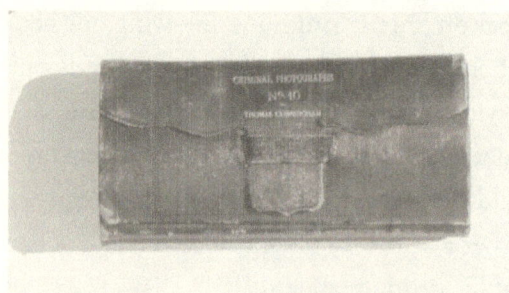

One of Cunningham's mug books, labeled No. 10. Books like these contained photographs of arrested suspects and were often known as rogues' galleries.
[*R. Tod Ruse*]

"Confronted by his own image, every scar and deformity on his body read to him without an examination, his record exposed as if by magic, the criminal, overcome with his utter vulnerability against such overwhelming testimony, sinks beneath its preponderance. He pleads guilty. This does not seem much, but every time a criminal pleads guilty to an offense, the county is saved $150. That is only a fair average. Sometimes it is $300 or $500. There are no fees for witnesses, no voluminous documents, etc., attendant upon a long trial. Sixteen of these cases in a few months just passed means $2,400 to this county.

"It is the duty of the county to keep these records up during all these years, but the county has not done so. The present cannot alter the past, but may atone for it. It has cost Sheriff Cunningham from between $15,000 to $20,000 to do this. There are 14,000 pictures and as many records of men. These are offered to the people for $5,000. Are they worth it in the light of the situation divested of all sentiment? Assuredly, they are. Los Angeles County wants them, but Sheriff Cunningham offers them to us. It is in justice to Sheriff Sibley (Cunningham's successor) that they be purchased, that he may receive the support and aid that will come from them.

"The Merchants and Manufacturers' Association, representing much vested property rights, did well in resolving that it be the sentiment of the body that the gallery be purchased. Safety to our women and children in repelling the criminal element from the community; safety to property and economy in county government demand that the gallery by procured..."[15]

The rogues' gallery of photographs and criminal records was widely praised by lawmen. Each criminal arrested in San Joaquin County was assigned a local arrest number, with detailed identifying information listed and a photograph of the criminal attached. Records were gathered from the state's prisons and from departments around the country. These records were cross-indexed in several different ways, such as category of crime and race of criminal, which made it a much easier task to locate a wanted person. The records later became the basis for the Identification Bureau, which was established in 1908 by Sheriff Walter F. Sibley.

At Christmas time, the officers of the Stockton Police Department made a presentation to Thomas as a token of their esteem for him. In front of all of the police officers, as well as all of his deputies, Thomas was presented with a gold watch and a fine gold-headed cane, inscribed with "Merry Christmas," and his initials, "T.C." Chief John Gall made the presentation:

> "Sheriff Cunningham, the members of the police department, on the eve of the great festival of Christmas, deem it a most fitting and appropriate time to congratulate you on the successful manner in which you have conducted the affairs of your office, and to wish you all the happiness the season can bring. The relations between the Sheriff's Office and Police Department have always found yourself and assistant ready whenever and wherever we have called upon you, and the members of this department, appreciating the many courtesies extended to them by yourself, desire to present you with this token of their esteem. Take it and wear it, and may success and prosperity always attend you, is our earnest wish."[16]

Newspapers in Stockton and San Francisco ran stories about Thomas as his time in office came to an end. The *Stockton Record* had this to say on December 31st, 1898:

> "THE MAN AND THE OFFICER—Official Career and Personal Characteristics of Thomas Cunningham—Sheriff— For the past few days, Sheriff Cunningham has been engaging in moving. After incumbency of nearly twenty-seven years, over

half a lifetime of an ordinary man, the Sheriff is about to retire to private life. For twenty-six years and ten months, Thomas Cunningham has been the sheriff of San Joaquin County, and today his is one of the best-known names in the State. Especially is it a name known and feared by those pre-disposed to crime and infraction of the law.

"Sheriff Cunningham leaves the office with a bald head, but this is no particular evidence of his being burdened with age, for the top of his head was minus hair when he went into office nearly twenty-seven years ago, and he was not thirty-three years of age then.

"When in a reminiscent mood, Mr. Cunningham is fond of talking about the barren spot on the top of his head, and ascribes his initial success in politics to that false evidence of age. Those who had preceded him in the office of sheriff of San Joaquin County had all been elderly men, and he maintains that he would never have been elected at so young an age had he not been bald. As a matter of fact, he was bald when he was twenty-five years of age.

"Mr. Cunningham drifted into politics quite naturally. All the old-time residents of Stockton will remember the days of the old volunteer fire department, with all its rivalry and wrangles. Mr. Cunningham was one of the most active members in the department. He was foreman of the old Eureka company, which served as a stepping stone to the office of chief engineer of the department.

"In those days, there was more of politics in connection with fire matters than there is in the election of a President of the United States, and it was quite natural that Mr. Cunningham should be a candidate for sheriff after having been chief engineer. Twelve times did Mr. Cunningham make the race for sheriff against some of the ablest men that the Democratic party could name for the position, but each succeeding election proved that

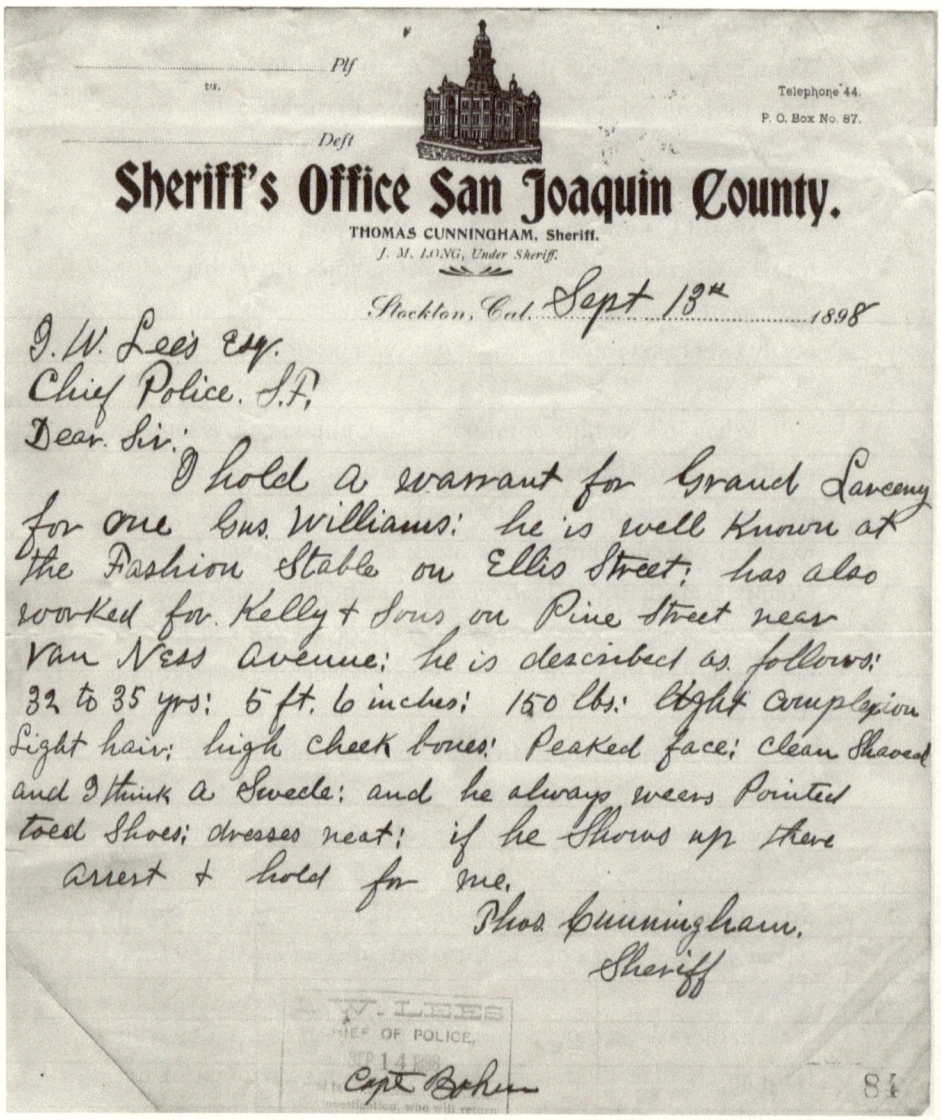

Letter from Sheriff Cunningham to Isaiah Lees, San Francisco Chief of Police, dated just a few months before he left office. Lawmen often communicated with each other through letters such as this one.
[Ray Moreno]

Mr. Cunningham was invincible. During the first four years of his official career, Mr. Cunningham had as his undersheriff A. B. Bennett, and since that time, J. M. Long has served him continuously in that capacity.

"In talking a few days ago with one of Mr. Cunningham's old friends, the writer was told this: 'Did you ever stop to think to what controlling factor Mr. Cunningham owes his success? He is not a brilliant man in the ordinary acceptation of that term, so his success cannot be ascribed to unusual talent. I will tell you what it is—It is that quality so rarely possessed—everyday common horse sense.'

"This just about expresses it, but it does not go far enough. My informant should have added that Mr. Cunningham was a keen judge of human nature, an instinct so valuable in nosing crime and ferreting out criminals.

"His unerring judgment of men, Mr. Cunningham has well exemplified in the selection of his deputies. The men who have served under him have been competent in their positions, but in connection with that competency they have been distinguished by faithfulness and devotion to their chief. Allowing all due credit to Mr. Cunningham's ability, as sheriff he could never have achieved anywhere near the success he has, had it not been for the men who were so loyal to his leadership.

"Thomas Cunningham has a dual character. There is Tom Cunningham, the man, and Thomas Cunningham, the officer. The man possesses a heart almost womanly in its softness. He is easily touched by a recital of trouble, and his generosity and kindness are boundless. The officer is stern, unyielding, uncompromising. No consideration could swerve him one particle from duty. His heart might bleed for the misfortune of some poor devil whom it should become necessary to incarcerate, but there would be no faltering when duty called…

"…In a chat recently, Mr. Cunningham expressed himself

as glad that he would soon have an opportunity to have a little rest and leisure. He made the statement that during his term of office, he had only been off duty once, and that was for a period of about a week, when he attended the conclave of the Knights Templar. He said that when he returned to his office, it took him several weeks to catch up with the routine of his professional duties. From this it will be seen that eternal vigilance has been the price of Mr. Cunningham's success…

"…Mr. Cunningham has made it an invariable rule never to accept any reward or private compensation of any nature for doing his duty. Illustrative of this fact may be told a little incident which happened in the earlier years of his official career. A prominent farmer, recently deceased, had suffered a considerable loss by theft, and had offered a reward of $50 for the apprehension of the criminal and the return of the goods. The thief had covered his footsteps very cleverly, and for several days Mr. Cunningham was perplexed and balked in his search. Finally, he succeeded in his quest. The farmer, glad to receive his property again, tendered Mr. Cunningham the $50 and was surprised when the Sheriff refused it…"[17]

The article went on to speak of instances of Thomas Cunningham's generosity and charity. It ended by saying:

"Now that Thomas Cunningham is about to retire from the stage of official life, even those who have been his enemies or political opponents can unite in a recognition of his manifold virtues. Brave, fearless, honest, generous, faithful, tender—in short, an exemplification of Pope's ideal that 'worth makes the man.'"[18]

The presents and proclamations to Thomas continued after the ringing in of the new year. On January 2nd, 1899, the day before he officially left office, Thomas was honored by his deputies.

Cunningham's first undersheriff, Abraham Bennett, made the presentation of a pair of gold-rimmed field glasses and a pair of gold opera glasses.

Thomas relinquished his office to Walter Sibley on January 3rd, 1899. A ceremony was held in one of the courtrooms, officiated by Judge James H. Budd.

The *Stockton Record* said:

> "Tom Cunningham was ordered into court at 10 o'clock this morning. There he found about 150 spectators. Information had been filed charging him with being true to the trust of the people. He was found guilty, and Judge Budd sentenced him to receive a solid silver dinner set consisting of knives, forks, plates and spoons, in an elaborate rosewood case, from Charles Haas & Sons. It was presented by the Stockton Bar and public officials.
>
> "Sheriff Cunningham responded feelingly. He said he had always tried to do his duty and the attorneys and officials had always aided him.
>
> "Then took place a touching scene, which caused the tears to come to the veteran sheriff's eyes. Unbuckling his pistol belt, he placed it about the body of Sheriff Sibley and turned over to him his handcuffs. In presenting the pistol, he used these peculiarly significant words:
>
> "'Never use this pistol to shoot down a man unless you find it absolutely necessary to the welfare of the people; and always protect a prisoner with your life, if need be.'"[19]

The *Hanford Journal* had this to say about Cunningham:

> "Last Tuesday at noon, Sheriff Tom Cunningham stepped out of the Sheriff's Office of San Joaquin County, after having completed the longest and one of the most successful administrations of the office of sheriff ever conducted in

California.

"For twenty-six years he had been in charge of the office, having been successful in twelve elections before the people. Though he has been a 'peace officer' for more than a quarter of a century, he has never shot anyone or been shot, never wounded anyone or been wounded. Offenders against the law avoided the county, over which he had the strictest watch, and none cared to know that the veteran Sheriff of the State had joined in the hunt for them. Nevertheless, there were none ever captured by a posse of which Sheriff Cunningham was a member but seemed to prefer the honor of capitulating to the veteran.

"In all of twenty-six years of his service as Sheriff, he lost but two prisoners, and in his efforts to recapture them he spent more than his salary for three years amounted to. Those two were William Clifton and Thomas McKenna, and nothing is known or has been known of their whereabouts, as far as knowledge of officers is concerned, since the morning of the 22nd of February 1877, when they were missing from their cell in the old county jail.

"He is probably the only sheriff that was ever called upon to arrest, and did arrest, a United Stated Supreme Court Justice, but that is what he did when he took Justice Field into custody in San Francisco shortly after the killing of David S. Terry at Lathrop by Deputy Marshal David Nagle. The marshal seemed to want to hide behind the robes of the Supreme Court, and Justice Field seemed willing that his authority should be tested against that of the Superior Courts...

"In twenty-six years, Cunningham had but two men to hang, but he and his deputies have accompanied upwards of eight hundred prisoners to the two penitentiaries. He retired for the office he has filled so long with the best wishes of all classes of the people of that county."[20]

16

AN HONORABLE NAME

Thomas stayed active in retirement. He was in San Francisco a few days after leaving office, visiting his old friend, retired Chief of Police Isaiah Lees. There was speculation that the two might start a private detective business, but Thomas threw water on that idea:

> "'I just called on Chief Lees to talk to him. Perhaps we could form a detective agency that might pay, but I don't like this idea of hunting up people's crimes and sins unless it is for the good of the country. It is wonderful what a difference it makes when you've got the people behind you in such ways.
>
> "'I might do something in a private detective agency business, but I have a few dollars left, and I believe I have enough not to start out in that direction. I feel very grateful to the people of San Joaquin County. There was one noticeable difference between my going out of office and Chief Lees' resignation. He was jumped on and harassed on all sides, the papers saying many unkind words about him. On the other hand, I don't know of a single paper which said anything about me that did not give me perhaps a better notice than I deserved.'"[1]

Thomas remained interested in politics and stayed active in the Republican party. He and his daughter Margaret were in Sacramento in the second week of January as interested spectators in a heated senatorial race.[2]

In October, Thomas was voted president of the board of directors of the Union Safe Deposit and Loan Company, a Stockton banking institution that lasted for over 100 years. The company was three years old at the time Cunningham was made president.[3]

In the early morning hours of November 26th, 1900, Thomas was traveling in Tuolumne County, headed to Sonora to catch a train back to Stockton, when he suddenly succumbed to a heart attack. Newspapers around the state reported Cunningham's death and eulogized him. The *Amador Ledger* gave a good account of the circumstances surrounding what led up to Thomas' death:

> "Ex-sheriff Cunningham left Stockton Saturday afternoon for Angels Camp. He had been importuned to be present and went against his own will. He had come home Friday from a stay of several days in San Francisco and was tired. His daughter Lillian awoke him Saturday morning and asked him if he was going to Angels. He said he did not know, but he arose and ate breakfast. Leaving the house, he took his long coat with him, stating that he might not be back, words which, in the light of subsequent events, bore a significance little dreamed of.
>
> "He did go to Angels and was present there Saturday night. From there, the drive was made over to Jamestown and then to Tuttletown. Tonight, there was to have been a big ratification at Sonora, and it was there he was going when overtaken by the grim messenger, Death.
>
> "Word was immediately sent to this city to his family and to the Sheriff's Office, when arrangements were commenced to

prepare for receiving the body. Congressman Woods arranged for a special train on the Sierra road from Oakdale to Jamestown and for the proper transfer at Oakdale on the return to this city."⁴

An article in the *Stockton Daily Record* of November 27th, 1900, detailed the circumstances around Cunningham's death:

"More details of the death were brought down on last evening's train. As stated yesterday, the death took place in Tuttletown. Mr. Cunningham had decided on Sunday to come home rather than attend the meeting at Sonora Monday night. He left W. C. Ralston, his host, and S. M. Shortridge, with whom he had been, at about 5 o'clock yesterday morning, at Mr. Ralston's home, Robinson's Ferry. Mr. Ralston arose and ate breakfast with his guest and saw him off. The first word he received was when his driver returned from Tuttletown to tell him that Mr. Cunningham had died.

"It appears that the veteran Sheriff complained to the driver of being unable to breathe easily, while they were driving over. Arriving at Tuttletown, Sheriff Cunningham started to walk to the hotel, but the driver, seeing that he needed assistance, went to his aid and helped the then dying man to a chair on the porch, while he went to arouse someone. When he returned, the sinking man had fallen from the chair. Aid was summoned hastily and he was removed to the parlor of the hotel, where he expired without speaking. A physician was summoned, but to no avail..."⁵

Thomas' obituary read:

"Ex-sheriff Thomas Cunningham of San Joaquin County died suddenly this morning in Tuttletown.

"Thomas Cunningham was a native of County Longford, Ireland, born August 17, 1838, and came to the United States

Illustration by Ralph O. Yardley of Cunningham's home as it appeared in 1900.
[*R. Tod Ruse*]

when 10 years of age, locating at Brooklyn. There he served an apprenticeship at the harness maker's trade with a brother-in-law. He worked there until 1855, when he removed to California, via Panama. He arrived in San Francisco June 16, 1855. He came at once to Stockton.

"In 1871, he was elected sheriff of San Joaquin County, took the office in March 1872, and a year later closed out his harness business. He was married in this city in 1861.

"He leaves an estate valued at $50,000. Three married daughters, Mrs. Confer (Lillian), Mrs. Boggs (Katherine) and Mrs. Higginbothem (Margaret) survive him.

"Both departments of the Superior Court adjourned today out of respect to his memory, and a committee of attorneys was appointed to arrange for his funeral. The body will arrive here on a special train and the obsequies will probably take place Tuesday under Masonic auspices."[6]

Words of condolence came in from lawmen around the country on notification of Cunningham's death. His family received telegrams from the most prominent lawmen and politicians from across the country, including a telegram from William Pinkerton, head of the Pinkerton National Detective Agency in Chicago. The *Fresno Republican* wrote, "It is not saying too much to declare that he was the best sheriff California has known," and, "Not only has San Joaquin County sustained a loss, but the State of California has as well."[7]

Former San Francisco Chief of Police Isaiah W. Lees, a legend in his own right, said this of Thomas:

"Cunningham arrested some of the most desperate criminals in the State, and exhibited coolness and a nerve possessed by few officers. In all of his career, he never hurt a man, nor was he wounded himself. This was due to the remarkable tact with which he arranged the plans for capture. Many of the desperadoes, when brought to bay, showed fight, but they never had a chance to do any damage, for they were quickly disarmed and handcuffed.

"The Sheriff possessed a persistency in tracking criminals, which made his fame. He would follow a crook thousands of miles, and generally land him. Stage robbers held him in terror and nearly all of them that committed crimes in San Joaquin or adjacent counties were eventually landed to San Quentin. The farmers never lost faith in Cunningham. His strong forte, which won their favor, was his skill in catching horse thieves.

"Many of the famous cases of this county were prosecuted successfully by the assistance of the Sheriff. This is also true of many cases in other counties of California. The principal witnesses in the Patterson-Dorsey murder case were found in Stockton through his efforts."[8]

Thomas' funeral took place on November 29th at his residence, which at that time was located at 1009 N. El Dorado Street, at the corner of Acacia Street. Cunningham's old friend and mentor, Harry Morse, gave the eulogy. Morse shared what he had written with a reporter from the *Stockton Daily Independent* the night before the service:

"Last evening Harry N. Morse, ex-sheriff of Alameda County, who for a quarter of a century has been a particular friend and comrade of Mr. Cunningham, arrived in Stockton. They followed criminals together, remained in the saddle for days, and between them there was the strongest ties of friendship. Mr. Morse rose from a sick bed to attend the funeral. He sent out the following tribute to his old friend to the *Independent*:

"'All must die. It is wisdom to submit with patience to the common lot, for death is the common lot of all. And so, death has come suddenly to our dear friend, Tom Cunningham. What a flood of reminiscence flashes upon my mind at the mention of that honored name! We were boys together and comrades for years and years. None knew the man better nor had more varied and exciting experiences with my old-time friend than I did. In the saddle, over mountain passes or through swamps, about the camp fire and midst the stealthy watch of the silent night, when on guard for the good of the common-wealth, Tom was always the courageous, sensible, vigilant officer of the law. To my idea of manhood, a grander character than Tom Cunningham, as we endearingly called him, did not exist in our broad State.

"Honest as the day, always truthful, never a selfish thought, ever seeking opportunity to do good and kind acts toward his fellow man, as hundreds can testify to, brave as man could possibly be, and yet with the caution necessary not to do a nasty or unmanly act, or a wrong to the humblest human being on God's earth. Always generous to his friends, his purse open at all times to the poor and needy, a sense of honor, right and justice so acute that no power on earth could swerve him from it when in the performance of official duty. What more could the Redeemer exact of mortal man? No man is absolutely perfect, and yet, to my thinking, no man came nearer being that than Tom Cunningham. I don't believe that dear old Tom had an enemy, for cause, in the wide world.

"If ever a plain, common mortal existed that was truly lovable in character, then that man was our departed friend, Thomas Cunningham. I know that I have honored and respected him all my life, and I also know that he was worthy of the respect of every man, woman and child in California, because his great heart went out to them all.

"There was no malice in Tom for anyone, not even his enemies. The dear old companion of yore has gone before me over the river. The gates are ajar; he has passed from time to eternity. If Tom had any sins recorded against him, I hope that the Recording Angel will blot them out, that no more will be known of them forever, and that the good he has done in mortal life may live after him. May the dear old boy rest in peace, is the earnest prayer of his old comrade.

Harry N. Morse'"[9]

Many peace officers from throughout the state of California attended Thomas' funeral. All of the fraternal organizations that Cunningham belonged to were well represented, as was his old volunteer fire company, Eureka Engine Company 2. Thomas had belonged to a number of organizations and lodges, including the Morning Star Lodge of the Masons, Knights Templar, Red Men, Odd Fellows, Elks and Knights of Pythias.[10]

It was estimated that over 500 people marched from Thomas' home to his place of interment, next to his wife Catherine in the Stockton Rural Cemetery.[11]

When Sheriff Walter Sibley took office, he retained every one of Cunningham's deputies as his own, a true testament of their value to San Joaquin County at a time when it was customary for new sheriffs to bring in their own people.

Joseph Long remained Sibley's undersheriff until January 1911. He had served in the position for almost 35 years when he retired, and had been a law officer for almost 45. Joe started his career in the Sheriff's Office in 1865, the year the Civil War ended. By the time he retired, Sheriff Sibley and his deputies were responding to calls in automobiles and Orville and Wilber Wright had made their historic airplane flight.

The *San Francisco Call* ran a story on January 5th, 1911, marking the occasion of Joe's retirement:

"STOCKTON, January 4—A touching incident occurred at the Sheriff's Office last evening when Under Sheriff Joe M. Long, who has been connected with the office almost continuously since 1865, called on Sheriff Sibley to turn over his badge. The officer visibly was affected, and as he unwrapped the tissue paper in which he had placed the badge, he remarked:

"'I don't think I tarnished this badge. It must have been done by the elements.'

"The sheriff accepted the badge, and, returning it to the retiring official, told him to retain it as a keepsake. He was also presented with a gold mounted cane bearing the inscription: 'Presented to J.M. Long by the boys in the Office—1911.'"[12]

Joe Long died at the age of 76 on January 20th, 1911, only 16 days after his retirement.[13]

Deputy Bernard "Barney" Cassidy remained with the Sheriff's Office for nearly 40 years. He worked through Sheriff Sibley's administration and into that of Sibley's successor, Sheriff William Riecks. He was still working as a court bailiff in 1923. Cassidy died in January 1926.[14]

Billy Wall became sick and was hospitalized with tuberculosis in 1901. Sheriff Sibley held Billy in very high esteem and kept him on as a deputy, even when he became too sick to work. Billy died of the disease on February 11th, 1902.[15]

Deputy George Black went on to head the sheriff's Identification Bureau when it was created in 1908. He stayed with the San Joaquin County Sheriff's Office until 1914, then served as a guard at San Quentin for several years.[16]

Tom Benjamin served as the chief jailer in the early 1900s. He and his family lived in an apartment on the top floor of the jail in Stockton, and the newspaper often reported the sounds of children's laughs and screams coming from the jail during birthday parties for one or the other of Benjamin's kids. He resigned his position in 1907 and became a farmer.[17]

Robert Hanks retired as a jailer in January 1903. The *Stockton Daily Record* marked the occasion by running a story about Hanks' nearly 50 years in law enforcement.[18]

Mark Smith served until his sudden death during a hernia operation on February 2nd, 1910. He was in charge of the chain gang at the time of his death.[19]

Sheriff Cunningham's collection of criminal curiosities remained in the Sheriff's Office for many years, and it is believed that it was dismantled and disposed of in the 1930s. The San Joaquin County Sheriff's Foundation Historical Preservation Committee recently received a number of these museum items back from the Haggin Museum in Stockton, but most of the collection is lost forever.

Thomas Cunningham's memory is kept alive in some of the public facilities in San Joaquin County. The Criminal Justice building on the campus of San Joaquin Delta College in Stockton is named in his honor, and the road leading into the present sheriff's complex in French Camp is named after Thomas.

Today, the members of the San Joaquin County Sheriff's Office strive to uphold the foundational ideals and traditions that Sheriff Thomas Cunningham and his deputies established 150 years ago: service to the public, hard-work, honesty, courage, diligence, humility, discipline and loyalty.

Thomas Cunningham's final resting place in the Stockton Rural Cemetery
[*SJSO photo by P.J. Ruiz/Julie Book*]

NOTES

INTRODUCTION

[1] *San Luis Obispo Morning Tribune*, November 15, 1899.
[2] *San Francisco Call*, December 9, 1890.
[3] *Sacramento Daily Union*, November 25, 1882.
[4] *Sacramento Daily Record-Union*, June 13, 1891; *San Francisco Call*, September 2, 1898.
[5] Statutes of California, Twenty-Ninth Session of the Legislature, 1891, Chapter CXCI, *An Act to Establish a Penal Code,* approved February 14, 1872, amended Section1, 1217 (approved March 31, 1891), State Office of Printing, Sacramento, 1891; *Morning Press*, April 12, 1891.
[6] Blansett, Eual Desmond, Jr., *Death Without Honor, Legal Executions in the History of San Joaquin County,* unpublished, Stockton, California, 1994, page 79.

1. LEATHER CRAFTER BECOMES LAWMAN

[1] Tinkham, George H. *History of San Joaquin County,* Historic Record Publishing Company: Los Angeles, 1923. pages 385-386
[2] *San Joaquin Republican*, October 11, 1857, June 19, 1859.
[3] *San Joaquin Republican*, October 11, 1857, November 4, 1857, June 19, 1859, August 22, 1860, July 2, 1861.
[4] *Stockton Daily Independent*, January 1, 1872;
https://www.bls.gov/data/inflation_calculator.htm.
[5] *Stockton Daily Independent*, August 13, 1861, November 5, 1862, October 24, 1864.
[6] *San Joaquin Republican*, January 18, 1866.

[7] *Stockton Daily Independent*, December 7, 1870.
[8] *Stockton Daily Independent*, April 22, 1865, May 2, 1865.
[9] *Ibid.*
[10] *Stockton Daily Independent*, March 4, 8, 20, 1872.
[11] Houston Gun Collector's Association, hgca.org
[12] *Stockton Daily Independent*, March 7, 1872; *Daily Alta California*, March 11, 1872.
[13] *San Joaquin Republican*, April 22, 1872; *Daily Alta California*, March 24, 1872.
[14] *Evening Mail*, January 8, 1896.
[15] *Stockton Daily Independent*, March 11, 1872.
[16] *Ibid.*
[17] *Evening Mail*, July 3, 1872.
[18] *Stockton Daily Independent*, April 13, 1872.
[19] *Stockton Daily Independent*, May 20, 1872.
[20] *Stockton Daily Independent*, May 22, 1872.
[21] *Stockton Daily Independent*, May 20, June 11, 22, 1872.
[22] *Stockton Daily Independent*, May 20, June 11, June 19, June 22, 1872.
[23] *Stockton Daily Independent*, June 22, 1872.
[24] *Stockton Daily Independent*, August 1, 2, 1872.
[25] *Daily Alta California*, September 26, 1872; *Stockton Daily Independent*, September 26, 27, 28, 1872.
[26] *Stockton Daily Independent*, October 19, 1872.

2. One Year In

[1] *Stockton Daily Independent*, January 3, 1873.
[2] Cal 49, 323; *Stockton Daily Independent*, February 19, 1873; *Sacramento Daily Union*, February 4, December 29, 1874.
[3] *Stockton Daily Independent*, March 4, 1873.
[4] *Stockton Daily Independent*, February 27, March 6, May 17, 1873.
[5] *Ibid*
[6] *Sacramento Daily Union*, March 26, 27, 28; *Stockton Daily Independent*, April 2, 1873.

[7] *Stockton Daily Independent*, March 27, 1873.
[8] *Marysville Daily Appeal*, March 29, 1873; *Sacramento Daily Union*, March 28, 1873.
[9] *Stockton Daily Independent*, April 2, 1873.
[10] *Sacramento Daily Union*, April 1, 7, 1873; *Stockton Daily Independent*, May 28, 1873.
[11] *Sacramento Daily Union*, May 27, October 23, *Stockton Daily Independent*, November 6, 1873.
[12] *Stockton Daily Independent*, April 14, 1873.
[13] *Stockton Daily Independent*, October 15, 1868.
[14] *Stockton Daily Independent*, October 15, 1868, February 27, March 1, 1869.
[15] *Stockton Daily Independent*, October 15, 16, 1868; February 4, 27, March 1, April 16, 1869; August 17, 21, September 11, 1871; January 12, June 29, July 22, 1872; March 1, 1873.
[16] *Stockton Daily Independent*, April 26, 1873.
[17] *Stockton Daily Independent*, April 24, 1873.
[18] *Stockton Daily Independent*, April 26, 1873; *Daily Alta California*, April 26, 1873.
[19] *Stockton Daily Independent*, April 26, 1873; *Daily Alta California*, April 26, 1873.
[20] *Stockton Daily Independent*, April 26, 1873; *Daily Alta California*, April 26, 1873.
[21] *Ibid.*
[22] *Sacramento Daily Union*, May 7, 1873; *Stockton Daily Independent*, May 13, 20, 1873.
[23] *Sacramento Daily Union*, May 16, 1873.
[24] *Stockton Daily Independent*, May 23, 1873.
[25] *Stockton Daily Independent*, July 29, 31, 1873, February 15, 1875.
[26] *Stockton Daily Independent*, August 25, 26, 27, 1873, May 14, 1880.
[27] *Ibid.*
[28] *Stockton Daily Independent*, September 2, 3, 1873; *Sacramento Daily Union*, September 3, 1873.
[29] *Stockton Daily Independent*, July 23, August 6, September 9, 1873.
[30] *Stockton Daily Independent*, June 2, November 3, 1868, March 3, April

2, May 3, 1869, February 8, 1871, March 4, 1874.
[31] *Stockton Daily Independent*, October 20, 1873.
[32] *Sacramento Daily Union*, November 22, 1873; *Stockton Daily Independent*, November 22, 1873.
[33] *Stockton Daily Independent*, March 14, 1871, January 12, 1874.
[34] *Ibid.*
[35] *San Jose Mercury News*, January 15, 1874.
[36] *Stockton Daily Independent*, February 17, 18, March 19, 21, 1874.
[37] Statutes of California, Nineteenth Session of the Legislature, 1871-1872, Chapter DXCII, Section 5, *An Act to regulate the salaries and fix the compensation of the county officers of San Joaquin County*, passed April 1, 1872, page 875, State Office of Printing, Sacramento, 1872.
[38] *Stockton Daily Independent*, February 18, 1874.
[39] *Sacramento Daily Union*, March 5, 1874; *Stockton Daily Independent*, March 11, 1874.

3. Hunting Bandits

[1] *Stockton Daily Independent*, December 11, 1869; *Daily Evening Herald*, December 20, 1869.
[2] *Los Angeles Herald*, January 3, 1874.
[3] *Sacramento Daily Union*, May 28, 30, 1870.
[4] *Stockton Daily Independent*, October 13, 15, 1870.
[5] *Stockton Daily Independent*, May 21, 1872.
[6] *Daily Alta California*, June 27, 1859.
[7] *Los Angeles Star*, November 17, 1860; *Sacramento Daily Union*, December 22, 1866; *Sonoma Democrat*, December 22, 1866.
[8] *San Jose Mercury News*, April 26, 1872.
[9] *Fresno Expositor*, March 19, 1873.
[10] *Sacramento Daily Union*, March 20, 1873.
[11] *Stockton Daily Independent*, July 26, 1873.
[12] *Daily Alta California*, August 28, 1873.
[13] *Daily Alta California*, August 28, 30, 1873.
[14] *Sacramento Daily Union*, September 3, 1873.

[15] *Sacramento Daily Union*, September 8, 1873; *Marysville Daily Appeal*, September 11, 1873.
[16] *Santa Barbara Morning Press*, September 18, 1873.
[17] *San Jose Mercury News*, January 1, 1874.
[18] *San Jose Mercury News*, November 15, 1873; *Daily Alta California*, November 16, 1873; *Sacramento Daily Union*, November 15, 18, 1873.
[19] *Sacramento Daily Union*, November 15, 1873; *Daily Alta California*, November 16, 1873.
[20] *Marysville Daily Appeal*, December 28, 1873.
[21] *Los Angeles Herald*, January 3, 1874
[22] *Sacramento Daily Union*, January 20, 1874; *San Jose Mercury News*, January 27, 1874.
[23] *Los Angeles Times*, December 29, 1889.
[24] *Daily Alta California*, December 10, 1860, November 24, 1861; *Sacramento Daily Union*, April 5, December 12, 13, 1862, March 26, 1872; *Sacramento Daily Record-Union*, June 2, 1898.
[25] *San Diego Union*, April 22, 1874.
[26] California State Archives, letter of Harry N. Morse to Governor Newton Booth, March 21, 1874.
[27] *San Francisco Chronicle*, May 18, 1874.
[28] *Ibid.*
[29] California State Archives, letter of H.N. Morse to Governor Newton Booth, April 12, 1874.
[30] *Stockton Daily Independent*, April 17, 1874.
[31] *Ibid.*
[32] *Ibid.*
[33] *Los Angeles Herald*, April 22, 1874.
[34] *Stockton Daily Independent*, April 23, 1874.
[35] *Stockton Daily Independent*, May 13, 1874.
[36] *Sacramento Daily Union*, May 15, 1874.
[37] *Daily Alta California*, March 20, 1875.
[38] Greenwood, Robert, *The California Outlaw*, Los Gatos, California, Talisman Press, 1960. pages 42-43.

4. A Dark Time

[1] *Stockton Daily Independent*, April 6, 1874.
[2] *Stockton Daily Independent*, June 3, 1874.
[3] *Daily Alta California*, July 4, 1874.
[4] *Sacramento Daily Union*, August 10, September 3, 1874.
[5] *Daily Alta California*, September 17, 20, 1874.
[6] *Sacramento Daily Union*, December 18, 1874; *San Jose Mercury News*, February 12, 1875.
[7] *Daily Alta California*, December 19, 1874.
[8] *Stockton Daily Evening Record*, May 23, 1918.
[9] *Los Angeles Herald*, January 22, 1875.
[10] *Stockton Daily Evening Record*, May 23, 1918.
[11] *Daily Alta California*, February 20, 1875; *Sacramento Daily Union*, February 20, 1875.
[12] *Stockton Daily Independent*, March 5, May 5,1875; Ruse, R. Tod, *Stockton Police Department, A History 1850-1990*, Graphic Publishers, 1991, Santa Ana, California, pages 46, 48-51.
[13] *Grass Valley Morning Union*, March 30, 1875; *Stockton Daily Independent*, March 24, 1875.
[14] *Daily Alta California*, April 3, 1875.
[15] *Stockton Daily Independent*, April 5, 6, 7, 1875; *Daily Alta California*, April 3, 1875.
[16] *Sacramento Daily Union*, April 12, 1875; *Stockton Daily Independent*, April 16, 1875.
[17] *Daily Alta California*, May 18, 1875.
[18] *Stockton Daily Independent*, May 24, 1875.
[19] *Ibid*.
[20] *Sacramento Daily Union*, June 22, 1875.
[21] *Stockton Daily Independent*, August 1, October 9, 1861,
[22] *Stockton Daily Independent*, January 8, 1865, April 4, 1866, May 28, 1867, March 3, 1868, June 10,1869.
[23] *Stockton Daily Independent*, April 4, 1866.
[24] *Stockton Daily Evening Record*, January 3, 21, 1911; *Stockton Daily Independent*, January 25, April 4, 1866; *Stockton Daily Evening Herald*,

January 25, April 4, 1866.
²⁵ *Ibid; Stockton Daily Independent,* March 26, 1862, January 8, 1865, March 19, 1868, June 10, 1869, April 5, 1870, June 6, 1870, April 17, 1872, December 2, 1872; *Sacramento Daily Union,* January 29, 1873.
²⁶ *Daily Alta California,* September 4, 1875.
²⁷ *Sacramento Daily Union,* October 9, 1875.
²⁸ Hume, James and Thacker, John, *Wells, Fargo & Co Report of Losses, 1870-1884,* 125th anniversary edition edited by R. Michael Wilson, Las Vegas NV, RaMa Press, 2007, pages 254-256, 259-260; *Sacramento Daily Union,* July 9, 1860.
²⁹ Hume, James and Thacker, John, *Wells, Fargo & Co Report of Losses, 1870-1884,* 125th anniversary edition edited by R. Michael Wilson, Las Vegas NV, RaMa Press, 2007, pages 254-256; *Stockton Daily Independent,* November 3, 1875.
³⁰ *Stockton Daily Independent,* March 2, 1875.
³¹ *Stockton Daily Independent,* March 24, 1875.
³² *Stockton Daily Independent,* March 29, 1875.
³³ *Marysville Daily Appeal,* August 4, 1875; *Sacramento Daily Union,* August 7, 1875.
³⁴ *Marysville Daily Appeal,* October 7, 1875; *Daily Alta California,* October 8, 1875.
³⁵ *Ibid.*
³⁶ *Marysville Daily Appeal,* October 7, 1875; *Daily Alta California,* October 8, 1875.
³⁷ *Sacramento Daily Union,* October 13, 1875.
³⁸ *Daily Alta California,* December 2, 1875.
³⁹ *Sacramento Daily Union,* January 3, 1876.
⁴⁰ *Sacramento Daily Union,* December 22, 23, 1875.
⁴¹ *Sacramento Daily Union,* December 23, 1875.
⁴² *Marysville Daily Appeal,* December 24, 2875.
⁴³ *Sacramento Daily Union,* December 22, 23, 27, 29, 1875, May 1, 1876; *Placer Argus,* December 25, 1875,
⁴⁴ *Sacramento Daily Union,* May 1, 24, November 16, 21, 1876; *Marysville Daily Appeal,* November 18, 1876.
⁴⁵ Hume, James, and Thacker, John, *Wells, Fargo & Co Report of Losses,*

1870-1884, 125th anniversary edition edited by R. Michael Wilson, Las Vegas NV, RaMa Press, 2007, page 226.

5. BURGLARS, ROBBERS AND MURDERERS

[1] *Sacramento Daily Union*, January 3, 1876; *Daily Alta California*, January 9, 1876.

[2] Ruse, R. Tod, *Stockton Police Department, A History 1850-1990*, Graphic Publishers, 1991, Santa Ana, California, page 39; *Stockton Daily Independent*, June 2, November 3, 1868, March 3, April 2, May 3, 1869; *San Joaquin Republican*, May 4, 1858; *Daily Alta California*, November 6, 1890.

[3] *Daily Alta California*, February 24, 1876.

[4] *Sacramento Daily Union*, July 24, 1875; *Santa Barbara Morning Press*, July 25, 1875.

[5] *San Jose Mercury News*, July 25, 1876.

[6] *Ibid.*

[7] *Sacramento Daily Union*, July 24, 1876; *Grass Valley Morning Press*, July 25, 1876; *San Jose Mercury News*, July 25, 26, 1876.

[8] *Ibid.*

[9] *Sacramento Daily Union*, July 24, 1876; *Grass Valley Morning Press*, July 25, 1876; *San Jose Mercury News*, July 25, 26, 1876.

[10] *Sacramento Daily Union*, November 25, 1876.

[11] *Ibid.*

[12] *Sacramento Daily Union*, January 9, 1877.

[13] *Daily Alta California*, February 23, 1877; *Sacramento Daily Union*, April 29, 1864; *Hanford Journal*, January 6, 1899.

[14] *Sacramento Daily Union*, September 20, 1877; *Daily Alta California*, September 9, November 24, 1877.

[15] *Sacramento Daily Union*, January 30, 31, February 6, 1878.

[16] *Stockton Daily Independent*, April 10, 1878.

[17] *Sacramento Daily Union*, March 22, 1878; Daily Alta California, March 22, 1878.

[18] *Daily Alta California*, July 17, August 3, 1878.

[19] *Sacramento Daily Union*, May 27, 1878; May 4, 1880; *Stockton Daily Independent*, May 3, May 7, 1880.
[20] *Sacramento Daily Union*, September 5, 1878.
[21] *Grass Valley Morning Union*, September 28, 1878.
[22] *Sacramento Daily Union*, November 29, 1878.
[23] *Sacramento Daily Union*, February 28, 1879.
[24] *Sacramento Daily Union*, March 10, April 25, 1879.
[25] *Sacramento Daily Union*, May 30, 1879.
[26] *Stockton Daily Independent*, September 10, 1879.
[27] *Stockton Daily Independent*, August 9, 1879.
[28] *Stockton Daily Independent*, September 29, 30, 1879.
[29] Stockton Daily Independent, November 24, 1879; *Santa Barbara Morning Press*, November 25, 1879.
[30] *Stockton Daily Evening Heald*, July 1, 1880; *Stockton Daily Independent*, July 2, 1880.
[31] *Stockton Daily Independent*, December 1, 1879.
[32] *Stockton Daily Independent*, December 22, 1879.

6. THE DAILY GRIND

[1] 1879 California Constitution, passed and ratified May 7, 1879; *Daily Alta California*, January 2, 1880; *Stockton Daily Independent*, June 8, 1880.
[2] *Stockton Daily Independent*, February 13, 1880.
[3] *Stockton Daily Independent*, February 20, 21, August 3, 1880.
[4] *Stockton Daily Independent*, March 1, 1880.
[5] *Stockton Daily Independent*, March 1, 6, 16, May 22, 26, 1880.
[6] *Stockton Daily Independent*, March 10, 1880.
[7] *Grass Valley Morning Union*, April 1, 1880; *Stockton Daily Independent*, April 16, 1880.
[8] *Stockton Daily Independent*, May 3, 1880.
[9] *Sacramento Daily Union*, May 27, 1878, May 4, 1880; *Stockton Daily Independent*, May 3, May 7, 1880;
[10] *Santa Cruz Weekly Sentinel*, May 22, 1880; *Sacramento Daily Union*, May 15, 1880.

[11] *Ibid.*
[12] *Ibid.*
[13] *Ibid.*
[14] *Stockton Daily Independent*, May 28, 1880.
[15] *Sacramento Daily Union*, May 8, 31, 1880; *Stockton Daily Independent*, May 8,1880; Hume, James and Thacker, John, *Wells, Fargo & Co Report of Losses, 1870-1884*, 125th anniversary edition edited by R. Michael Wilson, Las Vegas NV, RaMa Press, pages 139-142.
[16] *Ibid.*
[17] *Stockton Daily Independent*, May 17, 1880.
[18] *Stockton Daily Independent*, May 24, 1880.
[19] *Stockton Daily Independent*, June 25, 1880.
[20] *Stockton Daily Independent*, June 11, 1880.
[21] *Stockton Daily Independent*, August 4, 19, 1880
[22] *Stockton Daily Independent*, September 27, 28, 1880.
[23] *Stockton Daily Independent*, October 23, November 13, 15, 1880.
[24] *Stockton Daily Independent*, December 30, 31, 1880.
[25] *Stockton Daily Independent*, January 1, 1881.
[26] *Stockton Daily Independent*, January 6, 15, 16, February 19,1881.
[27] *Stockton Daily Independent*, February 4, 1881.
[28] *Sacramento Daily Union*, March 15, 1881; *Stockton Daily Independent*, March 15, 1881; *Daily Alta California*, November 2, 1881.
[29] *Stockton Daily Independent*, May 26, July 21, 1881
[30] *Livermore Herald*, December 15, 1881.
[31] Hume, James and Thacker, John, *Wells, Fargo & Co Report of Losses, 1870-1884*, 125th anniversary edition edited by R. Michael Wilson, Las Vegas NV, RaMa Press, pages 205-215.
[32] *Placer Argus*, December 10, 1881.
[33] *Sacramento Daily Union*, April 26, 1878, January 28, September 14, 1880.
[34] *Sacramento Daily Union*, November 8, 1881.
[35] *Sacramento Daily Union*, December 8, 1881.
[36] *Ibid.*
[37] *Sacramento Daily Union*, December 8, 9, 10, 1881, *Grass Valley Morning Union*, July, 22, 1884.

[38] *Placer Argus*, December 10, 1881.
[39] *Sacramento Daily Union*, December 10, 1881; January 23, 1882; *Red Bluff Sentinel*, January 28, 1882

7. Trouble on the Moquelumnes

[1] *Sacramento Daily Union*, January 10, 1882; *Red Bluff Sentinel*, January 14, 1882.
[2] *Sacramento Daily Union*, February 27, March 1, 1882.
[3] *Stockton Evening Mail*, April 3, 1882.
[4] *Stockton Daily Independent*, April 16, December 13, 1880; *Sacramento Daily Union*, October 4, 15, 1881; Daily Alta California, April 18, 1882.
[5] *San Jose Daily Morning Times*, April 26, 1882; *Los Angeles Herald*, April 27, 1882.
[6] *San Jose Daily Morning Times*, December 9, 10, 1882; *Sacramento Daily Union*, December 11, 1882; *San Luis Obispo Tribune*, January 5, 1883; *San Jose Mercury News*, April 5, 1883.
[7] *Sacramento Daily Union*, November 25, 1882.
[8] *Marysville Daily Appeal*, March 11, 1883.
[9] *Sacramento Daily Union*, May 23, 1883.
[10] *Sacramento Daily Union*, July 16,19, 1883; *Placer Argus*, July 19, 1883; *Placer Herald*, July 28,1883.
[11] *Sacramento Daily Union*, July 27, August 18, 1883; *Placer Argus*, August 2, 1883.
[12] Ogden Hoffman, 1862, *Reports of Land Cases Determined in the United States District Court for the Northern District of California*, Numa Hubert, San Francisco.
[13] *Stockton Daily Independent*, April 8, 1880.
[14] *San Luis Obispo Morning Tribune*, September 5, 8, 1883; *Los Angeles Herald*, September 9, 1883; *Sacramento Daily Union*, September 8, 1883, November 16, 1883.
[15] *Sacramento Daily Union*, September 19, 1883.
[16] *Sacramento Daily Union*, September 19, 20, 1883.
[17] *Sacramento Daily Union*, September 23, 24, 1883; *Santa Barbara*

Morning Press, September 27, 1883; *San Luis Obispo Morning Tribune*, September 27,1883.

[18] *Sacramento Daily Union*, October 4, 17, 1883.

[19] *Stockton Daily Independent*, November 5, 1883.

[20] *Stockton Daily Independent*, November 5, 15, 1883; *Calaveras Weekly Citizen*, November 17, 1883; Wells, Fargo History Room, San Francisco, papers of James Hume; Dillon, Richard, *Wells, Fargo Detective, a Biography of James B. Hume*, University of Nevada Press, Reno, 1986, pg 175.

[21] *Ibid.*

[22] *Stockton Daily Independent*, November 5, 1883; Wells, Fargo History Room, San Francisco, papers of James Hume; Dillon, Richard, *Wells, Fargo Detective, a Biography of James B. Hume*, University of Nevada Press, Reno, 1986, pg 176.

[23] *Sacramento Daily Union*, November 15, 1883.

[24] *Stockton Daily Independent*, November 15, 1883.

[25] *Sacramento Daily Union*, November 2, 3, 8, 20, 1883.

[26] *Daily Alta California*, November 14, 1883; *Stockton Daily Independent*, November 15, 1883.

[27] *Stockton Daily Independent*, November 15, 1883.

[28] *Stockton Daily Independent*, November 16, 1883.

[29] *Sacramento Daily Union*, November 16, 19, 1883; *Calaveras Weekly Citizen*, November 19, 1883.

[30] *Sacramento Daily Union*, November 21, 26, 1883; *Los Angeles Herald*, November 23, 1883; *Daily Alta California*, December 2, 1883.

[31] *Daily Alta California*, December 8, 1883.

[32] *Grass Valley Morning Union*, January 27, 1884.

[33] Stockton City Directory, 1884-1885.

[34] *Sacramento Daily Union*, February 2, 1884.

[35] *Los Angeles Herald*, February 10, 12, 1884.

[36] *Sacramento Daily Union*, April 21, May 9, 1884.

[37] *Sacramento Daily Union*, April 30, May 23, June 6, 1884.

[38] *Sacramento Daily Union*, June 7, 1884.

[39] *Daily Alta California*, July 9, 10, 1884; *Sacramento Daily Union*, July 10, 1884.

⁴⁰ *Stockton Daily Independent*, October 24, 26, 28, 29, 1884; *Sacramento Daily Union*, October 24, 27, 1884.
⁴¹ *Sacramento Daily Union*, October 17, 1884; *Marysville Daily Appeal*, October 18, 21, 1884.
⁴² *Daily Alta California*, November 9, 1884.
⁴³ *Sacramento Daily Union*, November 26, 1884.
⁴⁴ *Daily Alta California*, December 7, 10, 1884, *Sacramento Daily Union*, January 1, 1885, June 22, 1886.
⁴⁵ *Stockton Daily Evening Mail*, December 13, 1884; *Daily Alta California*, December 13, 1884; *Sacramento Daily Union*, December 13, 1884; *Humboldt Times*, December 17, 1884.
⁴⁶ *Ibid.*
⁴⁷ *Sacramento Daily Union*, December 13, 1884; *Humboldt Times*, December 17, 1884; *Daily Alta California*, October 25, 1885.
⁴⁸ *Stockton Daily Evening Mail*, December 17, 1884; *San Jose Herald*, February 2, 1885.
⁴⁹ *Ibid.*
⁵⁰ *Morning Union*, December 28, 1884.
⁵¹ *Stockton Daily Evening Herald*, December 30, 31, 1884.

8. THE SHERIFF'S LAST EXECUTION

¹ *Sacramento Daily Union*, March 8, 1885.
² *Daily Alta California*, April 18, 1885.
³ *Daily Alta California*, September 4, 1885; *Sacramento Daily Union*, September 8, 9, 1885.
⁴ *Grass Valley Morning Union*, December 9, 1885.
⁵ *Daily Alta California*, January 9, 1886.
⁶ *Stockton Daily Evening Herald*, June 30, 1886; *People v. French*, 69 Cal. 169, pages 270-280.
⁷ *Santa Barbara Morning Press*, April 2, 1886.
⁸ *Daily Alta California*, May 9, 1886.
⁹ *Daily Alta California*, May 20, 1886; *Sacramento Daily Union*, May 27, 1886.

[10] *Stockton Daily Independent*, June 30, 1886.
[11] *Ibid.*
[12] *Ibid.*
[13] *Ibid.*
[14] *Stockton Daily Independent*, June 30, 1886.
[15] *Ibid.*
[16] *Ibid.*
[17] *Sacramento Daily Union*, November 16, 1886.
[18] *Daily Alta California*, January 20, 1887.
[19] *Sacramento Daily Union*, February 16, 1887.
[20] *Sacramento Daily Record Union*, March 15, 1887.
[21] *Sacramento Daily Union*, April 4, 9, 1887; *Santa Cruz Sentinel*, April 7, 1887
[22] *Sacramento Daily Union*, April 30, 1887.
[23] *Sacramento Daily Union*, April 16, 1887.
[24] *Los Angeles Herald*, April 21, 22, 1887.
[25] *San Jose Mercury News*, July 7, 1887; *Sacramento Daily Union*, July 8, 1887.
[26] *Daily Alta California*, August 27, 1887.
[27] *Daily Alta California*, September 9, 1887.
[28] *Sacramento Daily Union*, September 22, 1887.
[29] *Sacramento Daily Union*, September 23, 1887; *Grass Valley Morning Union*, September 30, 1887.
[30] *San Diego Union*, November 5, 1887.
[31] *Ibid.*
[32] *Mariposa Gazette*, December 3, 1887.
[33] *San Diego Union*, January 22, 1888.
[34] *Daily Alta California*, April 8, 1888; *Sacramento Daily Union*, April 14, 1888, *Daily Alta California*, January 2, 1889.
[35] *Daily Alta California*, August 5, 1888; *San Luis Obispo Morning Tribune*, August 5, 1888.
[36] *Sacramento Daily Union*, August 9, 1888.
[37] *Sacramento Daily Union*, September 17, 1888.
[38] *San Jose Mercury News*, October 21, 1888.
[39] *Daily Alta California*, October 21, 23, 1888.

[40] *Sacramento Daily Union*, October 24, 1888.
[41] *San Bernardino Courier*, October 26, 1888.
[42] *Daily Alta California*, November 2, 1888.
[43] *Sacramento Daily Union*, December 3, 1888.
[44] *Sacramento Daily Union*, January 23, 1889; *Daily Alta California*, January 23, 1889.
[45] *Sacramento Daily Union*, February 13, 16, 1889; *Daily Alta California*, February 13, 1889.
[46] *Los Angeles Herald*, February 23, 1889.
[47] *Daily Alta California*, February 24, 1889.
[48] *Ibid.*
[49] *Ibid.*
[50] *Madera Morning Tribune*, February 24, 1889; *Daily Alta California*, February 24, 1889.
[51] *San Bernardino Daily Courier*, February 26, 1889.
[52] *Los Angeles Herald*, March 5, 1889.
[53] *Daily Alta California*, March 12, 1889; *Grass Valley Morning Union*, March 14, 1889; *Marysville Daily Appeal*, March 14, 1889.
[54] *Sacramento Daily Record Union*, March 15, 1889.
[55] *Sacramento Daily Record Union*, July 3, 1889.
[56] *Sacramento Daily Record Union*, July 7, 1889.
[57] *Ibid.*

9. A HIGH-PROFILE CASE

[1] The American Law Register, 1852-1891, Vol 38, No. 10, University of Pennsylvania Law Review.
[2] bioguideretro.congress.gov;
http://www.onlinenevada.org/articles/william-sharon
[3] govtrack.us/congress/william_sharon
[4] Urie, Phillip R., Knife-Wielding Judge, article in the *Wild West Magazine*, February 1993.
[5] MacCracken, Brooks W., American Heritage Magazine, June 1967, Volume 18, Issue 4.

[6] *Daily Alta California*, March 11, 1884.
[7] *Ibid.*
[8] *Santa Rosa Press Democrat*, September 17, 1883; *Sacramento Daily Union*, October 5, 1883; *San Jose Herald*, November 1, 1883.
[9] *Stockton Daily Independent*, August 15, 1889; *San Joaquin Republican*, June 26, 1852.
[10] *Sacramento Daily Union*, June 2, 1856.
[11] *San Joaquin Republican*, June 25, July 25, August 17, 1856; Johnson, J. Edward, *History of the California Supreme Court: The Justices 1850-1900*, vol. 1, 1963.
[12] *Marysville Daily National Democrat*, September 13, 14, 1859; *San Joaquin Republican*, September 17, 1859.
[13] *Sacramento Daily Union*, September 22, 1863.
[14] *San Francisco Examiner*, January 1, 1886.
[15] *Daily Alta California*, January 8, 1886; *Los Angeles Herald*, March 2, 1886
[16] *Daily Alta California*, September 4, 1888.
[17] *Daily Alta California*, September 6, 1888.
[18] *Stockton Daily Independent*, August 15, 1889.
[19] *Daily Alta California*, August 15, 1889.
[20] Secrest, William B., *Lawmen and Desperadoes: A Compendium of Noted, Early California Peace Officers, 1850-1900*, Arthur H. Clark Company, Spokane, Washington, 1994, pages 252-256.
[21] *Ibid.*
[22] *Stockton Daily Independent*, August 15, 1889.
[23] *Ibid.*
[24] *Ibid.*
[25] *Daily Alta California*, September 5, 1889.
[26] *Stockton Daily Independent*, August 15, 1889.
[27] *Ibid.*
[28] *Ibid.*
[29] *Stockton Daily Independent*, August 15, 16, 17, 1889.
[30] *Stockton Daily Independent*, August 16, 1889.
[31] *Stockton Daily Independent*, August 15, 1889.
[32] *Ibid.*

[33] *Stockton Daily Independent,* August 16, 1889.
[34] *Ibid.*
[35] *Stockton Daily Independent,* August 17, 1889.
[36] *Ibid.*
[37] *San Jose Herald,* August 17, 1889.
[38] *Daily Alta California,* August 18, 1889.
[39] *Ibid.*
[40] *Daily Alta California,* August 28, 1889.
[41] *San Jose Herald,* September 16, 1889.
[42] *Daily Alta California,* October 15, 1889.
[43] *The American Law Register (1852-1891)* Vol. 38, No. 10, New Series Volume 29 (Second Series, Vol. 3) (Oct., 1890), pp. 658-719 (62 pages) Published by: The University of Pennsylvania Law Review.
[44] *San Jose Mercury News,* February 15, 1892; *San Francisco Call,* March 12, 1892; *San Francisco Call-Bulletin,* February 15, 1937.

10. ROUTINE

[1] *Sacramento Daily Record Union,* September 25, 1889.
[2] *Morning Union,* September 27, 1889.
[3] *Sacramento Daily Union,* November 8, 1889.
[4] *San Jose Mercury News,* November 19, 1889.
[5] *Daily Alta California,* November 29, 1889.
[6] *Los Angeles Herald,* March 18, 1890.
[7] *Sacramento Daily Record Union,* April 15, 1890; *Daily Alta California,* April 15, 16, 1890; *Placer Herald,* April 19, 1890.
[8] *Ibid.*
[9] *Los Angeles Herald,* April 19, 1890
[10] *San Francisco Call,* June 29, 1890.
[11] *San Francisco Call,* July 22, August 29, 1890.
[12] *San Francisco Call,* September 7, 1890.
[13] *San Francisco Call,* September 12, 1890.
[14] *San Francisco Call,* September 28, 1890.
[15] *Stockton Daily Independent,* November 14, 1890.

[16] *Stockton Daily Independent*, November 15, 1890.

[17] Stockton City Directory, 1891.

[18] *Daily Alta California*, February 7, 14, 1891; *San Francisco Call*, February 8, 14, 1891; *Los Angeles Herald*, February 8, 1891.

[19] Secrest, William B., *Lawmen and Desperadoes: A Compendium of Noted, Early California Peace Officers, 1850-1900*, Arthur H. Clark Company, Spokane, Washington, 1994, pages 108-110.

[20] *Sacramento Daily Record Union*, February 15, 1891.

[21] *San Jose Herald*, January 20, 1891; *Sacramento Daily Union*, February 15, 1891.

[22] Statutes of California, Twenty-Ninth Session of the Legislature, 1891, Chapter CXCI, *An Act to Establish a Penal Code*, approved February 14, 1872, amended Section1, 1217 (approved March 31, 1891), State Office of Printing, Sacramento, 1891; *Santa Barbara Morning Press*, April 12, 1891; *Santa Cruz Sentinel*, April 17, 1891.

[23] Ruse, R. Tod, *Stockton Police Department, A History 1850-1990*, Graphic Publishers, 1991, Santa Ana, California, page 55.

[24] *Daily Alta California*, May 14, 1891.

[25] *Sacramento Daily Record Union*, June 13, 1891.

[26] *Los Angeles Herald*, July 19, 1891; https://calsheriffs.org.

[27] *San Francisco Call*, August 23, 1891; *San Jose Mercury News*, August 24, 1891.

[28] *Sacramento Daily Record Union*, September 4, 1891.

[29] *Ibid*.

[30] *Ibid.*.

[31] *Los Angeles Herald*, September 6, 1891.

[32] *San Francisco Call*, September 5, 1891.

[33] *San Bernardino Daily Courier*, January22, 1890.

[34] *San Luis Obispo Morning Tribune*, February 24, 1889.

[35] *San Francisco Call*, September 6, 1891.

[36] *Los Angeles Herald*, September 6, 1891.

[37] *San Francisco Call*, September 8, 1891.

[38] *San Diego Union and Daily Bee*, September 13, 1891.

[39] *San Francisco Call*, December 27, 1891; *Sacramento Daily Record Union*, December 29, 1891.

[40] *San Francisco Call*, January 17, 1892.
[41] *San Francisco Call*, February 6, 1892.
[42] *San Francisco Call*, February 25, 1892.
[43] *Sacramento Daily Record Union*, February 27, 1892.
[44] *San Francisco Call*, April 9, 1892.
[45] *San Francisco Call*, June 23, 24, 1892
[46] *San Francisco Call*, July 14, 1892.
[47] Advertisement on cover of Cunningham's annual peace officer publication.
[48] *Santa Barbara Morning Press*, August 5, 1892.
[49] *Los Angeles Herald*, August 6, 1892.
[50] *San Francisco Call*, August 6, 1892.
[51] *Ibid.; Sonoma Democrat*, August 13, 1892.
[52] *San Francisco Call*, August 6, 1892; *San Diego Union*, August 7, 1892.
[53] *San Francisco Call*, August 7, 1892.
[54] *Hanford Journal*, September 9, 1892.
[55] *San Francisco Chronicle*, June 13, 14, 1893.
[56] *San Francisco Call*, October 20, 1892; *Sacramento Daily Record Union*, October 20, 1892.
[57] *Ibid.*
[58] *Sacramento Daily Record Union*, January 23, 1893.
[59] *Ibid.*
[60] *San Francisco Call*, March 13, 1893.
[61] *San Francisco Call*, March 24, 1893.
[62] Statutes of California, Thirtieth Session of the Legislature, 1893, Chapter CCXXXIV, Section 60, *An Act to establish a uniform system of county and township governments,* approved March 24, 1893, State Office of Printing, Sacramento, 1893.
[63] *Los Angeles Herald*, March 12, 1893; *San Francisco Call*, May 31, 1893.
[64] *Stockton Record*, January 6, 1903.
[65] *San Francisco Call*, June 2, 1893; *Colusa Daily Sun*, June 4, 1893; *Stockton Evening Mail*, February 12 1909.
[66] *Stockton Evening Mail*, February 12 1909.
[67] *San Francisco Call*, June 18, July 4, 1893.
[68] *San Francisco Call*, September 7, 1893.

⁶⁹ *Ibid.*
⁷⁰ *Ibid.; San Francisco Call*, September 8, 1893.
⁷¹ *Santa Cruz Sentinel*, October 19, 1893; *San Francisco Call*, October 20, 1893.
⁷² *San Francisco Call*, October 31, 1893.

11. DEALING WITH INDUSTRIALS

¹ *Sacramento Daily Record Union*, January 4, 1894.
² *San Francisco Call*, March 3, 1894.
³ *San Jose Mercury News,* March 3, 1894; *San Francisco Call*, March 3, 1894.
⁴ *Stockton Evening Mail*, March 17, 1894.
⁵ *Ibid.*
⁶ *Stockton Record*, April 9, 1894.
⁷ *New York Times*, March 25, April 6, 1894.
⁸ *San Francisco Call*, May 15, 1894.
⁹ *San Francisco Call*, April 18, 1894.
¹⁰ *Chico Weekly Enterprise*, May 4, 1894.
¹¹ *Sacramento Daily Record Union*, May 12, 1894.
¹² *Ibid.*
¹³ *San Francisco Call*, May 15, 1894.
¹⁴ *San Francisco Call*, May 16, 1894.
¹⁵ *San Francisco Call*, May 18, 1894.
¹⁶ *Sacramento Daily Record-Union,* June 7, 2894.
¹⁷ *San Francisco Call*, June 28, 1894.
¹⁸ *Stockton Evening Mail*, February 12, 1902.
¹⁹ *San Francisco Call*, October 24, 25, 30, 1894; *Los Angeles Herald*, October 30, 1894.
²⁰ *San Francisco Call*, November 8, 1894; Stockton Record, July 24, 1895; Ruse, R. Tod, *Stockton Police Department, A History 1850-1990*, Graphic Publishers, 1991, Santa Ana, California, pages 51, 54-55; *Stockton Record*, January 6, 1903.
²¹ *San Francisco Call*, March 1, May 9, 1895.

[22] *San Francisco Call*, March 4, 1895.
[23] *Ibid.*
[24] *San Francisco Call*, March 4, 1895.
[25] *San Francisco Call*, March 10, 1895.
[26] *San Francisco Call*, March 31, *Sacramento Daily Record-Union*, July 27, 1895.
[27] *San Francisco Call*, March 10, 1895.
[28] *Ibid.*
[29] Secrest, William B., *Lawmen and Desperadoes: A Compendium of Noted, Early California Peace Officers, 1850-1900*, Arthur H. Clark Company, Spokane, Washington, 1994, pages 142-145.
[30] *San Francisco Call*, March 31, 1895.
[31] *San Francisco Call*, March 31, 1895; California Peace Officers' Memorial Foundation page, https://camemorial.org.
[32] *Ibid.*
[33] *San Francisco Call*, April 1, 1895.
[34] *San Francisco Call*, April 5, 1895; *Stockton Record*, April 9, 1895.
[35] *Stockton Record*, April 22, April 27, 1895.
[36] *Stockton Record*, May 8, 1895; *Grass Valley Morning Union*, November 28, 1895.
[37] *Stockton Record*, June 28, 1895.
[38] *Stockton Record*, July 23, 24, 1895.
[39] *Sacramento Daily Record Union*, June 20, July 27, 1895.
[40] *Sacramento Daily Record Union*, July 27, 1895.
[41] *San Francisco Call*, July 29, 1895.
[42] *Los Angeles Herald*, July 30, 1895.
[43] *Marysville Daily Appeal*, May 6, 1914.
[44] *Stockton Record*, July 27, 1895.
[45] *Stockton Record*, August 2, 1895.
[46] *Stockton Record*, August 18, 1895.
[47] *San Francisco Call*, October 26, 1895; *Los Angeles Herald*, January 14, 1896.
[48] *San Francisco Call*, November 27, 1895.

12. Death of a Deputy

[1] *Stockton Daily Independent*, November 30, 1895.
[2] *San Francisco Call*, December 1, 1895.
[3] *Stockton Daily Independent*, November 29, 1895.
[4] *San Francisco Call*, December 1, 1895.
[5] *Stockton Daily Independent*, November 20, 1895; *Stockton Evening Mail*, November 29, 1895.
[6] *Stockton Daily Independent*, November 30, 1895.
[7] *Stockton Daily Independent*, November 29, 20, 1895.
[8] *Stockton Evening Mail.* November 29, 1895; *Stockton Daily Independent*, November 29, 1895.
[9] *Ibid.*
[10] *Ibid.*
[11] *Stockton Evening Mail*, November 29, 1895.
[12] *Stockton Evening Mail*, November 29, 1895.
[13] *Stockton Evening Mail*, November 30, 1895.
[14] *Ibid.*
[15] *Stockton Evening Mail*, December 1, 1895.
[16] *Stockton Daily Independent*, November 30, 1895, *Stockton Record*, December 8, 1895.
[17] San Francisco Call, December 3, 1895; *Stockton Daily Independent*, December 3, 1895.
[18] *Stockton Daily Independent*, December 4, 1895.
[19] *Stockton Record*, December 8, 1895.
[20] *Stockton Record*, December 10, 1895.
[21] *Stockton Record*, December 19, 1895.
[22] *Ibid.*
[23] *Ibid.*
[24] *Stockton Evening Mail*, December 19, 1895.
[25] *Ibid.*
[26] *Stockton Evening Mail*, December 19, 1895.
[27] *Stockton Record*, December 25, 1895.
[28] *Stockton Evening Mail*, January 8, 1896.
[29] *Ibid.*

[30] *Stockton Evening Mail,* January 8, 1896.
[31] *Ibid.*

13. EMBEZZLERS, STICK-UP MEN AND THUGS

[1] *San Francisco Call,* January 7, 1896.
[2] *San Francisco Call,* March 10, 1896; *Stockton Record,* March 41, 1896.
[3] *San Luis Obispo Morning Tribune,* May 7, 1896.
[4] *San Francisco Call,* May 20, 1896.
[5] *San Francisco Call,* May 20, May 21, 1896.
[6] *San Francisco Call,* May 20, 1896; *Los Angeles Herald,* November 24, 1897.
[7] *San Francisco Call,* June 7, 1896; *Stockton Record,* June 7, 1896.
[8] *Ibid.*
[9] *Hanford Journal,* September 18, 1896.
[10] *San Francisco Call,* October 9, 1896.
[11] *San Francisco Call,* December 20, 1896.
[12] *San Francisco Call,* December 23, 1896.
[13] *Stockton Record,* January 7, 1897; *San Francisco Call,* January 7, 1897.
[14] *Ibid.*
[15] *San Francisco Call,* January 13, 1897.
[16] *Sacramento Daily Record Union,* February 1, 1897.
[17] *Sacramento Daily Record Union,* February 3, 1897.
[18] *Ibid.*
[19] *San Francisco Call,* March 21, 1897; *Stockton Record,* July 26, 27, October 5, 21, 1897, April 16, 1898.
[20] *San Francisco Call,* April 7, 1897.
[21] *Stockton Record,* April 15, 1897.
[22] *Ibid.*
[23] *Santa Cruz Sentinel,* April 16, 1897.
[24] *San Francisco Call,* April 24, 1897.
[25] *Sacramento Daily Record Union,* May 5, 1897; *The Weekly Calistogian,* December 17, 1897.
[26] *San Francisco Call,* May 25, 1897.

[27] *Stockton Record*, May 28, 1897.
[28] *Ibid.*
[29] *Stockton Record*, May 29, 1897.
[30] *Stockton Record*, July 8, 1897.

14. THE TRAIN WRECKERS

[1] *Stockton Daily Independent*, September 7, 1897
[2] *Ibid.*
[3] *Stockton Evening Mail*, September 16, 1897.
[4] *Stockton Evening Mail*, September 10, 1897.
[5] *Stockton Evening Mail*, September 14, 1897; *San Francisco Chronicle*, September 10, 1897; *Stockton Daily Independent*, September 10, 1897.
[6] *Stockton Evening Mail*, September 9, 10, 1897.
[7] *Stockton Evening Mail*, September 10, 1897; *San Francisco Chronicle*, September 10, 1897.
[8] *Ibid.*
[9] *Ibid.*
[10] *Stockton Evening Mail*, September 10, 1897.
[11] *Stockton Evening Mail*, September 9, 10, 1897; *Stockton Daily Independent*, September 9, 1897; *San Francisco Chronicle*, September 9, 1897.
[12.] *Stockton Evening Mail*, September 13, 1897.
[13] *Stockton Evening Mail*, September 15, 16, 17, 1897.
[14] *Stockton Evening Mail*, September 16, 1897.
[15] *Ibid.*
[16] *Stockton Evening Mail*, September 14, 1897.
[17] *Stockton Evening Mail*, September 10, 1897.
[18] *Ibid.*

15. End of an Era

[1] *Stockton Record*, September 13, 18, 29, 1897.
[2] *San Francisco Call*, October 23, 1897.
[3] *Livermore Herald*, December 11, 1897.
[4] *Stockton Record*, January 4, 1898.
[5] *Stockton Record*, March 11, 1898.
[6] *Stockton Record*, March 25, 1898; *Sacramento Daily Record Union*, April 2, 1898; *San Francisco Call*, April 5, May 17, 1898.
[7] *San Francisco Call*, April 2, 14, 1898; *Stockton Record*, April 16, 1898.
[8] *San Francisco Call*, May 8, 1898; *Los Angeles Herald*, May 20, June 11, July 2, 1898; *Stockton Daily Independent*, July 21, 1898.
[9] *Stockton Daily Independent*, July 21, 1898.
[10] *San Francisco Call*, August 14, 1898; *Stockton Record*, August 15, 1898.
[11] *San Francisco Daily Morning Call*, November 23, 1898.
[12] *San Francisco Call*, September 16, 1898.
[13] *San Francisco Call*, September 16, 20, 1898.
[14] *Stockton Record*, November 25, 1898.
[15] *Stockton Record*, November 15, December 6, 1898.
[16] *Stockton Record*, December 24, 1898.
[17] *Stockton Record*, December 31, 1898.
[18] *Ibid.*
[19] *Stockton Record*, January 3, 1899.
[20] *Hanford Journal*, January 6, 1899.

16. An Honorable Name

[1] *San Francisco Call*, January 7, 1899.
[2] *Stockton Record*, January 12, 1899.
[3] *Stockton Record*, October 4, 1899.
[4] *Amador Ledger*, November 30, 1900.
[5] *Stockton Daily Record*, November 27, 1900.
[6] *Oakland Tribune*, November 26, 1900.
[7] *Fresno Republican*, November 29, 1900.

[8] *San Francisco Call*, November 27, 1900.
[9] *Stockton Daily Independent*, November 29, 1900.
[10] *Stockton Daily Record*, November 29, 1900.
[11] *Stockton Daily Record*, November 30, 1900.
[12] *San Francisco Call*, January 5, 1911.
[13] *Stockton Daily Evening Record*, January 21, 1911.
[14] *Santa Cruz Evening News*, January 21, 1926.
[15] *Stockton Evening Mail*, February 12, 1902.
[16] *Stockton Daily Independent*, February 11, 1914, March 15, 1919.
[17] *Stockton Daily Independent*, November 18, 1905, June 14, 1907, February 22, 1918.
[18] *Stockton Daily Record*, January 6, 1903.
[19] *San Francisco Call*, February 4, 1910.

BIBLIOGRAPHY

BOOKS

Dillon, Richard, *Wells, Fargo Detective, a Biography of James B. Hume*, University of Nevada Press, Reno, 1986.

Greenwood, Robert, *The California Outlaw*, Los Gatos, California, Talisman Press, 1960.

Hume, James and Thacker, John, *Wells, Fargo & Co Report of Losses, 1870-1884*, 125th anniversary edition edited by R. Michael Wilson, Las Vegas NV, RaMa Press, 2007.

Johnson, J. Edward, *History of the California Supreme Court: The Justices 1850-1900, vol. 1*, 1963.

Ruse, R. Tod, *Stockton Police Department, A History 1850-1990*, Graphic Publishers, 1991, Santa Ana, California,

Secrest, William B., *Lawmen and Desperadoes: A Compendium of Noted, Early California Peace Officers, 1850-1900*, Arthur H. Clark Company, Spokane, Washington, 1994.

Stockton City Directory, 1891.

Tinkham, George H. *History of San Joaquin County*, Historic Record Publishing Company: Los Angeles, 1923.

Unpublished Works

Blansett, Eual Desmond, Jr., *Death Without Honor, Legal Executions in the History of San Joaquin County,* unpublished, Stockton, California, 1994.

Wells, Fargo History Room, San Francisco, papers of James Hume

Court Records

The American Law Register (1852-1891) Vol. 38, No. 10, New Series Volume 29 (Second Series, Vol. 3) (Oct., 1890), pp. 658-719 (62 pages), The University of Pennsylvania Law Review.

Ogden Hoffman, *Reports of Land Cases Determined in the United States District Court for the Northern District of California,* Numa Hubert, San Francisco, 1862.

People v. French, 69 Cal. 169, pages 270-280.

Government Records

Statutes of California, Nineteenth Session of the Legislature, 1871-1872, Chapter DXCII, Section 5, *An Act to regulate the salaries and fix the compensation of the county officers of San Joaquin County,* passed April 1, 1872, page 875, State Office of Printing, Sacramento, 1872.

California State Archives, letter from Harry N. Morse to Governor Newton Booth, March 21, 1874.

California State Archives, letter from H.N. Morse to Governor Newton Booth, April 12, 1874.

California Constitution, passed and ratified May 7, 1879.

Statutes of California, Twenty-Ninth Session of the Legislature, 1891, Chapter CXCI, *An Act to Establish a Penal Code,* approved February 14, 1872, amended Section 1, 1217 (approved March 31, 1891), State Office of Printing, Sacramento, 1891.

Statutes of California, Thirtieth Session of the Legislature, 1893, Chapter CCXXXIV, Section 60, *An Act to establish a uniform system of county and township governments,* approved March 24, 1893, State Office of Printing, Sacramento, 1893.

Newspapers – California

Amador Ledger (Jackson)
Daily Alta California (San Francisco)
Calaveras Weekly Citizen (San Andreas)
Chico Weekly Enterprise
Colusa Daily Sun
Evening Mail (Stockton)
Fresno Expositor
Grass Valley Morning Press
Hanford Journal
Humboldt Times (Eureka)
Livermore Herald
Los Angeles Herald
Los Angeles Star
Los Angeles Times
Madera Morning Tribune
Marysville Daily Appeal
Marysville Daily National Democrat
Pacific Rural Press (San Francisco)
Placer Argus (Auburn)
Placer Herald (Rocklin)

Red Bluff Sentinel
Sacramento Daily Record Union
Sacramento Daily Union
San Bernardino Daily Courier
San Diego Union
San Diego Union and Daily Bee
San Francisco Bulletin
San Francisco Call
San Francisco Chronicle
San Francisco Examiner
San Joaquin Republican (Stockton)
San Jose Daily Morning Times
San Jose Herald
San Jose Mercury News
San Luis Obispo Morning Tribune
Santa Barbara Morning Press
Santa Cruz Evening News
Santa Cruz Weekly Sentinel
Santa Rosa Press Democrat
Sonoma Democrat
Stockton Daily Evening Herald
Stockton Daily Independent
Stockton Evening Mail
Stockton Record
Weekly Calistogian (Calistoga)

Newspapers – Other States

Carson Appeal (Carson City, Nevada)
Chicago Times (Chicago, Illinois)
Denver Tribune (Denver, Colorado)
New York Times (New York, New York)
New York Sun (New York, New York)
Tombstone Epitaph (Tombstone, Arizona)

Websites

bioguideretro.congress.gov

California Peace Officers' Memorial Foundation page, https://camemorial.org.

California State Sheriffs' Association
https://calsheriffs.org.

California State Library
https://www.library.ca.gov

CPI Inflation Calculator on-line
https://www.bls.gov/data/inflation_calculator.htm

govtrack.us/congress/william_sharon

historysanjose.org

Houston Gun Collector's Association, hgca.org

In Time and Place, intimeandplace.org

https://www.onlinenevada.org/articles/william-sharon

https://scvhistory.com

U.C. Berkeley, Bancroft Library
https://www.lib.berkeley.edu

United States Library of Congress
https://loc.gov

PERIODICALS

MacCracken, Brooks W., *American Heritage Magazine*, June 1967, Volume 18, Issue 4.

Urie, Phillip R., Knife-Wielding Judge, article in the *Wild West Magazine*, February 1993.

INDEX

A

Acampo, San Joaquin County, 101
Ackerman, Charles, 185-186
Adams, Augustus, 31
Adams County, Illinois, 273
Adams, John, ix, 44-45, 48, 55, 61
Ah Goon, 274
Ah Meng, 97
Ah Nam, 58
Ah Shoo, 58
Ah You, 105
Ahern, Detective, 237
Alameda County, California, ix, 16, 34, 39, 48, 53, 69, 80, 109, 125, 156, 173, 190, 292, 316
Aldridge, Albert (Bert), 136-137
Aldridge, J. M. (Lon), 136-137
Alila, Tulare County, 196, 202
Alta baseball club ("Alta's"), 146-147
Altaville, Calaveras County, 15
Amador County, California, 14, 40, 70, 111, 115, 134-135, 140, 205, 272
American Express Company, 277
Anderson, Alfred, 17-18
Anderson, Charles, 223
Anderson, Edward, 88
Andrus Island, Sacramento County, 84
Angels Camp, Calaveras County, 223, 312
Anson (railroad brakeman), 158
Antioch, Contra Costa County, 106
Antone (true name: Garcia, Antonio), 38
Arata, Joseph, 205

Arizona, 160, 177, 258
Arizona Bill (true name: Waite, William), 97
Arroyo Seco, Los Angeles County, 52-53
Ashe, Porter, 170, 173
Ashley, J. T., 111
Atkinson, William, 64
Atwood, Oscar F., 77, 85, 96, 101-102, 129, 141
Auburn, Placer County, 70
Aull, Charles, 108-110
Austin, Henry, 219
Austin, Mrs. Henry, 219

B

Bacon, E., 65
Bailey, A. W., 131
Bailey, Susan E., 85-86, 97
Bailey, William J., 213-214, 217-218, 227
Baker, Henry, 212
Baker, John (true name: Tison, Henry Sr.), 262
Bakersfield, Kern County, 44, 160
Baldwin, Barry, 276
Ballou, S. D., 268
Bank of California, 164
Bank, N. G., 162
Banks, C. P., 162
Banta to Grayson stage, 115, 132
Banta, San Joaquin County, 7-8, 55, 115, 132, 157, 221, 282
Bantas (see Banta)
Barker, (constable), 149
Barker, John, 225-228
Barker's army, 226
Barnes, Thomas, 14-15
Barton, Daniel, 97
Beach, Myron, 141, 145, 253, 279-280

Beal's Photography, 110
Beaver, Oscar, 209, 211
Beck, Henry, 120, 125
Beede, W. M., 157
Bellota, San Joaquin County, 39
Belmont, San Mateo County, 244
Ben Ali Switch, Sacramento County, 232, 238
Benjamin, Charles Dewitt, 1
Benjamin, Elizabeth (Cunningham), 1
Benjamin, Thomas, 141, 145, 153, 179, 190-191, 211-212, 223, 262, 276, 285, 295, 297, 319-320
Bennett, Abraham B., 4-6, 27, 33, 65, 307, 309
Bennett, George, 22-23
Benson's Ferry, 81, 84
Bentley (doctor), 265
Bentley, Ed, 158-160
Berenda, Madera County, 50, 274
Bertola's Saloon, 278
Beyer, Emma, 59
Beyer, George, 59
Bidwell (Superintendent of Streets), 279
Big Oak Flat, Tuolumne County (Groveland), 70
Biggs Station, Butte County, 97, 242
Bing, Lum, 105
Bissell (police officer), 129
Black Bart (true name: Boles, Charles), 124-128, 300
Black, George H., 195, 201, 236-237, 244, 253, 272-274, 279-280, 286-287, 289, 295-298, 301, 319
Blair, Sherman, 149-150
Blanther, Joseph E., 269-271
Board of Associated Charities, 259
Board of State Prison Directors, 234
Board of Supervisors, x, 10, 105, 198, 232, 241, 267, 277, 280, 300, 302
Bogard, John J., 239, 241, 243
Boggs, John, 111
Boggs, Katherine (Cunningham), 315

Boles, Charles ("Black Bart"), 125-127
Bolton, Charles (true name: Boles, Charles), 125, 129
Booker, Samuel, 40
Booth, Newton, 44, 48, 51
Borland, Alexander, 275
Bossenecker, John, ix, 66
Bowers, Mart, 242
Bowler, Miles, 283
Brady, Jack (true name: Williams, Henry), 240, 242-243
Bragg, C., 64
Brannon, John, 30
Breen, Jack, 298
Breeze, William, 130
Brennan (Father), 142-143, 145
Brewer (Judge), 187
Briggs, William, 36
Broderick, David C., 169
Brooke (General), 225
Brown, Charles, 192-193
Brown, Frank, 28
Brown, James, 232, 241
Brown, John (alias Douglas, alias Foster), 59
Brown, Mitchell (alias "Little Mitch"), 68, 70-71, 74, 76
Brown, Oscar (true name: Browning, Oscar S.), 240
Browning, Oscar S. (alias Brown, Oscar), 240
Bryant, Al, 33-34
Bryant, Harry, 274
Buckley (Justice), 60
Buckskin, 177
Budd, James, 49, 185-186, 265-266, 309
Buell and Company, 269
Burke, F. F., 60-61
Burnham, J. H., 212, 236, 256
Burnham, O. N., 102
Bush, U. G., 162
Bustamonte, Procopio, 41

Butte County, California, 72, 75-76, 97
Butts, George, 87
Buzzell, Joseph, 221, 244, 250-254, 256, 259-261, 263, 265-266
Buzzell, Mary, 255
Buzzell, Willard, 254
Byrnes, Maurice, 263

C

Cadwallader, Chales H. (alias Wilber, E. H.) 301
Calaveras County, California, 15-16, 63, 70-72, 75-76, 93, 97, 107, 111, 122-124, 127, 129, 134-136, 140, 157, 192, 205, 223
Calhower, Chales (true name: Hart), 140
California Navigation and Improvement Company, 301
California State Sheriffs' Association, 200
California Supreme Court, 19, 25, 49, 100-101, 130, 141, 167-168
Camanche, Calaveras County, 70
Campbell, J. C., 180-181
Campbell, James (alias Wright, E. C.), 130
Campbell, Joseph, 143
Campbell, Thomas, 193
Campbell, William, 140
Canyon Pass, San Bernardino County, 45
Cape Girardeau, Missouri, 165
Caroline Z, schooner, 17
Carpenter's Army, 227
Carrillo, Charles, 200-201
Carson City, Nevada, 87, 140
Carver's Wild America Circus, 206
Casey, James, 133
Cassidy, Bernard "Barney", 141, 145, 179-180, 194, 256, 262, 295, 297, 319
Castle Switch, San Joaquin County, 234, 238-239, 242
Castle, George H., 25-26, 68, 194
Castoria Township, San Joaquin County, 20, 139, 298
Castro, Jose, 41

Catholic Cemetery, 28, 145
Cavis, J. M., 25
Central Methodist Episcopal Church, 63
Central Pacific Railroad, 7, 23, 59, 87, 91
Ceres, Stanislaus County, 201-203, 207
Chaboya, Anastasio, 119
Chamberlin, John, 154-155
Chamberlin, Mrs., 154-155
Chandler, (outlaw), 158
Charles Haas and Sons, 309
Charley (see Everson, Charles), 33
Chavez, Cleodoveo, 41-42, 45, 47, 55
Childs (thief), 152
Chinese Camp to Copperopolis stage, 74
Chinese Camp, Tuolumne County, 15, 70
Cholame Valley, San Luis Obispo County, 196
Circus Jack, 152
City Mills of Sperry and Company, 114
Clark (doctor), 256
Clark, George, 87
Clear Creek, Shasta County, 242
Clements, San Joaquin County, 130, 192
Cleveland, Volney, 616
Cliff House, 237-238
Clifton, William, 83, 310
Coast Range mountains, 39, 47, 50-51, 53, 132, 156, 160, 196, 248, 299
Coast Stage Lines, 115
Cochise County, Arizona, 177
Coffeeville, Kansas, 196
Coggins, John, 115
Cogswell (cashier), 228
Coleman, H. B., 245-273
Collegeville, San Joaquin County, 149
Collins, Richard (alias Fighting Dick), 80
Collins, William H., 25, 33
Collis, Fresno County, 207, 209

Colorado, 107
Columbia, Tuolumne County, 15, 70
Colusa County, 148
Commercial Hotel, 96
Confer, Lillian M. (Cunningham), 315
Congregational Church, 259
Conroy, W. C., 200, 233
Contant, George (Sontag), 209296
Contra Costa County, California, 49, 69, 106, 296
Cook, Bernard, 267
Cook, George, 282, 286, 292
Cooper, Matthew, 30
Copperopolis, Calaveras County, 74, 112, 123, 127
Copperopolis Road, 23
Cornell, Mary, 102
Cornell, Richard, 102
Cornwall, William, 97
Cosgrove, (New York detective), 194
Cotta, Phillip, 62
Coulterville, Mariposa County, 223
County Court, 93
Courtland, Sacramento County, 84, 130, 242
Cox, George, 199
Coxey, Jacob, 224, 226, 229
Coxeyites, 224-225
Coxey's Army, 224
Coyne, Joseph, 153
Craig, John, 279-280, 296
Crandall, William, 129, 141, 145
Crist, Daniel, 35
Cross Creek, Tulare County, 298
Crossley, N. D., 190-191
Crow, John, 101
Crowley, James, 224, 240
Crowley, Patrick, 101-102, 139, 183, 186, 190, 204
Crows Landing, Stanislaus County, 289

Crum, Jim, 107-111
Cuneo, Andrew, 205
Cunningham, Catherine (Mrs. Littebrandt), 1
Cunningham, Catherine (Quirk), 3-4, 63-64, 318
Cunningham, Charles (true name: Everson, Charles), 34
Cunningham, Elizabeth (Mrs. Benjamin), 1
Cunningham, Lillian M. (Mrs. Confer), 4, 312, 315
Cunningham, Margaret E. "Maggie" (Mrs. Higginbothem), 4, 134, 312, 315
Cunningham, Thomas, boyhood, 1; move to California, 1; leather businesses, 1-2; citizenship, 2; Eureka Engine Company 2, 2-4; marriage, 3-4; Stockton Fire Department, 4-6; Stockton City Council, 5-6; election as sheriff, 5-6; Cunningham's Rangers, 299; retirement, 305, 308-310; death of, 312-313, 315-317
Cunningham's Castle, 214-215

D

Dalton, Bob, 196, 202
Dalton, Emmet, 196, 202
Dalton, Grat, 196
Dalton, Peter (alias Mountain Spirit, Nick of the Woods), 90-91
Dalton, William, 203
Dane, Charles (true name: Hart), 140
Davis, Yolo County, 110
Davisville, see Davis
Davis, William, 97
Dean, Henry, 233-234
Dean, Riley, 203
Deitrich, Julius, 120-121
Deitrich, Mrs., 120-121
Delano, Kern County, 158-159
Den, Chan, 157
Denig, William "Pony", 217

Denson, Richard, 91
Dent Township, San Joaquin County, 274
Department of the Platt, 225
Devin, Bennett, 204
Devries (deputy distrct attorney), 266
Dial, Charles H., 30-31, 192
Diarmid, Mathew, 296
Dickerson (burglar), 192
District Court, xv, 19, 40, 93, 170
Ditz Brothers, 207
Ditz, George Jr., 181
Dodge, Charles, 275
Doro, Emil, 192
Doty's Ravine, Placer County, 75
Dougherty, Lemuel (New Zealand Bill), 148, 153
Douglas, John (true name: Brown, John), 59
Douglass, David, 105
Douillard, Franck, 20, 28-29
Downey, John, 88,
Drew, M. M., 88
Drew, Warren F., 199
Dudley, Mr., 106
Dudley, P. W., 31
Duncan, James, 16
Dunham (outlaw), 279
Dunne, Charles, 296, 298
Durham, Thomas, 240
Durkin, Bob (alias Russell, John), 22
Durrant, Theodore, 296
Dutch Corners, Tulare County, 61
Dye, Troy, 88

E

Earl, Harry M., 275
Eastman, George, 79-80
Eaton, Edwin, 58
Edgerton, John, 30
Egan, E. M., 295
El Capitan Hotel, 202
El Dorado County, California, 100, 111, 117
El Tejon, Kern County, 55
Elizabeth Lake, Los Angeles County, 44-45, 53
Elk Grove, Sacramento County, 150, 227
Elks Lodge, 318
Elmore, Arthur "Al", 7, 14
Emmett Guard, 131
Ennis (San Joaquin County supervisor), 228
Estrada, Domingo, 62
Eubanks, Martin, 93-94
Eureka Engine Co 2, 3-6, 24, 28, 90, 97, 114, 305, 318
Evans and O'Brien, 62
Evans, Chris, 209, 211, 279, 288
Evans, James J., 31-32, 77-78
Everson, Charles (alias Charley), 34

F

Fagan, Frank, 60
Farish, A. D., 172
Farmers' Union Warehouse, 298
Farmington, San Joaquin County, 28, 60, 193
Farney (robber), 14
Faville, Ralph, 49
Fay's ranch, 161

Fick, H. L., 192
Fiddletown, Amador County, 76
Field, Stephen J., 169-176, 178-180, 182-185, 187-188, 310
Fields, Charles, 88-89, 103-105, 129, 138, 141, 212
Fighting Dick (true name: Collins, Dick), 80
Fillmore, J. A., 201
Finch (constable), 132
Finnegass, Henry, 172
Finnell, Michael, 212, 256
First National Bank, 243
Fitzgerald (constable), 296
Fitzgerald, Eli, 102
Folks, John H., 200
Folsom Prison, xiv, 93, 106, 113, 116, 118, 139, 145, 153, 155, 198, 205, 224, 240, 243
Forbestown to Oroville stage, 133
Forbestown, Butte County, 72
Forest Springs, Nevada County, 87
Fort Gunnybags, 168
Foster, John (true name: Brown, John), 59
Fox, C., 200
Frage, Antonio, 83-84
Frank, Charles E., 162
Franklin, Sacramento County, 161
Franks, John C., 172-174, 177-178, 180, 183-185, 187
Frazee, Ben, 110-111
Frazee, R. S., 157
French Camp, San Joaquin County, 14, 20, 23, 267, 278, 320
French, Uzza, xiv, 134-135, 138, 141-143, 145
Fresno, 175, 272
Fresno County, California, 20, 42, 47-48, 50, 111, 149, 207, 214
Fugitt, John, 133
Fulkerth, A. S., 111, 132-133
Funk Hill, Reynolds Ferry Hill, Calaveras County, 71, 122, 124
FX07 (laundry mark), 300

G

Gabart, Charles, 159
Gagliardo, Mr., 268
Gall, John, 295, 304
Galt, Sacramento County, 16, 86
Gamboa, Luis, 16, 86, 113
Garia, Antonio, 38
Garcia, L., 16
Garibaldi Mine, 108
Garwood's Ferry, 151
Georgetown to Placerville stage, 100
Gibbons, Patrick, 16
Gibson (Thomas, detective San Francisco police), 244
Gibson, E. D., 200
Gibson, Mary, 28
Gibson, William, 181-183
Gifford, George (true name: Hall, Ira), 22
Gilroy, Santa Clara County, 61
Ginn, John, 84
Glenn, Vincent, 203-204
Goodhue, Frank, 161
Goodwin, N. W., 131
Gorham, George C., 183
Goshen, Tulare County, 201-202, 298
Gossett, Hank, 87
Gottschalk, Charles V., 127
Graham (Robert, San Francisco police officer), 275
Graham, Monte, 231
Graham, William, 160
Grand Hotel, xii, 166
Grangers' Business Association of Lodi, 120
Grant Brothers, 248
Grant, Ulysses S., 89
Grass Valley, Nevada County, 140
Gray, John T., 240

Greek George, 55
Green, John R., 240
Greenhorn, Charles (true name: Everson, Charles), 34
Greenwood (thief), 15
Gregory, U. S., 272
Griffin, John, 199
Grimes, Frank, 132
Gould, John, 275

H

Haggin Museum, 320
Haight, Henry H., 34
Hailey, Idaho, 154
Hall, Ira (alias Gifford, George), 22
Hamilton, Albert, 100
Hamilton, Alexander E., 145
Hamilton, Alexander H., 145
Hammond, John, 292
Hancock, Charles (alias Little), 118
Hanks, Robert, 216-217, 220, 231, 280, 295, 297, 320
Harelson, D. O., 6, 16, 21, 33, 59
Harkey, William, 111
Harris, Len, 201
Harris, Nicholas R., 80, 205
Harrison, Benjamin, 237
Harrison, William, 148
Harrold, U. S., 32,
Hart, Charles (alias Calhower, Dane), 140
Harvey, Charles, 157
Hayden (constable), 201
Haywards, Alameda County, 296
Heid, Christopher, 120, 125
Helmore, J. (alias Hughes, John), 229
Henderson, A. B., 49, 51

Henderson, Robert, 130
Henry, Samuel, 228
Herlihy, Widow, 205
Hersom, W. J., 279-280
Hickey, Bill, 209
Hicks, William, 141-142
Higginbothem, Margaret (Cunningham), 315
Higgins (officer, Sacramento police), 229-230
Hill, Sarah Althea (Sharon, Terry), 163-166, 169-170
Hill's Ferry, 8
Hoffman (judge), 170, 184
Hoffman, John, 205
Hoffman, Mrs., 42
Hogan, J. M., 62
Holland, Denny, 295
Hollister, San Benito County, 41, 43
Hook, Thomas K., 66
Hopkins, A. S. and Brothers, 196
Hopkins, James, 87
Hopkins, Sterling A., 168
Horber, Frederick, 17-18
Horn, Henry F., 1-2
Hornitos, Mariposa County, 151
Hotel Marre, 268
House (express messenger), 235
Howe, Charles E., 279-280
Howell, M. D., 205-206, 220
Hulbert (rilroad brakeman), 85-86
Humbolt County, California, 109
Hume, James B., 100, 109, 122, 124-125, 137, 159-160, 202, 237, 240, 295
Hunt, Charles (true name: Everson, Charles), 34
Huppe, Phillip, 204-205
Hurley, Jim, 151-152
Hussey, Arthur, 57

I

Identification Bureau, 304
Independence Saloon, 21
Industrial Army, 225, 227
Industrials, 225-227
Ingle (railroad engineer), 234
Inglesode House, 237-238
Inman (colonel), 226
Ione, Amador County, 14, 76, 99
Irwin, William (governor), 90

J

Jackson, Amador County, 70, 205
Jacobs, Charles (alias Professor Charles), 78-80
James, Edward, 217-218
James, Hiram, 114-115, 147-148, 153-154
James, W. S., 149-150
Jamestown, Tuolumne County, 74, 312-313
Jennings, A. J., 200
Jenny Lind, Calaveras County, 99, 129-130
Jesurum (deputy constable), 201
Johnson (detective), 172
Johnson, Carrie (alias Strauss, Carrie), 104
Johnson, David, 150
Johnson, Frank T., 233-234, 236, 242
Johnson, Gordon, 145
Johnson, James H. E., 87-88
Johnson, Joseph, 274
Johnson, R. S., 284
Johnson, Richard, 17-18

Joice Island, Solano County, 17-18
Jones, George, 276-277
Jones, Stanton P., 107-108
Jones, William, 139
Jones's store, 46
Jorgenson (ranch family), 290

K

Kansas National Bank, 162,
Kay, Eugene, 196, 200, 203, 209
Keagle, A. G. "Del", 195, 199, 283
Kearnes (robber), 139
Kelly (robber), 139
Kelly, Robert, 193-194
Kennedy, William, 59
Kenney, William, 224
Kenyon, Brennis, 212, 279-280
Kern County, California, 160
Keyt, John, 106
Kingsberry, Charles, 120
Kingston, Fresno County, 47-48
Kleupfer, Charles F., 275-276
Knight, N. A., 245
Knight's Landing, Yolo County, 261-262
Knights of Pythias, 318
Knights Templar, 318
Kowalsky (attorney), 140-141
Kurth, Hiram or Herman, 150-151

L

La Porte to Oroville stage, 72
Lachman, Abraham, 87
Lacy, Theodore, 200
Lagunda, Claro, 63
Lamb, John, 146
Landeman and Noakes, 100
Lane, George, 133-134
Lang and Ball, 256
Langfeld, Philepena, 269
Langley, James, 61
Langmaid, Orrin, 15, 93, 101, 136
Langman, O. G., 199
Langwarth's, Stanislaus County, 38
Lastreto, Fernando, 57
Lathrop Hotel, 85, 97, 174
Lathrop train station, 50, 79, 85, 163, 174-175, 180, 282, 286-287, 289, 292
Lathrop, San Joaquin County, 81, 86-87, 100, 129, 139, 150, 160, 178, 182, 186, 190, 243, 285, 298, 310
Laumeister, Charles S., 200
Launcha Plana, Amador County, 14
Lawrence, lbert (true name: Luckhardt), 139
Lawton, W. D., 226-227
Leayan, J. M., 120-121
Lee, Timothy, 109, 130, 161
Lees, Isaiah W., 183, 186, 238, 240, 260, 269, 306, 311, 313
Leffingwell (leader of unemployed group), 277
Legrer, Gustav, 212-213
Leiva, Abdon, 45
Lemaister, George, 233-234
Lenaris, Jose, 68, 73, 76
Lentini, John, 113, 117
Levy, James, 177
Lewis (alias Roper), 59-61

Liebre Hills, Coast Range, 160
Lincoln, Fred, 175
Linden (Foreman ranch), San Joaquin County, 16, 30, 97, 270
Littebrandt, Catherine (Cunningham), 1
Littebrandt, Hartman, 157, 179, 216
Little Mitch (true name: Brown, Mitchell), 68, 70-71, 74, 76
Little Rock Creek Canyon, Los Angeles County, 54
Little, Charles (true name: Hancock), 118
Littlejohn, J. B., 151-152
Livermore, Alameda County, 16, 120, 156, 186, 190, 296
Lockeford, San Joaquin County, 28, 30-31, 192, 274
Lodi Bank, 228
Lodi, San Joaquin County, vi, 33, 35, 70, 114-115, 119-120, 134, 147, 204-205, 213, 217, 227-228, 230, 235-237, 240, 245, 273-274, 276-277
Londerback (judge), 183
Lone Tree Canyon, Coast Range, 132,
Long, C. C., 83
Long, Joseph M., 65-66, 68, 93-94, 106, 129, 141, 143, 145, 179, 194-195, 289, 295, 307, 318-319
Loomis, Boyd, 276-277
Loomis, William, 276-277
Lopez, Manuel, 51
Lord, George, 140
Los Angeles, 41, 52-55, 130, 149, 158, 174-175, 178, 196, 214, 237, 240, 285
Los Angeles County, 40, 45, 48, 50, 54-55, 69, 200, 221, 237, 283, 285, 303
Los Angeles Express, 201, 207, 286
Los Banos Creek, Merced County, 39
Los Banos, Merced County, 264
Los Gatos Canyon, Fresno County, 61
Love (thief), 278
Low, Walter, 298
Loy, Ten, 106
Luckhardt, Albert J. (alias Lawrence) 139
Lynch, James "Billy", 136-137

M

Mack, Harry (true name: McDonald), 149
Mackay, Walter, 267
Macville, San Joaquin County, 133-134
Maddix, Henry, 199
Madera County, 274
Magee, Thomas, 99
Magud, Michel, 223
Maloney (deputy U.S. marshal), 220
Mandorf, John, 108
Manly, George, 133
Margin, Ed, 288
Maria, Jose (alias "Kokimbo"), 68, 72-73, 76
Mariposa County, California, 90, 151, 223, 298
Market Street jail, 13, 15-16, 96, 142, 194
Markey, Samuel, 120-122, 125
Marshall, Oscar, 254, 280
Martin (Black Bart witness), 124, 127
Martin (horse thief), 190
Matin (justice of the peace), 18, 22
Martin, George, 242
Martin, William, 117
Martinez, Contra Costa County, 87
Marysville to Downieville stage, 73
Marysville, Yuba County, 38, 40, 73, 83, 113, 199, 239-240
Masonic, 315
Masterson (Calaveras deputy sheriff), 223
Mathews, David, 91
Maxwell, Colusa County, 148
McCann (deputy constable), 280
McCarthy, Charles (true name: Everson, Charles), 34
McCarthy, George, 93
McCarty, Dan, 115-116
McCarty, George, 97
McCarty, Thomas, 97
McClanahan, W. T., 93
McCloud, Alonso A., 62, 78, 84
McConnell, Reason, 122-124

McCormick, James, 75
McCoy, Henry, 40, 73, 109, 111, 113, 150
McCoy, James, 226
McCraney (Banta constable), 132
McCulloch, Andrew A., 276
McDonald, Harry (alias Mack, Harry), 149
McDougal, Giles E., 200
McDougald bridge, San Joaquin County, 257
McFee's Saloon, 31
Maguire, J. G., 185
McGuire, John (true name: Williams, Henry), 240
McGuire, Sam (true name: Browning, Oscar), 240
McIntyre (thief), 152
McKenna, Thomas, 83, 310
McKenzie, G. S., 200
McKenzie, James, 101
McKowan, Arthur, 199
McLaughlin (baseball player), 147
McLaughlin ranch, 248, 251-252
McMurray, Charles, 62
McQuaid, A. S., 111, 123-124
Meany, Anthony 64
Medina (store murders), 37
Mendocino County, California, ix, 124
Merced County, California, 20, 61, 64, 145, 262, 264
Merced River, 61
Merced, Merced County, 64, 150, 202, 262, 264, 298
Merchants' and Manufacturers' Association, 33
Meridian, Texas, 271
Messick's bridge, San Joaquin County, 60
Micheltorena, Manuel, 119
Michigan Bluff, Placer County, 16
Midway, Alameda County, 16
Miller & Company, 70
Miller, W. H. H., 178
Miller, William, 107-110
Millerton, Madera County (then Fresno County), 46
Mills, Freeman, 24, 38, 66, 194
Milner (justice of the peace), 152

Milpitas, Santa Clara County, 61
Milton, Calaveras County, 16, 70, 73, 93-94, 108-109, 124, 127, 136-137, 270
Miner, William "Billy", 66-67, 106-110
Mission San Jose, 61
Mitchell, H. M., 54, 149
Modesto, Stanislaus County, 80-81, 111, 143, 158, 203, 287, 289
Mohr's Landing, San Joaquin County, 186
Mokelumne Hill Road, 16
Mokelumne Hill to Ione stage, 99
Mokelumne to Lodi stage, 70
Mokelumne River, 14, 84, 204, 245
Monterey County, California, 40, 44, 47, 50, 115-116, 200-201, 231
Montgomery, William, 86, 90-91
Montpellier, Idaho, 225
Moore, Henry, 118
Moore, John D., 64
Moquelumnes, 119, 130-131
Moquelemos, 119, 125
Moran, Frank, 139
Morano Switch, San Joaquin County, 281, 286, 292
Morehouse, (William, San Francisco police officer), 68
Morehouse, Lewis, 39
Morning Star Lodge of Masons, 318
Morris, Amos, 115
Morris, Archie, 275
Morse Detective Agency, 125
Morse, F. N., 73
Morse, George, 49
Morse, Harry, ix, 34, 39, 44, 48-51, 53-55, 61, 80, 125, 127-128, 316, 318
Mortimer, Charles, 28
Moss, William, 193-194
Mossdale Crossing, San Joaquin County, 244, 248, 251, 253-254, 288
Mother Lode, iii, x, 15, 119
Mountain Spirit (true name: Dalton, Peter), 90
Mulligan, William, 167
Mullen, Dennis, 101
Mullins, Kevin, ix
Murphy, Eugene, 133

Murphy, John J., 24-28, 81, 143
Murphy, Tilly, 149
Murphy, William, 223
Murphys, Calaveras County, 15
Murray, Edward, 120
Murray, Frank, 211-212
Murray, Patrick, 24-25, 27
Murrietta, Joaquin, 37
Musuem (Cunningham's), xiii, 84, 199, 284, 300, 320
Myers, Jerome, 21, 28, 57, 62, 66, 75, 83, 106

N

Napa County, California, 41, 118
Napa, Napa County, 118, 200
National Guard, 80, 131-132
Neagle, David (also spelled Nagle by newspapers), 174-182, 185-188, 310
Neilson, E. C., 268-269
Nelson, Charles, 233-234
Nevada City, Nevada County, 87, 140
Nevada County, California, 86, 90, 133, 140
New Hope (Thornton), San Joaquin County, 81, 105, 113, 203-204, 275-276

New Idria, San Benito County (then Moneterey County), 47, 55
New Zealand Bill (true name: Dougherty, Lemuel), 148, 153
Newman, C. P., 162
Newman, Stanislaus County, 201, 289-290
Nicholas Canyon, Los Angeles County, 55
Nick of the Woods (true name: Dalton, Peter), 90
Nightengale, San Joaquin County, 20
Noriega, Cristobal, 97
Norton, Charles, 139
Nuey, Lin, 68
Nutley, Oliver, 271-272
Nutter, W. B., 302
Nye, John, 94

O

Oakdale, Stanislaus County, 14, 28, 313
Oakland, Alameda County, 49-50, 66, 118, 148, 186, 204, 224-225, 230, 270, 278, 295
O'Byrne's Ferry, Calaveras County, 74
Ogden, Utah, 154
Old Joaquin (true name: Savage, Antone), 68-71, 74
Old River, San Joaquin County, 106
Oleta, Amador County, 134
Olney, Richard, 224
O'Meara, Roger, 100
O'Neal Township, San Joaquin County, 273, 279-280
Opper, Julius, 255-256
Oregon Express, 239
Oroville, Butte County, 59, 64, 75
Otis, E. S., 225
Overall, Daniel, 211
Overland Express, 232, 238
Ozagaras, Jesus, 63
Pacheco Pass, Santa Clara County, 61
Packer (detective), 202
Padilla, Isodore (also Ysidoro, Isodoro), 38, 40, 46, 68, 72-73, 75-76
Padillo, (see Padilla, Isodore)

Page, James D., 183
Palace Hotel, 165
Pardillo (see Padilla, Isodore
Parker (justice of the peace), 265
Parker, Henry, 94, 96-97
Patterson, A. Van R., 138
Patterson-Dorcey, 316
Patterson, J. D., 217
Paynter, A. L., 279-280
Perez, Jesus (true name: Tejada, Jesus), 38
Perrazo, Dominico, 192
Perry, George, 6
Petaluma, Sonoma County, 41
Petty, John, 94, 96-97
Pico, Andres, 119
Pico, Jose, 83
Pinkerton National Detective Agency, 315
Pinkerton, William, 315
Pioche, Nevada, 177
Pixley, Tulare County, 158-159, 202
Placer County, California, 70, 75, 107, 111, 117-118, 145, 150, 192, 200, 233
Placerville, El Dorado County, 71
Pocatello, Idaho, 153
Port Costa, Contra Costa County, 185
Port Harford, San Luis Obispo County, xi, 268-269
Porter (robbery victim), 66
Portland, Oregon, 145, 240
Pounce (train burglar), 87
Presidio at San Francisco, 298
Professor Charles (true name: Jacobs, Charles), 78
Pullman (train car), 230
Purvis, R. B., 289, 298
Pygall, Frank, 115

Q

Quirk, Catherine (Cunningham), 3
Quinn, Michael, 20-21
Quincy, Plumas County, 113

R

Racardo (jail escapee), 23-24
Rahm, Frank, 109
Ralston, W. C., 313
Ramage, Louis, 25
Rancho Sanjon de Los Moquelmnes, 119
Randolph, County, Indiana, 301
Rangers (Cunningham's), 299
Ransom, Samuel, 129
Ratovich, Mitchell (alias Big Mitch), 68, 70-71, 74, 76
Red Antone (true name: Valacca, Antone), 68, 72, 75
Red Men, 318
Redford (teamster), 43
Reed, George, 158
Reed, Mack, 158
Reed's Station, Yuba County, 239, 241
Regan, Cliff, 298
Remington, E. L., 251, 253
Reno, Nevada, 88, 140
Reparto, Alexander, 52
Resley, William, 64
Reynolds and Turner stables, 274
Reynolds Ferry, Calaveras County, 122
Reynolds Ferry Hill (also Funk Hill), 71
Reynolds ranch, 129
Rice, W. H. (true name: Scott, Bob), 148
Richardson, E. T., 219
Riecks, William, 294, 319
Ringer, George, 133

Ripon, San Joaquin County, 135, 274, 281-282
Rix, Alfred, 183
Roberts (burglar), 192
Roberts Island, 136, 181
Robinson, Isaac, 231, 236, 253, 256, 295
Robinson's Ferry, Tuolumne County, 313
Rockwell, J. W., 244-245
Rodgers, John, 80, 109
Rogers (Rowland posse member), 52
Rolf, (Israel, Stockton fire chief), 114
Rolleri, Jimmy, 123-124
Romero, Ramon, 49-50
Roper (true name: Lewis, gambler, con man), 59
Roscoe, Los Angeles County, 221-222, 285
Rossi, Frank, 278
Roth, A. H., 273
Rothschild (store clerk), 270
Rowell, Leonard F., 159
Rowland, William, 45, 48, 52-55
Ruiz, Ramon, 68-75
Russell, James (alias Slim Jim), 59
Russell, John (true name: Durkin, Bob), 22
Rynerson, C. C., 66, 194

S

Sabin, George M., 170, 173, 184, 187
Sacramento County, California, 233, 241-242
Sacramento River, 261
Sacramento, Sacramento County, 189-190, 192, 196-197, 199, 201, 205-206, 212-213, 221, 225-227, 230-233, 236-237, 241-242, 261, 270, 301, 312
Salinas, Monterey County, 150-151, 200-201
Salt Lake City, Utah, 23, 59, 161
Salt Spring Valley, Calaveras County, 15, 70, 135
Sampson, Emma J., 28-29
Sampson, G. W., 20, 24, 28
San Andreas, Calaveras County, 63, 97, 99, 136
San Andreas to Stockton stage, 107

San Benito, San Benito County, 41-44
San Benito River, 43
San Bernardino County, California, 45, 133
San Diego, California, 50, 151, 153, 200
San Fernando Pass, 52
San Fernando Road, 283
San Franciscco, California, x, 1, 7, 11, 14, 17-18, 23, 58-59, 61, 67-68, 78-80, 83, 87, 97, 101-102, 109, 118, 125, 127, 1132, 134, 137, 139-141, 145, 149, 158, 164-169, 174-175, 180, 182-183, 185-187, 190-193, 196-197, 199-200, 204-205, 212, 214, 219-220, 224-245, 260, 269, 275, 277, 295-296, 298, 304, 306, 310-312, 315
San Gabriel Mission, 52
San Gorgonio Pass, 54
San Joaquin Catholic Cemetery, 28, 145
San Joaquin City, San Joaquin County, 132, 222, 284-285, 288
San Joaquin Fair Association, 189
San Joaquin River, x, 17, 24, 42, 50, 80, 111, 151, 156, 160, 244, 248, 250-251, 254, 258, 287-289
San Joaquin Valley, x, 20, 44, 160
San Jose, Santa Clara County, 34, 55, 61, 79, 149, 190-191, 197, 200-201, 244, 299
San Juan Bautista, San Benito County, 43
San Lucas, Monterey County, 201
San Luis Obispo County, California, 55, 191, 268
San Luis Rancho, 55
San Mateo, California, 169, 200, 244
San Quentin Prison, xi, xiv, 20, 30, 36, 40, 49, 59, 61, 63-64, 67, 69, 76-78, 86, 90-91, 97, 99-102, 105-106, 109, 114, 118, 129-130, 133, 138, 140, 153, 162, 193, 198, 204, 219, 224, 232, 240
San Rafael, Marin County, 218-219
Sansome, John, 113-114, 150
Santa Clara County, California, ix, 44-45, 48, 55, 61, 80, 145, 190, 200, 205
Santa Cruz County, California, 49, 198, 200
Santa Lucia Mountains, Coast Range, 51
Saterlee, James, 7
Savage, Antone (alias Old Joaquin), 68-71, 74, 76
Sawyer, Lorenzo, 170, 173
Schaffer (deputy, Alameda deputy sheriff)
Scheld's Brewery, 233

Schlegel, George, 221-222, 282-293
Schmidburg, F. C., 65
Schofield, (John, General), 225
Schultz, Theodore, 151
Schuyler, J., 145
Scott, Bob (alias Rice, W. H.), 148
Scott, Joseph W., 2
Scott, Robert T., 194-195
Sedgwick, Charles, 88
Sell (deputy), 202
Sepulveda, Andronice, 155-156
Seymour, John, 231
Sharon v. Sharon, 163, 174
Sharon, William, 163-167, 169-171, 188
Shasta Butte, 54
Shasta County, California, 241
Sheldon, James, 80
Shepard, J. A., 85-86
Shepherd, George, 298
Shepherd, J. A., 131
Shepherd, James, 273-274
Sheridan, Michael, 102-103
Shine, J. C., 70
Shine, John H., 276
Shippee, L. U., 189
Shortridge, S. M., 313
Shultz, F. W., 91
Sibley, Walter, 68, 303-304, 309, 318
Sierra Madre, Los Angeles County, 45
Sierra Nevadas, x, 140, 282
Silvey, Raymond, 295
Simmons (sheriff), 301
Simpson, (William, captain Stockton police)
Sinclair, John, 66-67
Sink (reverand), 259
Skipa, Nicholas, 223
Slim Jim (true name: Russell, James), 59
Smith, Anne Mrs., 227-228
Smith, Clinton R., 240

Smith, J. H., 36
Smith, James, 20-22
Smith, Jesse, 160
Smith, Mark, 295, 297, 320
Smith, Peter, 133
Smith, Sam, 74
Smith, Will, 202, 209
Smith, W. T., 119
Snedigar (doctor), 256
Snyder (detective), 237
Snyder, Mr. (store owner), 43-44
Snyder, Mrs. (store owner), 43-44
Soderberg, Peter, 245
Solano County, California, 18
Soledad Canyon, Los Angeles County, 53
Soledad, Monterey County, 115-116
Soloman, Matt, 87-88
Sonoma County, California, 40-41
Sonora to Milton stage, 70-71, 73, 108, 122, 135
Sonora, Tuolumne County, 20, 108, 283, 312-313
Sontag, John, 209, 211, 279,288
Southern Pacific Railroad, 158, 160, 196, 201, 209, 230, 237, 269, 277, 281-282, 286
Spaulding, T. Z. (true name: Boles, Charles), 125
Spellman (Catholic priest), 27
Spiegel, Phillip (true name: Huppe), 204
Spooner, J. Pitcher, 127
St. Louis, Missouri, 100, 164, 277
St, Clair, Chauncey, 101
St. Clair, Walter, 101
St. John's Episcopal Church, 182
St. Mary's Catholic Church, 145, 169
Stackpole, Mr. (restaurant proprietor), 175-176
Stagg, Cornelius, 238
Staiger, John, 249, 251-253, 258-260, 265
Standard Oil Company, 129
Stanislaus County, California, 14, 20, 60, 80, 109, 111, 115, 132, 201, 223, 289, 298
Stanislaus River, 38, 60, 71, 77, 80, 122

Sterns, Cicero, 130
Stevens, A. B., 78
Stockiard (deputy), 202
Stockton City Council, 56
Stockton Coronet Band, 3
Stockton fair, 150, 155, 189, 194, 220, 295
Stockton Fire Department, 34, 243, 305
Stockton Guard, 131
Stockton Insane Asylum, 17, 146, 188
Stockton Savings Bank, 243
Stokes Mountain, Tulare County, 211
Stone, Appleton, 83, 127-128, 134
Stoneman, George, 130, 142
Strauss, Carrie (alias Johnson, Carrie), 104
Stringham, Clark, 108
Suisun City, Solano County, 18
Sullivan, Daniel M., 150
Sullivan, Jim, 256
Summers, Alfred, 120-121
Superior Court, 93, 127, 134, 138, 167, 181-182, 265, 310, 315
Sutter County, California, 111
Sutter's Fort, Sacramento, 227
Sutterville, Sacramento County, 227
Sutton, E. F., 149
Swain, H. V. J., 182
Swan's Ferry, Merced County, 61
Sweem, Ed, 249, 251-253, 258-259, 260, 265
Sweeney, J. J., 132
Swift, Charles, 223
Swift, Frank, 192

T

Tacoma, Washington, 275
Taggert (deputy U.S. marshal), 172
Talbot (officer, Sacramento police), 229-230
Tehachapi Mountains, Kern County, 51
Tehama County, California, 239
Tejada, Jesus, 38-40
Terry, Clinton, 180
Terry, David S., 100, 167-170, 172-178, 180-182
Terry, Sarah, 170-173, 175-176, 182, 188
Texas, 117, 167, 271
Thacker, John, 108-109, 127-128, 132-133, 136-137, 209, 211, 221-222, 240, 284-285, 289-290, 292
The Army of the Commonwealth of Christ, 224
The Pocket, 111
Thomas, Harry, 49
Thorn, Benjamin K., ix, 71-72, 75-76, 94, 109, 111, 123, 125, 127-128, 134, 136, 193
Thornton, see New Hope
Tibbetts, A. J., 6, 14, 23, 33-34, 57, 62
Tipton, John S., 28
Tison, Henry Jr., 247-248, 250, 255-256, 258, 260, 262, 266
Tison, Henry Sr., 247-249, 252-253, 258-266
Tison, Julius, 248, 260, 262, 266
Tison, Moses, 248, 260, 262, 266
Todhunter, William, 107, 111
Tombstone, Arizona, 177
Tomka, Frank, 97
Tracy, San Joaquin County, 248, 259, 282, 284-285, 288
Trahern and Dudley, 106
Traver, Tulare County, 203
Trenton, New Jersey, 192
Tres Pinos, San Benito County (then Monterey County), 43-44, 55
Troia, Margaret, 113, 117
Truckee, California, 301
Tulare County, California, 20, 117, 139, 158, 160, 196, 200, 202-203, 209, 211, 272, 288, 298
Tuolumne City, Tuolumne County, 33

Tuolumne County, 15, 33, 74, 109, 111, 123, 217, 223, 276, 312
Tuolumne River, 33, 60
Turcott, Abraham, 120-122, 129-130
Turner Saloon, 254
Turner, W. E., 185
Tuttletown, Tuolumne County, 312-313

U

United States Supreme Court, x, 119, 163, 169-170, 174, 187-188, 310
United States citizenship (Cunningham), 2
Utzrath, John, 43
Utah, 59-61, 154, 162
Utah State Penitentiary, 61
Union island, San Joaquin County, 84-85, 130
Urbano (murder victim), 97
U. S. marshal, x, xv, 60-61, 134, 174, 217, 220, 237
United States Circuit Court, 185
Union Pacific Railroad, 225
Union Township, San Joaquin County, 276
Union City, Indiana, 301
Union Safe Deposit and Loan Company, 312

V

Valacca, Antone (alias Red Antone), 68, 72-73, 75-76
Vallejo, Solano County, 80, 225
Valley Springs to Mokelumne Hill stage, 192
Van Horn (murder victim), 83-84
Van Vlear (gunsmith), 181
Vance, D. M., 120,125
Vancouver Barracks
 Vasquez gang, 45, 52

Vasquez, Tiburcio, 40-42, 44-49, 51-55, 68
Vermont Lodging House, 286
Vinelli (deputy constable), 280
Visalia, Tulare County, 44, 64, 117, 196, 211, 272
Vogan, John, 111
Volta, Merced County, 264

W

Western Pacific Railroad, 119
Weston, Harry, 156-157
White, Avery C., 180, 182
White, Clifford, 295
Whittier Reform School, 213, 221-222, 283-284
Wichita Clearing House Association, 161
Wichita, Kansas, 161-162
Wilber, E. H. (true name: Cadwallader, Charles H.), 301
Wilkens, J. P. D., 21-23
Wilkens, Lizzie, 23
Williams, George (burglar), 101
Williams, George (train wrecker), 282-288, 290-294
Williams, Henry "Harry" (alias Browning, Jack, alias McGuire, John), 240-243
Williams, J. Q. A., 35
Williams, Jim, 32
Williams, N. E. (true name: Williamson), 161-162
Williams ranch, 130
Williams, Samuel, 130
Williams, Thomas, 84
Williamson, W.E. (alias Williams, N. E.), 161-162
Willow Creek, San Benito County, 44
Wilson, Parker D., 241
Wilson, Parker J., 241
Windmiller, L. D., 233-234
Winters, Jim (true name: Walsh, Michael), 85
Winters, Lee, 223
Witty, George, 203, 209

Woodbridge, San Joaquin County, 14, 31, 67
Woodland, Yolo County, 97
Woods (congressman), 313
Woods, C. L., 26
Woods, Lafayette, 31
Woodward bill, 35
Woolf, Edmund, 83
Wright, Charles (true name: Hancock, Charles), 118
Wright, E. C. (true name: Campbell, James), 130

X

Y

Yancey, T. M., 109
Yolo County, California, 109-110, 116, 261
Yosemite Hotel, 242
Yosemite Stables, 140
Yosemite Theater, 243

Z

Zamansky's Pawnbrokers, 229
Zapato Chino Cree, Coast Range Mountains, 55